MW01222057

FIRST EDITION

Siva Nara
and
Priya Raghavan

Wise
Pen
Corp

Published by:

Wise Pen Corp.
2613 Plaza drive
Woodbridge, New Jersey
Email: author@dollarwisepennyfoolish.com
Website: www.dollarwisepennyfoolish.com

ISBN: 0-9753208-0-7

Manufactured in the United States of America

DEDICATION

Dedicated to our friends, relatives, and colleagues who hate the word "stocks". If every one of our close associates were a knowledgeable investor, we would never have dreamed of writing a book about stocks.

Siva Nara
Priya Raghavan

Disclaimer:

This book (Dollar Wise Penny Foolish)'s goal is to provide the reader personal finance and investment ideas. The contents of the book should NOT be construed as investment advice, nor does their appearance imply an endorsement by the authors of any specific security or trading strategy. An investor's best course of action must be based on individual circumstances.

You are responsible for your own investment decisions. The authors of this book will NOT be responsible for any errors or omissions. The authors will not be liable for any loss or damage caused by a reader's reliance on information obtained in our area. Data and information is provided for informational purposes only, and is not intended for trading purposes. The authors are NOT liable for any errors or delays in the content, or for any actions taken in reliance thereon.

Data Source Disclaimer

All of the data represented in the charts and tables in this book (1) are proprietary to Morningstar and/or its content providers; (2) may not be copied or distributed; and (3) are not warranted to be accurate, complete or timely. Neither Morningstar nor Wise Pen Corp. is responsible for any damages or losses arising from any use of this information. Past performance is no guarantee of future results.

Neither Morningstar nor Wise Pen Corp. is liable for the accuracy, integrity, completeness or timeliness of the data.

Contents

Acknowledgements

"The spirited horse, which will try to win the race of its own accord, will run even faster if encouraged."
Ovid

We would like to first thank our family members, **Ram Nara, Sona Ram, Saradha Raghavan and J S Raghavan,** for extending all the support and encouragement a loving family could possibly give.

We extend our sincere thanks to the following people, who helped us make this book what it is today.

Christopher Cobb:
We may have written a good number of pages on finance and blended it with fiction. But all the words in this world are not sufficient to thank Chris for his superb editing. He zealously read every word, scrutinized every sentence and corrected every mistake. His tremendous confidence in our endeavor to educate every reader made us work even harder to produce a great book. We owe you BIG time, Chris.

Kavitha Manley:
Editing is Kavitha's profession, but she reviewed this book with passion. She gave every word great attention and came up with amazing observations.

C G Rishikesh:
Despite an ocean separating us from this veteran editor of leading newspapers in India, Rishikesh reviewed the book in great detail and fine-tuned it.

Pamela Tompkins:

A mother of two young children rarely has time even to look after herself. But our dear friend Pam, in addition to being a great mother, made the time to edit and review this book. Her remarkable observations and suggestions have vastly refined the work you see before you.

Parameshwar Iyer:

We owe a big thanks to the design whiz kid from India, who designed and created the cover page.

Reviewers:

We would like to thank Kenneth Schafer, for reviewing the financial aspects of the book.

We would also like to thank Patricia Pepe, Diwakar Ram and Stephanie Waynant, who reviewed every chapter and offered excellent suggestions.

Finally, big thanks to all our friends.

Do-It-Yourself!

What do you do when the light bulb burns out? What do you do when you decide to paint your room? You do it yourself! You have learned the art of fixing things involved in your life. However, when it comes to investing, why do you run to someone else to fix it? It is that you do not fully understand the concepts of investing. Choosing the right company in which to invest becomes quite a challenge.

You think understanding finances or reading company reports requires special education and training. You think it requires an expert to make your financial decisions. You prefer to read fiction and skip finance books.

How useful it would be if you had the nitty-gritty details of *investment, particularly in stocks* taught through the form of narrative non-fiction? How useful would it be if the book explains each and every formula that helps in choosing the right companies in which to invest? What a great gift it would be to have the keys to unearth stocks that return at least 20% or more on an average in the long run!

The Idea:

Anything simplified is demystified! The goal of the book is to present 'investing in stocks' in the form of fiction. Non-fiction reading takes a lot of time, effort and dedication, whereas fiction reading is considered to be entertainment. The readers will consume the vital medicine of financial concepts wrapped in a capsule of fiction.

Understanding finance is like eating dry toast. If the toast has the right spread, it becomes delectable. The book explains that **stocks** are a form of investment that can reap rewards, as long as the right companies are chosen at a bargain. The art of picking the right companies in which to invest is taught to the readers using a simple approach. Even a fifth grader who understands basic arithmetic can master the techniques discussed in the book.

The book helps readers of all ages to conquer the fear of investing in stocks. Each criterion involved in picking the right company is explained chapter by chapter. The complex financial concepts involved in evaluating companies are broken down to simple fragments, so that any reader can understand them with ease.

A blend of finance and fiction:

Sam, the central character of the book, is a young finance whiz who has achieved a lot of knowledge in the field of investing. He has spent all his teenage life meeting several wise investors, reading a lot of books and attending classes.

A chance discussion in his class opens the topic of 'making money in the field of stocks'. A love interest also develops between Sam and Jessica.

Sam's friends, including Jessica, learn several vital concepts:

> Why should one invest in stocks?
> How to make millions by investing only $125 a month.
> What are the effects of inflation?
> What are the costs of retirement and raising children?
> How to beat inflation and prepare for college education and retirement.
> The step-by-step approach of evaluating a company.
> How can one identify a company that is in financial trouble?
> How can a person be an astute investor in the stock market?
> How to detect accounting scams.
> How to buy a great stock at a bargain price.

Sam illustrates the methods with numerous easy-to-understand examples, charts and various "homework" assignments. The friends attend parties, go on a road trip to Las Vegas, enjoy camping, and engage in several activities. During these events, they learn all the essential concepts of investing in stocks.

Chapter I

Who is Dollar Wise, Penny Foolish?

Knowledgeable investor or risk avoider?

Change is automatic but progress is not
Anthony Robbins

Random Thoughts

You see things; and you say, "Why?"
But I dream things that never were; and I say, "Why
not?"

George Bernard Shaw

Sam entered the class, which was very popular on the campus for its bright students. "Hello Sam, take a seat," the professor welcomed amiably. He introduced Sam to the class. Sam said a quick hello to everyone and occupied the seat nearest the window. The professor continued, "Sam, we have a 15-minute discussion every day on a random topic. As you've joined us today for the first time, why don't you suggest one?"

Sam happily agreed. "What is the easiest way to make lots of money?" he asked.

Someone yelled, "New York Lotto," while another said, "Las Vegas, man."

Sam interrupted: "Let me rephrase the question. What is the *easiest and surest* way to make lots of money?"

The professor said, "Bank deposits."

Someone else joined in with, "Stocks."

Joe, the self-proclaimed smart aleck of the class, said, "Yeah, right! Investing in stocks is no different from gambling. You think you have invested in a solid company, and the next year your money either doubles or it goes down the drain. Just look at *Enron*!"

Sam was quite taken aback. "Can I interrupt?" He rose and asked the professor, who gave a quick nod, smiling. "Joe, I think your opinion is quite common among many people. With all due respect, I disagree. Let me just ask you a few questions to prove my point.

"Joe, when you start your car in the morning, what are your thoughts?"

"Well," Joe answered, taking a moment to recollect, "I think about getting to class on time or planning an alternate route based on the traffic advisory, or which cd to play."

Sam asked, "Do you think about any accidents you might encounter, or about getting stopped by the police?"

Joe replied quickly, "Sure, I had those thoughts when I first got my license, but not any more. I didn't know to drive very well back then."

Sam continued, "Okay Joe, how do you spend your evenings after school?"

Joe was quick to answer this time. "I try to keep fit, so I work out in the gym and usually swim for about an hour."

Sam asked, "What thoughts do you get while swimming? Are they about splashing in the water and having fun, or about gasping for breath and drowning?"

Joe laughed. "I sure do have a great time swimming and never once think about anything bad happening. Thoughts of drowning did of course come to my mind when I first learned how to swim, but that was a long time ago."

The whole class wondered where Sam was going with this.

Sam turned to address the class, "Well, investing in stocks is no different from driving a car or swimming. The reason Joe has radically different thoughts about the same activities within a few years is that he had 'LEARNED' to do them correctly. When you don't know, you think of risks; when you learn, you appreciate the rewards. So, any individual who learns the art of investing will master it and eventually will make lots of money."

Another student joined the discussion, "Assuming I learn to invest, I don't think I can be another Warren Buffet or Peter Lynch. It is not easy to become Warren Buffet, who started with an investment of $100,000 and went on to become the second richest man in the world. As of July 2003, he made 26 billion dollars. Or Peter Lynch, the ex-manager of *Fidelity Magellan Investments*, who consistently produced a whopping 30% annual returns."

"Why not?" said Sam. "Even Peter Lynch in his book *One up on Wall Street* says that anyone who made it through the fifth grade can become a great investor."

Bankruptcy – Not an Overnight Delivery

America's business is Business
Anonymous

Joe asked, "What about situations where companies file for bankruptcy? How do you differentiate between robust companies and the fly-by-night ones?"

Sam cleared his throat to begin his stocks sermon. "Let's take an example.

"John and David work for a pharmaceutical company. They are colleagues earning about $40,000 per year. David is a spendthrift and leads a luxurious life. He rents an apartment in Manhattan for $2,000 a month and drives a Corvette, paying high insurance premiums as well as a hefty monthly auto loan payment. In addition to this, he eats at expensive restaurants more often than he cooks at home. He unwinds after a hard day by watching movies or hitting the bar scene in the city that never sleeps.

"John, on other hand, lives in a small condo that he owns and pays a much lower mortgage of $800 a month. He drives a used Honda Accord on weekends but commutes to work by train every day. After reaching home, John reads books on management, and whenever possible, talks with his friends and colleagues about various corporations or the latest happenings in the business world."

Sam asked the professor's permission to use the board and drew the following table:

Figure 1.1:   Net worth of John and David

(Income/Expense or Assets/Liabilities)	John	David
Salary	$40,000	$40,000
Credit card debt	Pays his bills on time and has no debt	$30,000
Monthly mortgage/Rent	$800	$2,000
Auto loan (Monthly)	$150	$650
Auto insurance (Monthly)	$80	$300
Bank savings (CDs, checking accounts, savings account, money markets)	$15,000	$150
Investments in stocks	$20,000	$0
Other personal loans	$0	$20,000

Sam addressed the class, "Now look at this chart carefully and tell me who between John and David is the better handler of finances?"

The answer was obvious.

Sam continued, "Between John and David, who is more likely to file for bankruptcy if he got the pink slip? Isn't it David, our carefree spender? A public company is no different from individuals like David and John. Don't you agree that David's lifestyle is not a clear indicator of his financial health? If you come to the conclusion that David is financially well off because he has an expensive apartment and a nice car, then you are clearly wrong.

"Similarly, a corporation's success does not depend solely on the total income it is capable of producing in a year. A public company's growth does not depend only on what it produces or what the analysts say about it. A corporation's success also depends upon various other factors, including how much debt it has to repay in the long term and short term, its assets, and the profits it makes each year."

Sam paused for breath and then resumed: "The first and most important step in investing is to understand a company's fundamental business. Let me give you an interesting example. Anyone who has not set foot in a *McDonald's* can punch me right now." The whole class laughed.

"Ray Kroc, the founder of *McDonald's (Public company, Ticker: MCD),* once addressed a group of college students. He led a discussion on the key elements for a business to succeed in a competitive world.

"He asked a very simple question to the students: 'What business do you think *McDonald's* is in?' Without any hesitation the students answered, 'Selling burgers and fries.' Ray Kroc then stunned the audience by saying that *McDonald's* is not in the business of selling burgers and fries, but is in the business of real estate.

"*McDonald's*, now a very big public company, owns most of the buildings in which their food is sold. The franchisee not only has to share the profits but also has to pay a huge rent to *McDonald's* Corporation. So, even if burgers and fries are not sold, *McDonald's* will continue to make money by leasing the real estate they own.

"It appears that McDonald's is in the business of making burgers, when in reality, real estate is the fundamental business of *McDonald's.*"

Ray Kroc opened the 100th Store of *McDonald's* in 1959 and the first overseas store in 1967.

Ray Kroc bought the rights for *McDonald's* from his customers Mac and Dick McDonald.

The discussion ended on an abrupt note, with the students having mixed thoughts about stocks and companies. They had more questions, but Sam promised he would enlighten them over a cup of coffee at the local *Starbucks (Public company, Ticker: SBUX).*

Rise of the Phoenix

Common people think that stocks are left to millionaires. What they don't realize is they became millionaires only by investing in stocks
John Slatter

"Son, how was your day?" Sam's dad James asked with keen parental interest.

Sam briefed him on the class discussion. He chuckled and added, "You wouldn't believe how apprehensive people are when it comes to investing in stocks."

James thought for a moment and said, "I kind of share that feeling. I understand how the stock market works and the fact that stocks provide fantastic returns, but what about those bankruptcy stories we hear? People losing millions and turning insane? I, for one, am reluctant to invest in stocks, son."

Sam pondered for a moment on the fact that the fear of investing in stocks spans every generation. He proceeded, "Dad, bankruptcy is not an overnight occurrence. A solid company does not file for bankruptcy overnight. For example, let's take *Microsoft*, the software giant. As of July 4th, 2003, *Microsoft* was a company holding approximately $40 billion in cash assets. It is like having a bank balance of $40 billion with absolutely no debt. Anyone can vouch that *Microsoft* wouldn't file for bankruptcy within the next two years, even if it does not generate another single dollar of income. Let me give you another example along similar lines.

"The payroll processing company *PayChex Inc.* has total current assets of $750 million with a debt of only $11.4 million. You don't have to be a John Nash to know that *PayChex* wouldn't file for bankruptcy within at least the next couple of years.

"The only thing that is not in our hands is nature. But haven't we developed the technology to forecast the weather? We have means of predicting rainfall, hurricanes and snow. If the human brain can develop a superior technology to prepare for the weather, it is entirely possible to differentiate between great public companies and the rest."

Sam's dad interrupted: "Are you saying that big companies never face problems?"

Sam replied, "Definitely not. Even big companies go through tough situations. For instance, on July 1st 2003, the *Six Flags (Public company, Ticker: PKS)* operations at Virginia experienced a setback; a mechanical failure occurred in the roller coaster while it was operating at full speed. Can you imagine the plight of the people who were enjoying the ride? *Six Flags* stopped the roller coaster immediately and, after two nerve-racking hours, the emergency squad rescued the people. Do you think because *Six Flags* of Virginia experienced a mechanical hiccup, no one would ever visit *Six Flags* again?"

"Likewise, every company is likely to experience pitfalls. *Pfizer (Public company, Ticker: PFE)* might not get one of its drugs approved by the FDA. *Microsoft (Public company, Ticker: MSFT)* might experience security flaws in its operating systems. *Intel (Public company, Ticker: INTC)* might experience defects in its chips when used under certain conditions. *Altria (Formerly Philip Morris, Public company, Ticker: MO)* might receive lawsuits from cigarette addicts."

In the year 2000 alone, *Wal-Mart* was sued 4,891 times. That is nearly one lawsuit every two hours.

Wal-Mart is sued more often than any other company in the U.S.

"But what differentiates a regular company from a great company is the capacity to rise again. Let me explain to you the ways to understand the difference between great companies and the not-so-great ones.

"Before we go on a long trip, don't we check the tire pressure in our car? Similarly, it is important to analyze a public company's health before we invest in it.

Can You Avoid Public Companies?

Whoever said money can't buy happiness, didn't
know where to shop
Anonymous

"No, Sam, I am not convinced yet," said James. Sam expected this from his dad. So he got up from his chair and plugged in his laptop.

"Okay dad, can you spend 15 minutes with me? Even though I know your daily routine, I would like you to list what products you use on a typical day."

James was amused. He pulled at his beard to fire up his recollection of the mundane things his son seemed to be interested in.

He began, "I brush my teeth in the morning with *Colgate*. Then I make a pot of coffee with *Folgers* and down it while watching *CNN*. That reminds me, I have to send a check to *Comcast*. Anyway, the next thing I do is read the *New York Times*."

Sam smiled and shook his head, with an all-knowing look.

James continued, "Then I trim my beard, using a *Gillette* razor."

Sam interrupted, "Where did you buy it?"

"From *Target,* of course", replied his dad and went on. "Then I don a pair of slacks and shirt which I got from *Ralph Lauren*.

"I mostly eat cereal for breakfast as you know."

Sam interrupted again, "That must be from *General Mills*."

"Then", James continued, "I start my *Ford* Explorer. If I am out of gas, I usually stop at the *Exxon* around the corner. They accept *American Express,* by the way. I go to work and first check my emails using *Microsoft Outlook.* Since I am a very careful man and still believe in the written word, I take a printout of the most important emails – using my new *Hewlett-Packard* laser jet printer.

"For lunch I generally eat a salad at *Wendy's* and usually have a *Coke.* After a typical day, I see you at around 7 pm at home. If it's a Friday, we eat out, mostly at your favorite restaurant *Outback Steakhouse.* I take the doctor-recommended *Lipitor* to keep my cholesterol down, 'choLESStrol' as they advertise.

"This is my regular day, son, even though you know it like the back of your hand."

Sam took a deep breath and told his Dad, "OK Dad, here is the table of products you use almost every day and the companies associated with them."

Figure 1.2: List of products used in every day's life

Product	Brand	Owned by	Ticker
Toothpaste	Colgate	Colgate Palmolive	CL
TV channel	CNN	AOL Time Warner	AOL
Cable provider	Comcast	Comcast	CMCSA
Coffee	Folgers	Procter & Gamble	PG
Newspaper	New York Times	New York Times	NYT
Shaving gel and blades	Gillette	Gillette	G
Retail store	Target	Target	TGT
Shirts	Ralph Lauren	Polo Ralph Lauren	RL
Trousers	Ralph Lauren	Polo Ralph Lauren	RL
Cereal	General Mills	General Mills	GIS
SUV	Explorer	Ford	F
Gas	Exxon Mobil	Exxon Mobil	XOM
Credit card	American Express	American Express	AXP
LaserJet printer	Hewlett Packard	Hewlett Packard	HP
Software package	Microsoft Outlook	Microsoft	MSFT
Soda	Coke	Coca-Cola	KO
Salad	Wendy's	Wendy's	WEN
Restaurant	Outback Steakhouse	Outback Steakhouse	OSI
Drug	Lipitor	Pfizer	PFE

James was peering over the list.

Sam explained, "Whether you invest in stocks or not, public companies are part and parcel of your daily life. Except for the oxygen you breathe, the sunshine during the day and the moonlight you enjoy in the evening, everything else is given to you by public companies. It is up to you whether you just want to use their products or grow with them. It is that simple, and the decision is yours. This is why I wanted you to spell out your daily routine."

Sam continued, "We cannot live for even a day without the products churned out by public companies. So there is absolutely no way for all public companies to evaporate or go out of business. Can you imagine companies like *GE, Procter and Gamble, Coca-Cola, Pfizer, IBM, Microsoft* or the *New York Times* going out of business? The average market value of the companies traded in the New York Stock Exchange alone is 28 trillion dollars. Can you imagine all this money evaporating? It is certainly not possible."

Market value is equivalent to number of shares multiplied by the price of the share.

The market value of *Johnson and Johnson* was $153 billion as of August 9th, 2003.

"At any given moment, there are 1,800 thunderstorms occurring around the world. When it is raining in Tokyo, do you protect yourself with an umbrella as you walk the streets of New York? If it is very cold in Sydney during July, do we wear winter jackets in Florida? Definitely not! Similarly, if *K-Mart* filed for bankruptcy, that doesn't mean *Wal-Mart* is next in line. If every company goes bankrupt, we wouldn't be able to drink water or get electricity. In the U.S., every service is provided by public and private companies, be it an electronic store like *Circuit City (Ticker: CC)* or a utility like *Exelon Corporation (Ticker: EXC)*."

James was quite impressed. "That's a refreshing and different outlook. I did not look at it from that angle."

Wisdom Mocha

Wealth is the product of a man's ability to think
Ayn Rand

Sam met Joe and a couple of other students at *Starbucks* later that evening for the promised cup of a tall mocha in exchange for financial knowledge. Sam first showed them the chart and briefed them on the discussion he had with his dad. He added, "More than banks, public companies are in need of your money. Corporations like *IBM*, *Microsoft* and *General Electric* need money to expand their horizons, and they turn to the public for it. When you deposit your money in banks, you are in need of their services. However, when you invest in corporations, they are in need of your money. Why should banks pay you more when you are in need of their services? That is why banks are more profitable businesses, because they get money from the public and have no obligation to provide great returns. On the other hand, corporations need money from you, and naturally they have to provide excellent returns for your money to stay in business".

One of the students, Bill, asked Sam, "Do you think public companies are safe to invest in because we use their products every day?"

"Absolutely," said Sam. "In fact, the U.S. is one of the very few countries that promotes capitalism. A capitalistic country provides the fullest opportunity both to corporations and to the public to use their talents and capacity to make money. The only business run by the federal government is the *United States Postal Service.* The Founding Fathers learned much earlier that the only way the country could prosper was by providing individuals every opportunity to make use of their talents. No other country encourages and provides more opportunities than the U.S. That is why it is possible for Bill Gates, Warren Buffett, or maybe even you and me to become the richest people in the world.

"Even the President of the U.S. earns much less than the CEO of many companies. It is left to you to decide whether you want to use this opportunity to make yourselves rich."

"Whoa!" Joe said, "The CEOs earn more than the President? I thought the President of the U.S. is the most powerful man in the world."

Sam said, "Hey, I never mentioned anything about power here. We are talking about just the green stuff. Take a look at this chart if you believe in numbers."

The President's annual salary is just $400,000 and the Vice President makes around $190,000 per year.

Figure 1.3: Salaries of CEOs of major corporations

Company	Ticker	CEO as of 2003	Salary for 2002
DELL	DELL	Michael Dell	$16 million
Best Buy	BBY	Richard Schulze	$20 million
General Electric	GE	Jeffrey Immelt	$23 million
IBM	IBM	Samuel Palmisano	$25 million
Pfizer	PFE	Henry McKinnell	$34 million

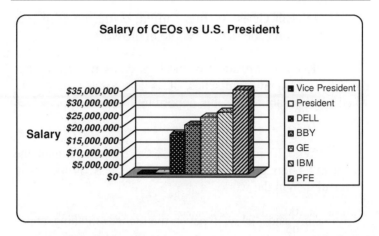

Salary of CEOs vs U.S. President

Facts, Not Just Fate

Knowledge is Power; but only if used
Anonymous

Joe told Sam, "You know, I am all for public companies being part of my life and bankruptcy not happening overnight. But I need more solid facts for you to convince me to invest in stocks."

Sam teased, "I thought what I explained was convincing enough! You want more facts, huh?"

"Of course," insisted Joe. "Let me give you an example, since you seem so fond of them.

"In ancient times people used to believe the earth was motionless. They explained the succession of day and night and the changing position of the stars by saying the sky moved around the earth. We now know that the earth completes its rotation in approximately 24 hours. How did someone come to that conclusion?

"The French physicist Jean Bernard Leon Foucault performed several experiments and proved with facts that the earth itself must be rotating. Today, we all agree with Foucault's findings. To prove any finding, it is best done with solid facts", concluded Joe.

"Okay Joe. I have tons of facts to prove it," said Sam.

Solid Facts, Not Just A Gamble

There is no security in life. There is only opportunity
Mark Twain

"First of all, let's compare the average stock price of some of the better companies during 1996 compared with September 2003. Don't you agree that 1996 was a great year for stocks and that 2001 to 2003 were not? But for great stocks, it doesn't matter whether the market is doing poorly. We'll find out what percentage we would have gained if we had invested in these stocks and what the value of each of these would have been if we had invested $10,000 in 1996.

"Let us look at the growth of each stock if we had invested in 1996 and sold them in September 2003. Even if we had invested in *Intel*, a stock that faced a huge loss during the recession in 2002, we would have still gained substantial returns over the period.

"All these prices are based on the assumption that you had not reinvested the dividends. If you had reinvested the dividends, it would have grown even more than this. Dividends are the share of profits given by companies to shareholders. Dividends are calculated on a per-share basis. So the more shares you own, the more dividends you get.

"The only way you can make your money work for you, even when you are asleep, is with stocks," concluded Sam, showing the chart to his friends.

Figure 1.4: Comparison of few companies's stock price between 1996 and 2003

Source: Morningstar, Inc.

Company	Ticker	1996		2003*		Growth of $10,000 invested in 1996 as of September 2003	
		Low	High	Low	High	Value	Growth %
PayChex	PAYX	$6.02	$12.57	$21.82	$37.50	$57,663	447
Pfizer	PFE	$10.04	$15.21	$27.00	$36.92	$33,214	232
Home Depot	HD	$9.22	$13.22	$20.10	$34.99	$33,014	230
Kohl's	KSS	$6.33	$10.50	$44.00	$73.06	$91,578	816
Wal-Mart	WMT	$9.55	$14.13	$46.25	$60.10	$52,917	429
Microsoft	MSFT	$9.98	$21.53	$21.55	$29.48	$49,286	393
Bed Bath and Beyond	BBBY	$4.09	$7.88	$29.98	$45.00	$97,710	877
Dell	DELL	$0.72	$4.02	$22.95	$34.52	$331,315	3,213

* Indicates the high and low price for the past 52 weeks as of September 2003.

Each stock has undergone multiple splits. If a stock had not split, the actual prices would have been much higher than what is shown above.

Joe took a detailed look at the chart and confirmed his conclusions with Sam.

"So Sam, if I had invested $10,000 in *Dell* in 1996, as of September 2003 I would be worth a little over $330,000?"

Sam laughed, "Yes, and you wouldn't be sitting here in the dead of night discussing this with me. You would probably be vacationing in Hawaii."

If you compare the price of these stocks versus the growth, it might not show the actual growth. The reason is that the stocks had multiple splits between 1996 and 2003.

If you really want to know what the price of a stock would be if it had never split, look at the price of *Berkshire Hathway (BRK.A)*. As of July 3ᵈ 2003, the price was $72,500, whereas it was a mere $18 when Warren Buffett took over the company in 1965.

2 and 1 is 21

The greatest discovery of the 20th century is compounding
Albert Einstein

"What do you get when 2 and 1 are put together? One said 3 and the other said 21. The one who said 21 is none other than Warren Buffett." Sam continued, "The coffee we drink has the single most important ingredient for success, which is the finest quality beans. Similarly, the single most important factor contributing to multiplying your money is the mantra known as 'compounding'. In a nutshell, compounding describes how numbers can grow. There are two ways by which numbers can grow. One is linear or arithmetic progression, and the other is exponential progression.

"In linear progression, each unit is added in each step, and the action provides the growth; for example, 2, 4, 6, 8, 10, 12 or 3, 6, 9, 12, 15, 18, etc. When numbers grow exponentially, the increase comes by doubling the number at each step in the progression, like 2, 4, 8, 16, 32, 64 or 3, 6, 12, 24, 48, etc."

Sam said, "Let me consider two fictitious characters and their investing habits to illustrate the power of compounding."

Billionaire's Secret – Invest a Dollar Day

The only constant thing in the world is Change
Heraclitus

"Michael and John are good friends. Michael's father is very conservative and old-fashioned. John's dad is modern and forward-looking, and he keeps himself up-to-date by reading business magazines and management books. When Michael was young, his dad raised him like any other boy by teaching him the ABCs, taking him to Disneyland, etc. John's dad also taught his son everything, but in addition to regular stuff like reading and arithmetic, he taught him the power of compounding. Both parents wanted to help their boys, so that when they grew old they would have enough money to retire. Michael was taught how to keep money safely in a bank, whereas John's dad taught his son how to multiply his money by analyzing stocks using some common principles and simple arithmetic. At the age of five, both Michael and John were ready to save money for their respective futures, with their fathers' help.

"Michael and John requested their respective parents to give them one dollar each per day. Both of them started saving, but they used two very different approaches.

"Michael, being very conservative, invested every dollar in the local bank as soon as he got the money from his dad. John learned some basic fundamentals from his dad and knew the art of picking stocks that grow annually at 20% compounded. So whenever John received the money from his dad, he would invest in the right stocks at the right price. Michael's money was safe, but it was in the checking account that was practically dormant, never gaining interest. John decided to leave the money in stocks, which grew annually at 20%.

"After they reached 18, their dads informed them that they would no longer continue the practice of giving them one dollar a day, but both of them continued their same investing habits. As the old adage reads, 'Old habits never die'. They continued this habit until they reached 70. They invested $1 per day for 65 continuous years. The only difference was that Michael saved in the bank, whereas John invested in public companies.

"Shall we look at the net value of each of their investments? Michael, who saved each dollar in the bank, retired at 70 with a net value of $24,000, whereas John, who invested in stocks that grew at 20%, retired with one billion dollars. Yes, that is true! One dollar a day at a 20% annual compounded rate would grow to one billion dollars in 65 years. Do you want to retire with $24,000 or one billion? The choice is yours.

"Money grows exponentially and not linearly. If you invest $10,000 in an account that offers an interest rate of 5%, after 20 years your original investment would earn $17,126. What do you think the same $10,000 would earn if you place your money in an investment that grows 10% annually? Isn't it $17,126 x 2, which is $34,252? It is not. Instead, it would be $63,281. How is that possible? Every time you get returns from your investment, is the returns are reinvested. For example, at the end of year one, a $10,000 investment with 10% return would become $11,000. However, in the next year we will not be getting 10% on $10,000. Instead, we will be getting 10% on $11,000. That is the power of compounding.

"Historically, great stocks provide an average compounded return of 20 to 25%."

5% or 20%

Why make money? It is the American thing to do
Anonymous

Sam said, "Take a look at this chart."

Figure 1.5: Interest earned from $10,000 in 20 years at various percentages

Percentage of annual return	Interest earned from $10,000 at the end of 20 years
5%	$17,126
10%	$63,281
15%	$187,155
20%	$518,275

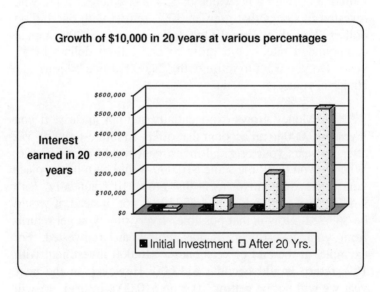

Joe said, "Sam, I don't have ten thousand dollars to invest." The entire group agreed that they didn't have that much money, either.

"You don't have to," Sam went on.

"Here is a proven method to become more than a millionaire. Look at this:"

Figure 1.6: Growth of small monthly investments at various percentages

Monthly invest-ments	Number of years	5% (Compo-unded)	10% (Compo-unded)	20% (Compou-nded)
$125	25	$ 74,438	$165,854	$1,060,660
$150	25	$ 89,326	$199,025	$1,272,793
$150	30	$124,838	$339,073	$3,446,675

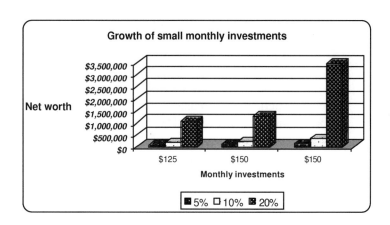

Millionaire – Different Routes But Same Goal

People spend more time on explaining their view
than accepting the truth
Anonymous

"We'll do the same calculations in a different way," Sam said to his friends.

"How many of you want to have a million dollars?" Everyone raised their eyebrows along with their hands. "If our goal is to get a million dollars in 25 years, how much do we need to save every month? The answer depends upon the average annual return you get from your investments."

Figure 1.7: Monthly investment required to make one million dollars in 25 years

Annual compounded interest	Monthly investment required to get a million dollars in 25 years
5%	$1,679.23
10%	$ 753.67
20%	$ 117.85

"So, which one is easier? Is it easier to invest $117.85 per month or $1,679.23? The choice is yours. By the way, if you can afford to invest $1,679.23 a month you can have a net worth of $14 million dollars by getting an annual return of 20%."

"Well," one of the guys asked, "How do I get a 20% return?"

The Magic Behind the 20%

*Whether you believe you can, or whether you believe
you can't, you're absolutely right!*
Henry Ford

Sam said in a serious tone. "Invest in stocks!

"Stocks that are proven to be solid and financially
stable. How do we find such stocks on our own? Are they
hidden and known only to Peter Lynch and T.Rowe Price?
Not really. Anyone of you can find stocks easily, as long as
you have time to hear me out. Hey, if you wanted to find the
simplest and most well established method to make your
money work for you, wouldn't you spend time to learn it? I
think you would."

"Wait a minute", asked Joe, "I almost forgot about
bank deposits. Aren't they 100% safe?"

Sam said, "Any money you don't need for the next
three to six months should not be lying dormant in banks.
Bank deposits are to be treated as cash reserves and not as a
means for growing your money.

"Why do great investors love to hate bank deposits?
Ask yourself a question: Are bank returns constant or
volatile? Is there a huge difference among interest rates
offered by each bank? *Bank of America* may provide a return
of 2% while *Bank of New York* may provide 2.1%. Is that a
big difference? Also, these interest rates are not constant.
They are based on various other factors, and they change
almost every week. Those who argue that stock prices are
volatile should first check interest rates every day before
making that statement.

"Great investors like Benjamin Graham, Warren
Buffett and Peter Lynch know very well that no other
investment has provided a better return than stocks."

Focus on Facts, Not Myths

I realized that most of the average salaried people
became millionaires by investing in stocks
Charles Carlson

Joe interrupted Sam again, "Can you prove that stocks can return an average of 20% annually?"

Sam said, "Sure, let's look at average returns of certain stocks for the past five years."

Figure 1.8: Average annual return of companies in the past five years

Source: Morningstar, Inc.

Company	Ticker	Average annual return % in the past five years as of 1st July 2003.
Lowe's	LOW	20.0
Bed Bath and Beyond	BBBY	24.4
Eaton Vance	EV	25.4
United Health Group	UNH	27.1
Best Buy	BBY	28.0
Cheese Cake Factory	CAKE	29.6
CDW Corporation	CDWC	31.2
Apollo Group	APOL	31.7
Hovnanian Enterprises	HOV	42.0
NVR	NVR	57.7

Source: Morningstar, Inc.

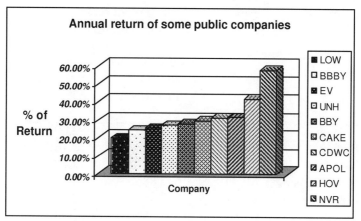

"Even during the recession that started in 2001, the stocks of big companies have performed consistently. So irrespective of the index, what ultimately counts is which stocks are doing really well, and whether we can identify and invest in them."

You May Have To Pinch Yourself

God doesn't give a lick of an ice cream without
wanting you to have the whole cone
Marshall Thurber

Joe asked, "Sam, can you draw one of your charts, assuming that my dad had invested $3,000 in some public companies 25 years ago?"

"Sure", said Sam. He started punching in some numbers while the rest of the group went for a refill. When they came back, they just couldn't believe what they saw.

Figure 1.9: Growth of $3,000 investment in 25 years
Source: Morningstar, Inc.

Company	Ticker	Growth of $3,000 investment in 25 years	
		Net worth of $3,000 investment as of 3/23/03	Growth %
DuPont	DD	$63,066	2,002
Boeing	BA	$66,859	2,129
Nike	NKE	$71,314	2,277
McDonalds	MCD	$72,886	2,330
Concord EFS	CE	$92,564	2,985
Citigroup	C	$92,585	2,986
American Express	AXP	$98,156	3,172
Lowe's	LOW	$98,255	3,175
Pfizer	PFE	$114,816	3,727
Wells Fargo	WFC	$138,732	4,524
Exxon Mobil	XOM	$142,144	4,638
PayChex	PAYX	$152,550	4,985
Colgate Palmolive	CL	$158,400	5,180
General Electric	GE	$186,586	6,120
United Health Group	UNH	$222,732	7,312
Home Depot	HD	$234,747	7,725
Altria	MO	$238,868	7,682
Best Buy	BBY	$420,390	13,913
Microsoft	MSFT	$481,512	15,950
Wal-Mart	WMT	$2,459,843	81,895

Wal-Mart is the largest retailer in the world.

If Wal-Mart continues to grow at the same rate it grew in 2003, it will become the first company to reach one trillion dollars of annual sales within 15 years.

Sam began, "Some of the companies in the table might not have gone public 25 years ago. In such cases, the calculations are done from the date they went public.

"Keep in mind that these stocks also underwent a major crash on October 19, 1987. This day is known as 'Black Monday' in the stock market. The *Wall Street Journal* called it 'The most perilous day in 50 years.'

"This is a clear indication that great stocks will outperform every other investment in the long run, even though they might lose value in-between."

"Okay", Joe asked, "What if my dad had put the same $3,000 in a bank CD?"

Sam replied, "If your dad had invested the same $3,000 in a bank certificate and assuming it provided an annual return of 5%, his net worth at the end of twenty five years would be $10,159.06."

"Do you enjoy earning just 5% in the name of financial security, or 20% in really secure stocks?

"When compared to all of the stocks in my chart, even the worst one, *DuPont*, performed 500% better than bank returns. Bank deposits would have grown to only $10,159.06, whereas investment in *DuPont* would have grown to $63,066."

"Here are the interest rates from various banks as of July 7, 2003, along with how a $3,000 investment would have grown (meagerly, of course) at the end of 25 years."

Figure 1.10: Growth of $3,000 invested in bank instruments

Bank	Method of investment	Interest rate	The net worth of $3,000 after 25 years
Bank of America	Savings account	0%	$3,000.00
PNC Bank	Money market	0.30%	$3,233.29
MBNA Bank	Money market	1.5%	$4,352.84
ING Direct	Certificate of deposit	3.60%	$7,262.98
Net Banking	Certificate of deposit	3.51%	$7,106.88

"The maximum return you would have received would be $7,100 after 25 years. Now, would you like $3,000 to grow to $7,100 or to at least $100,000?

If you had invested $10,000 in Berkshire Hathaway when Buffett bought control of it in 1965, you would have more than $50 million today.

Double Shot Please!

*Stocks may be volatile. But as long as the business is
not volatile, I would invest*
Warren Buffett

One of the guys asked, "Let me ask you a different
but related question. How do I know how long it will take to
double my money?"

Sam said, "That's simple: apply the rule of 72. It is
the easiest way to determine the number of years it might take
for your investment to double. Just divide 72 by the interest
rate. For $10,000 to double with an interest rate of 5%, it
would take 72 divided by 5, which is 14.4 years. For a stock
that returns an average of 20%, $10,000 would take 72/20,
which is 3.6 years, to become $20,000. So in three and a half
years, I would surely double my money by investing in
stocks."

The group was visibly impressed.

Sam went on, "Let me ask you guys another question.
Do you think even the 5% returns from a bank savings
account is a very safe form of investment?"

"No doubt in that," Bill said.

Sam corrected him, "Absolutely not! Bank
investments are not safe because of a very important factor. I
need more time to explain. Would you be interested in
investing that kind of time?"

Joe answered, "Sam, since I spend about three hours
watching a movie and a couple of hours playing video games,
and neither of them gives me any monetary benefit, I would
definitely like to spend some time with you to understand the
nuts and bolts of investing. What do you say, guys?"

Bill teased, "Where is my friend Joe, and what have you done with him?"

Sam got up and collected his papers. "All right then!" He gave a dramatic pause and said, "Those of you who seek financial nirvana, meet me here the same time tomorrow."

Sam's Sprinkles

- Stocks are safe investments.

- Good stocks grow at an average of 20%.

- Public companies are part and parcel of your life. You cannot live without them.

- Public companies don't go bankrupt overnight.

- Bank interest rates are more volatile than a stock's growth.

- Think exponentially and not linearly.

- The earlier you invest, the more your money will grow.

- Don't forget the rule of 72. Divide 72 by the interest rate and you will know the number of years it will take for your money to double.

Self Explorer

- Find the meaning and purpose of NASDAQ.

- Why are stock tickers commonly used to represent a stock?

- Can you identify the products you use in your day-to-day life that are not manufactured / distributed by public companies?

Chapter II

Who is Dollar Wise, Penny Foolish?

Conservative Returns or Optimum Returns?

I am easily satisfied with the very best
Winston Churchill

Are You The Next Millionaire?

There is always a limit to save but there is no limit to earn.
Anonymous

Sam looked up from the book he was reading when he heard someone call his name. Joe and his cohorts were punctual. Joe's eyes suddenly shifted focus. "Wait a minute! What is she doing here?" he asked and dashed off. He returned with someone who swept Sam's feet away. He playfully introduced her, "This is Jessica, born to create new meaning to sibling rivalry in my house." Jessica laughed and shook hands with everyone.

Jessica asked, "What are you guys doing here?"

Joe volunteered, "Sam, our city's answer to Warren Buffett, is leading us down the path of financial deliverance."

Jessica raised her eyebrows and said, "Wow! Mind if I join in?"

Sam said, "No, not at all," and gave her a brief overview of what they had been discussing and debating so far.

Jessica said, "You guys seem to be having an interesting discussion. Personally, I think the easiest and safest way to make money is by investing in the tools that banks provide. I worked in a bank briefly, and I certainly like the certificate of deposits and money market tools banks provide. You are guaranteed never to lose that money. There is no other secure way to make your money grow."

Sam asked, "Okay, but what is the average return on these investments?"

Jessica replied, "Well, as of now, about two percent."

Sam continued, "So, let's assume you had invested $10,000. Your investments of $10,000 in a bank's certificate of deposit would have grown to $12,189.94 in 10 years, assuming it yielded two percent annually."

Jessica said, "Exactly. But your money grows, right?"

Sam said, "Yes, but I am not finished yet. How much do you think the same $10,000 would have grown to if you invested in a company like *Best Buy* for 10 years starting in 1993?"

Jessica replied, "I am not sure. I don't follow the market."

Sam continued, "Never mind. Let me spell it out for you. $10,000 invested in *Best Buy* in 1993 would have grown to $685,000 in 10 years. It would be silly of me to ask which figure you like better."

Jessica hesitated. "That's impressive, but I don't want my original $10,000 to vanish either, if I make a wrong investment choice."

Sam nodded his head in agreement. "My point exactly. I am here to unravel the safest and surest ways of not only retaining the $10,000, but also making it grow exponentially. The answer is just one mantra: 'Stocks'. You must be aware that Warren Buffett made more than 30 billion dollars from $100,000 in 45 years. He neither won the lottery every year nor gambled. The genius from Omaha was lucky enough to learn that the only investment vehicle that can provide excellent growth in the long term is 'stocks'.

"Allow me to convince you with numbers. Let's compare various investment vehicles like Certificate of Deposits and checking accounts with stocks. This will show the monthly deposits or yearly contributions required to make one million dollars."

Jessica exclaimed, "Wow! One million dollars?"

Sam went on. "That's right, Jess, give me a few minutes. I will prove it to you."

Awaken the Millionaire within You

Every one thinks of changing the world, but no one thinks of changing himself
Leo Tolstoy

Jessica and Joe stepped out for a while. Joe said, "I am beginning to think that I had tunnel vision when it came to investing."

His sister disagreed, "No, you didn't. I still believe that bank investments are the best bet for your future."

Joe laughed, "Wait until you see the amazing charts Sam comes up with. They are real eye openers. I bet you will feel differently after you hear his lectures." They went back in, and Sam was already showing a chart to the group. Jessica politely asked to see the chart.

Figure 2.1:   Goal: To reach one million dollars in 10 years

Type of investment	Checking account	Certificate of deposit or money market with 2% return	Solid stocks
Monthly deposit required	$8,333.33	$ 7,610.54	$ 3,210.23
Yearly contribution	$100,000	$91,326.53	$38,522.76
Average annual returns compounded	0%	2%	20%
Feasible for common investors	No	No	Yes

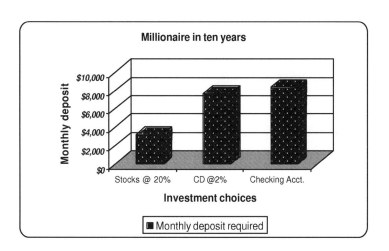

Sam began, "In other words, either deposit $8,333.33 in the bank, $7610.54 in CDs or money market funds, or invest $3,210.23 in stocks, which are solid and provide excellent growth. Now, which of these will help you make a million dollars at the end of ten years?"

Jessica said, "Well, hello? Don't you think $3,000 is a huge amount to invest every month?"

Sam said, "Okay, let's do it in a different way. Assuming you have 20 years to retire, would you be able to save at least $500 dollars every month?" She nodded. Sam continued, "Take a look at this chart, which shows how to save a million bucks before you retire, assuming you have 20 years before retirement."

Figure 2.2:   Goal: To reach one million dollars in 20 years

Type of investment	Checking account	Certificate of deposit or money market with 2% return	Solid stocks
Monthly deposit required	$4,166.66	$ 3,429.72	$ 446.38
Yearly contribution	$50,000	$41,156.72	$5,356.53
Average annual returns compounded	0%	2%	20%
Feasible for common investors	No	No	Yes

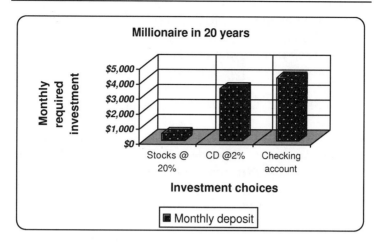

"Which is easier? Investing $446.38 every month or saving $3,429.72 a month?"

Banks – Having Your Cake and Eating it Too

Business, that's easily
defined; it's other people's money
Anonymous

Sam said, "I have another theory to prove my point. What do you think is the surest way to buy a product at its lowest price?"

Jessica volunteered, "Well, I would go to *Wal-Mart (WMT)* or *Dollar Tree Stores (DLTR)*, or even better, bid on it at *www.ebay.com (eBay)*."

Sam continued, "Right, but do you agree that *Wal-Mart* and *Dollar Tree Stores* buy these products at a lower price and sell them to you at a higher price? In a way, *Wal-Mart* makes a profit from every dollar you spend."

She said, "Of course, that's business."

Sam went on, "Companies like *Procter & Gamble (PG), Johnson & Johnson (JNJ), Clorox (CLX)* and *Kimberly-Clark (KMB)* produce these products and sell them to *Wal-Mart.* So naturally these companies hike their prices before selling their products to stores. A cereal box costs $2 from *Wal-Mart*, but it costs the manufacturer only around fifty cents, including the labor costs. By the time it reaches the store, we pay an extra $1.50 for the same product, which we could have bought for fifty cents. In other words, the consumer pays around 300% more than the wholesale cost."

Jessica asked "So you are saying that the only way to buy a product at its lowest price would be to buy it directly from the manufacturer before they add any profit to it."

Sam said, "Correct, but it is not possible to buy directly from the manufacturer. It would be great if that were an option. Don't you agree?"

She hesitantly said, "Yeah, but I still don't see your point."

Sam asked, "When you deposit your savings in the bank, invest in a money market or in mutual funds, what do you think they do with your money?"

She answered, "Well, banks lend the money to individuals and corporations."

Sam said, "You are right, these financial institutions lend money to the public and to big corporations. Do you know how much profit they make from the money you keep in the bank?"

She just shrugged. Sam continued, "Anywhere between 200% to 500% profit from the money you lend to them. These financial institutions lend your money to corporations. When you invest in a certificate of deposit or a savings account in a bank, the bank doesn't keep your money in its safe. They in turn invest your money by lending it to major corporations and make bigger profits from your money.

"This is like letting someone else make more money out of your savings. It may not be possible to buy a product directly from *Procter & Gamble, Kimberly-Clark* or *Clorox*. However, it is definitely possible for us to invest in stocks, which the banks do with our savings anyway. A bank ultimately invests in stocks and gets a much better return. Similarly, individuals like you and me can directly buy these stocks and reap the entire returns and profits. This allows us to get the maximum returns for the money we invest. Now do you see my point?"

"So," Joe asked, "You mean to say every one of us has invested in stocks either directly or indirectly, because each one of us here has deposited at least a dollar in a bank?"

Sam said, "Yes, you have already loaned your money to the corporations. Your money is already invested in stocks. In fact, banks buy thousands of shares at a time at the same price available to you."

Jessica pointed to Sam. "You are good! You certainly look at things from a very different angle."

Sam masked with a faint smile the somersault his heart made, and he continued, "Thanks. All I am saying is your bank deposits or mutual funds are in turn invested in stocks. If you think for a minute about who gets the maximum returns, you will know it is the bank and not you. You have the choice of being an active or a passive investor."

Jessica tried to sum it up. "Let me get this straight. As an active investor, if you are directly buying stocks of solid companies, you get maximum returns. However, if you are a passive investor and just allow your money to sit in the bank or in mutual funds, then you let the financial institutions play the active investor role. So they make much higher returns than what they actually pay to you."

Sam laughed, "Now that's a role reversal. You joined the discussion swearing on a stack of CDs. You learn fast, I must say."

Joe winked, "Runs in the family, buddy!"

Sam went on. "Everything we own should be utilized for maximum returns. Not investing in stocks is like owning a supersonic jet and occasionally using it to fly between New York and Boston. Not investing in stocks is like having the latest computer that is not connected to the Internet. Not investing in stocks is like visiting Orlando without going to Disney World and Universal Studios.

"By investing, you make your money work for you. The money you earn should be put to work from the time it is in your hands. When you get a hefty raise every year, don't you want the money you invest to get maximum returns? The only secret to getting better returns is to invest in stocks."

911 – Corporations Need Money

> *A bank is a place where they lend you an umbrella in fair weather and ask for it back when it begins to rain*
> Mark Twain

Bill, who was silent until now, said, "Tell me something, Sam. You are slowly beginning to convince me that investing in stocks is the way to go. You were telling us earlier that corporations need money from investors. My first question is, why? Second, how do I know which corporation I should lend my money to?"

Before Sam could answer, the waiters at the coffeehouse politely told the group that it was time to close the shop. Sam invited them to his house. As they were walking, Bill pointed to a sprawling house. "You know, I would give anything to live in a house like that with a gorgeous woman."

Sam laughed, "I don't know about the gorgeous woman, but if you listen to my advice, you can own a house like that. So do you think the people who bought the house paid for it entirely in cash, or do you think they got help from a mortgage company?"

Bill said, "How do I know? I assume they are paying a hefty mortgage eve ry month."

Sam asked, "Why do you think they borrowed the money from either a bank or a mortgage institution to buy the house? How did the bank or the financial institution know that they were capable of repaying the loan? Or to take a simpler example, f you decide to buy a car, I am sure you will not be paying the entire amount up front. You would get a loan, right?"

Bill said, "Naturally."

Sam continued, "Banks and mortgage institutions provide loans because they want to make money from us in the form of interest, and they know by verifying our credit history that we are capable of returning the money along with interest. If you had filed bankruptcy or if you had been paying inconsistently with multiple late payments, do you think banks and financial institutions would still loan you money? Definitely not!

"Similarly, every corporation and company needs money to raise capital for its growth. If companies were not growing, the world would remain stagnant, even after millions of years. If you believe the world would benefit from new products, better facilities and much more comfort and speed in every product that is produced, then there must be new technologies, innovations, methods, processes, etc., In other words, every major and minor company must gr ow. That includes every company from *Boeing (BA), Johnson and Johnson (JNJ)* and *Wal-Mart (WMT)* to *Microsoft (MSFT)* and *United Parcel Service (UPS)*. For a company to grow, it needs more capital than it has invested currently. Sometimes a company like *GE* may need millions or even billions of dollars for its expansion. In order to raise this kind of money, corporations borrow directly from the public. This allows common investors like us to own part of the company without physically managing it."

Banks and financial institutions provide only one-fifth of the money required by corporations. Initial Public Offerings (IPOs) raise the rest.

The Good, the Bad and the Ugly

Ready money is Aladdin's Lamp
Lord Byron

Bill said, "Fine, I agree with you. But you have still not answered my earlier question. How do you decide which corporation is going to produce great returns from the money you lend it?"

Sam said, "Let's take a hypothetical situation.

"Joe and Jessica are your friends. You know both of them quite well. Jessica works for a major corporation and is earning a very good salary, whereas Joe is now in-between jobs. Jessica is very honest and always keeps her promises, even in simple things.

"Joe does not take life seriously. Even for interviews, he is known for showing up at least 30 minutes late. Since Joe is in-between jobs, he has already borrowed a huge sum of money from another common friend of yours. Now, Jessica needs to buy a laptop to complete certain assignments, and she approaches you for $1,000. On the other hand, Joe wants to throw a birthday party and approaches you for $1,000. Now, to whom would you lend the money? Would you lend it to Jessica or to Joe? Wouldn't you analyze their habits before you decide? Given their lifestyles, I am sure you would be able to decide who is more worthy of your money."

Joe interrupted, "Sam, I take offense. Why did you paint me in such a bad color? Of all the names, you had to pick mine, huh?"

Jessica teased him. "I think Sam is just giving us a realistic example." Everyone laughed.

Sam went on, "I said 'hypothetical', Joe. Anyway, when a company needs money to grow, it issues stocks to the public. *General Electric (GE)* may be building a new factory in Arizona or *Pfizer (PFE)* may be finding a new AIDS drug or *Comcast (CMCSA)* may be doing research on increasing the speed of the Internet.

"Since these companies need billions of dollars, they approach common investors like you and me and ask, 'Hey, my friend, please give us some money, because we are starting a new project. We'll issue stock certificates as proof of our borrowing from you.' Common investors like us buy the shares and provide them the money required for their expansion. Since we are loaning the money to the company, it is our responsibility to find out whether we are loaning to companies like Joe or to companies like Jessica."

Sam added, "If your question is why I should lend my money to them, then think about why institutions should lend to you when you need a car or a house. Why do credit card companies lend you money when you need to fill gas or rent a video? Financial institutions lend you money to provide the comforts and growth you need in personal life, and in turn they make money by collecting interest from you. Similarly, companies need money from common investors in order to grow. If you do not invest, others will, and they will make both themselves and the companies rich"

Jessica asked, "Sam, I understand that companies need money to grow, and I also want my money to work for me. Tell me how to differentiate between the Joes and Jessicas of these companies, since they are not my personal friends."

Sam replied, "Well, I am going to be spending the entire week with you all" (*'hopefully more time than that with you, Jess'* he thought to himself), "and I will show you different techniques that will help you identify the right companies, as well as how to sidestep certain landmines carefully."

The oldest corporation being traded in New York Stock Exchange is *Bank of New York*; their ticker symbol is BK.

Ask and You Shall Receive

Have the courage to be ignorant of a great number of things, in order to avoid the calamity of being ignorant of everything
Sydney Smith

Joe said, "I have a suggestion: why don't we go on a road trip somewhere? We can have fun while we learn something that might change our lives."

Sam replied, "Sure, why not? We could do that."

Joe turned to Bill, "You are definitely not driving, buddy. Remember last year, you nearly had us killed by your antics in your SUV."

Sam said, "You know, this reminds me of something. In 2002, around forty thousand people died in traffic accidents because of SUVs alone."

Bill asked, "Really? I didn't know that."

Sam said, "Something that occurs every day gets the least attention, whereas something that occurs once in a while gets more attention."

Joe said, "Hold on, I know what's coming. Let me wrap this up for you. The few companies filing for bankruptcy get more attention than the many companies that are almost consistently doing well."

Sam was impressed. "You sure are a great mind reader! How did you know I was going to say that?"

Joe said, "Elementary, my dear Sam, you can't say one sentence without the word 'companies' or 'stocks' or 'consistency'." The whole group laughed.

INFLATION – The Silent Killer

Inflation - Being broke with lots of money in your
pocket
Anonymous

They reached Sam's house, and Sam was surprised to see a group of his father's friends at the dinner table.

Sam's dad James called out, "Come on in."

Sam apologized, "Dad, I totally forgot it's your poker night."

James said, "That's all right son, we were just about to stop. Looks like you have made some new friends." Introductions were made.

Joe said, "Sam's been doing a great job convincing us to invest, especially in stocks."

James agreed, "I am not surprised. In fact, I had an interesting discussion with him yesterday regarding that."

One member of the poker group, Steve, rose and moved to the couch. He said, "That's interesting. I have been quite an investor myself and have made a decent amount of money."

James exclaimed, "Really! I thought you had inherited a fortune from your father, and I was honestly quite jealous of you."

Steve replied, "I thought you were jealous of my Marlon Brando looks." The entire group laughed. He continued, "It's true that I inherited quite a sum, but that was 20 years back. Even if I had inherited a million dollars 20 years back, it would be worth a mere $250,000 now, assuming I hadn't invested it wisely."

Joe was taken aback. "Sir, forgive me if I am being impolite for saying this, but I think you're exaggerating."

Steve answered, "No son, I am telling you the plain truth."

Sam added, "Actually, this reminds me of a disease I have to tell to you about."

Bill recoiled. "What disease? Do you have it?"

Sam replied, "We all have it. It's called 'inflation'."

Joe interrupted. "I think I speak for everyone, when I say, 'What do you mean by inflation?'" Everyone listened attentively.

Sam began, "In a nutshell, *inflation is the increase in price of every commodity, or to put it another way, a decline in the purchasing power of the dollar*."

Bill said, "Of course we know prices increase over time! You are using a frightening term for something we all know about."

Sam went on, "True, but very few people realize its impact."

Jessica added, "I remember my manager saying that the average inflation rate for the past 25 years was 6%."

Bill asked, "In layman's terms, please?"

Sam began, "Sure, let us assume the price of servicing your car is $100 today. However, next year it wouldn't be $100. Instead, it would be $106. The following year it would be $112.36, and the year after that it would be $120. After 20 years, servicing your car would cost $350. That, in a nutshell, is inflation.

"Inflation is something people do not like to believe and blissfully live in denial of the truth. I have an idea. We have people in this room here who remember the prices of everyday products 20 years ago. Let's ask them, and we will compare them to today's prices. Fair enough?"

Bill pulled up a chair. "I'm game!"

Sam asked Steve, "Sir, if you don't mind, can you tell me how much you spent to buy a gallon of milk or a postage stamp 20 years ago?"

Steve smiled. "Now that's stretching my memory a little bit. Anyway, I think it might have been about $1.10 or $1.20 for a gallon of milk and about 20 cents for a stamp."

Sam turned to Joe, "Ok, Joe, what's the current price of a gallon of milk and a postage stamp?"

Joe thought for a moment and said, "$2.75 for a gallon of milk and 37 cents for a stamp."

Sam asked Steve, "Let me ask you for the price of a bigger commodity. How much did you pay for your car 20 years ago?"

Steve said, "About $4,000."

Bill interrupted, "Wow, I think a decent new car would cost around $20,000 now."

Sam continued, "Give me a piece of paper and we'll put down the price of these products in the past, present and future." Sam took a few minutes and then showed them the figures.

Figure 2.3: Comparison of common product's price
Note: A 6% inflation is assumed in these calculations

Product	20 years back ($)	Current price (As of 2003) ($)	20 years later ($)
Stamps	0.20	0.37	1.25
Gasoline	0.32	1.45	4.65
Gallon of milk	1.20	2.75	8.82
Movie ticket	1.50	8.00	26.00
Automobile	4,000	20,000	72,671

Sam continued, "Let me put it this way. If your monthly expenses are, for example, about $4,000 today, then after 20 years, assuming there is no change in your monthly expenses, it would be $13,000. To look at the bigger picture, if your yearly expenses are $48,000, in 20 years you will need $156,000 per year."

Steve said, "We seem to have some math whiz kids out here. It's good to see young people showing a keen interest in their future, especially their financial future! The truth is, the more we earn the harder it is to save, because our needs grow every day."

The first record of inflation was when Alexander the Great introduced a uniform coinage to all the territories he conquered. He confiscated the gold and silver in these countries and minted coins from them.

Money in Banks – A Sleeping Beauty

A little inflation is like a little pregnancy; it keeps growing
Leon Henderson

Steve continued, "Actually, this reminds me of an incident. One of my schoolmates was born with a silver spoon in his mouth. He led a luxurious life, and when his father died, he inherited around a million dollars from him. He thought he had a comfortable nest egg from his dad, so he never bothered to put the money to work and happily retired at 60. He had deposited most of his money in the local bank earning a paltry interest rate. He thought he could happily live for the next 20 years with the inherited money, but then he realized he had only $250,000. Yes, the million dollars automatically diminished to two hundred and fifty thousand dollars. You know how?" He paused.

Bill nodded, "Yeah, I know that now. The 'I' word!"

Steve continued, "Even though his net worth in the bank was a million dollars, he lost 6% every year due to inflation and another 40% due to taxes for the interest he earned. In a nutshell, he lost around 8% every year. Even though his net worth on paper is a million dollars, as of today it is worth only $250,000."

Sam said, "I remember a funny but very true quote on inflation. It goes like this: 'Inflation is when you pay fifteen dollars for the ten-dollar haircut you used to get for five dollars when you had hair.'" Everyone laughed.

Joe asked, "Out of curiosity, why does inflation occur?"

Steve volunteered to answer. "Inflation occurs because people expect an increase in their salary, and the only way companies can increase salaries i by increasing the price of the products they sell. Even though we might get pay raises every year, we pay around 30% of the increase in taxes, and the rest goes to match the increased price of every product. If as an employee you are happy with the increase in your salary, then as a consumer you lose the entire hike you receive every year."

"Wow! I never realized this. You hear about it or read about it, but like a disease you always feel that you are the last person who will be affected by it," Jessica acknowledged.

Joe opened a soda can and said, "I know! I was thinking all along that if I want to be rich, I need to invest in stocks. Now it looks like if I want to lead the same lifestyle I am enjoying today, I need to save, and more importantly, invest my money in the right way."

Jessica said, "I have an idea. Instead of panicking about the future, why don't we make a list of our requirements for the future, financially speaking of course, how much we need to save, so that we can go in the right direction? I'm sure our 'charts guru' will produce some colorful solutions."

Sam said, "Of course guys, but I need some fuel for that. You can help yourselves too." He headed to the kitchen to make a tuna melt sandwich for himself while the others concocted their own personal favorites.

Steve and James were having a discussion of their own. "You should be very proud of your son."

James admitted, "He is something, isn't he?"

One of the other men joined them, "You know, some of my friends still work two jobs just to maintain a decent lifestyle. They never thought about retirement, and we were blind to concepts like inflation."

Sam declared that he was ready.

Bill started, "I thought of three things about the future I feel are important. First and foremost, I want to retire at, say, 55 or 60. Second, I want to provide a good education for my children. Third, I would like to go on a good vacation once a year."

Sam said, "Why don't we first see how much it would cost you to raise children."

Joe teased. "Now, some of the charts Sam comes up with are not for the faint-hearted, so I am warning you guys in advance."

Costs "R" US

A father is someone who carries pictures where his
money used to be
Lion

Sam laughed. He said, "According to the *United States Department of Agriculture (USDA)*, a baby born in 1995 would cost around $350,000 before he or she enters college. If you decide to provide money for their education, then you need to think of their college and tuition fees.

"So let's compare the costs of different colleges in the next 18 years."

Figure 2.4:
Cost of college education for the year 2003 vs. Cost of college education 18 years from 2003

Expense description	Annual cost as of 2003 ($)	Annual cost in the next 18 years ($)	Total cost in 18 years to complete four year graduation (Annual cost * 4) ($)
Average tuition fee for a private college	23,700	67,648	270,592
On campus stay (room & board)	6,500	18,553	74,212
Books and supplies	800	2,500	10,000
Total	31,000	88,701	354,804

"The average cost of raising a child including college education is $700,000. If you have two children, you need to be a millionaire just to raise them and provide their college costs. So the biggest question that remains to be answered is, how are you going to raise a million dollars to provide the basic needs and education for your children?"

Bill exclaimed, "I'm actually about to pass out. Do I need a million dollars to raise two children? I declare I'm going to take a solemn vow of celibacy."

Sam laughed. "It's not that bad. The amount varies a little based on the income group and type of college you decide to send your children to. The bottom line is, it is quite an expense to raise children. Let's see what can be done to raise that kind of money."

Bill said, "Now you're talking."

Inflation rate is calculated from the consumer price index or CPI. CPI is calculated by the U.S. Department of Labor based on approximately 400 frequently purchased items.

Raising Half a Million Dollars - Solution 1

People begin to be successful the minute they decide to be
Harvey McKay

Sam said, "There are two ways to raise half a million dollars. One method is to invest yearly so that the contribution grows over a period. This also allows the entire returns to be used for college education purposes."

Bill asked, "Okay, can you tell us how much we need to invest if we have maybe 15 or 18 years?"

Sam continued, "Sure, we'll find out how much we need to contribute every year with various percentages to raise half a million dollars."

Figure 2.5: Goal: To raise half a million dollars for college education purposes

Num- ber of years	Annual compounded growth			
	At 15% growth		At 20% growth	
	Yearly investments ($)	Monthly investme nts ($)	Yearly investments ($)	Monthly investm ents ($)
15	10,508.00	875.66	6,941.06	578.42
16	8,973.85	747.82	5,718.07	476.50
17	7,683.43	640.28	4,720.07	393.34
18	6,593.14	549.42	3,902.69	325.22

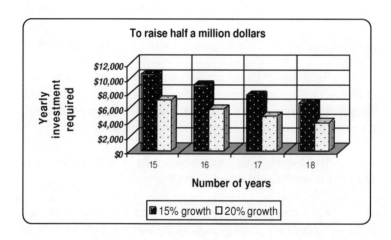

Raising Half a Million Dollars – Solution 2

"The second method is to invest once in stocks and allow it to grow until your child gets into college.

"So, we'll find out how much we need to invest initially, with various percentages and years to raise half a million dollars."

Figure 2.6: Goal: To raise half a million dollars for college education purposes

Number of years	One time investment / Initial investment required	
	At 15% annual compounded growth	At 20% annual compounded growth
	Initial investment ($)	Initial investment ($)
15	61,447	32,452
16	53,432	27,044
17	46,462	22,536
18	40,402	18,780

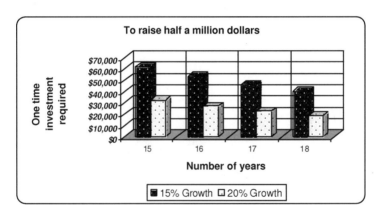

Facts - Just Not Words

The trick is to make sure you don't die waiting for prosperity to come
Lee Iaccoca

Joe said, "Since we are talking in millions here, let me ask a million dollar question. How do you get 20% or even 15% consistent returns?"

Sam began, "Here is a list that explains what your net worth would have been as of July 2003, if you had invested in some of the best stocks 15 years before. Be aware that the U.S. had been facing a recession from 2000 until this time.

"This is just an illustration and a proof to show you that great stocks perform very well regardless of recessions or great economic conditions. It clearly shows that any great stock performs very well in the long run."

Figure 2.7: Investment growth of some stocks in 15 years.
Note: Initial investment is taken from Figure 2.5

Initial invest-tment	Number of years	Company	Net worth as of 14th July 2003	Average annual compo-unded interest %
$61,447	15	General Electric	$0.64 million	16.91
		Johnson and Johnson	$0.78 million	18.47
		Bed, Bath and Beyond	$1.05 million	20.83
		Dollar General	$1.90 million	25.70

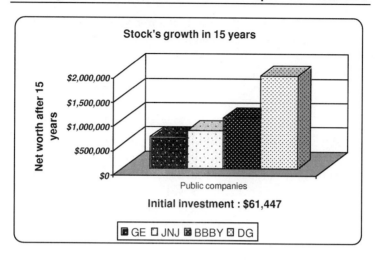

Jessica noted something in the chart. "Hmm, the companies don't belong to a specific industry. For example, *General Electric* is a company that is into every business, whereas *Bed, Bath and Beyond* specializes in retail stores. That's interesting. Hey, why don't we take a smaller amount?"

Sam said, "Well then, let's check the growth of $27,044 in approximately 16 years. Some stocks might not have been issued to the public until the early 1990s, so a few companies may have grown only for a fewer number of years."

Figure 2.8: Investment growth of some stocks in 16 years
Note: Initial investment is taken from Figure 2.5

Initial investment	Number of years (IPO year)	Company	Net worth as of 14th July 2003	Average annual compounded interest %
$27,044	11 (1992)	Fair Isaac & Co	$0.5 million	30.36
	16	Wells Fargo & Company	$0.74 million	22.97
	13 (1990)	United Health Corp.	$0.95 million	31.50
	13 (1990)	Pay Chex	$1.28 million	34.55

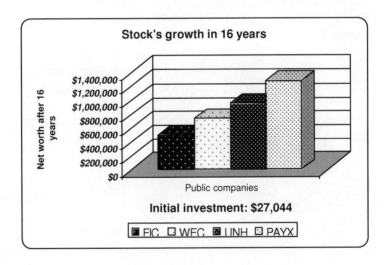

Jessica was impressed. "Wow, if we had invested $27,000 in *PayChex* in 1990, we would have been millionaires in 2003."

Sam showed them another one. "Take a look at this. Here are some comparisons of stocks earning an average 15% return per year and growing for 17 years with an initial investment of $46,462."

Figure 2.9: Investment growth of some stocks in 17 years
Note: Initial investment is taken from Figure 2.5

Initial invest-tment	Number of years	Company	Net worth as of 14th July 2003	Average annual compo-unded interest %
$46,462	17	Merck & Co	$0.605 million	16.30
		Procter & Gamble	$0.610 million	16.35
		Gillette & Co	$0.617 million	16.43
		Altria (Formerly Philip Morris)	$0.695 million	17.25
		Colgate Palmolive	$0.768 million	17.95
		Medtronic Inc.	$2.038 million	24.90

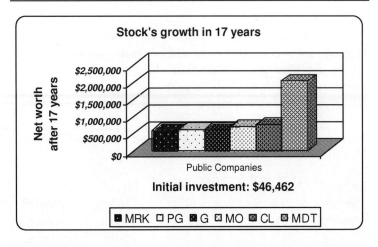

"Again, let's go back to a smaller amount. If you thought $18,780 could never grow into half a million, here is proof that shows the growth of stocks that had averaged 20% for the past 18 years. This growth would have made our initial investment of $18,780 half a million or much more than that."

Figure 2.10: Investment growth of some stocks in 18 years
Note: Initial investment is taken from Figure 2.5

Initial investment	Number of Years	Company	Net worth as of 14th July 2003	Average annual compounded interest %
$18,780	18	Wal-Mart	$0.59 million	21.10
	18	Lowe's Corporation	$0.67 million	21.96
	13	Eaton Vance Corp	$0.86 million	34.20
	18	Best Buy	$1.6 million	28.01
	16	Harley Davidson	$2.11 million	34.33
	18	Home Depot	$2.42 million	30.99
	18	Microsoft	$3.07 million	32.73
	15	Dell	$6.07 million	47.00

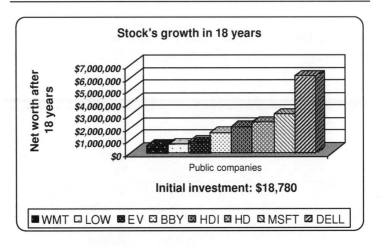

James commented, "I can also see the companies you mentioned here manufacture products we use day-to-day. Hmm, very interesting!"

The Mystery Behind the Charts

There was a hushed silence in the room as everyone studied the charts. They seemed to show that making a million dollars is not a Herculean effort after all.

Sam continued, "I'm sure you must be convinced that the best way to raise money for your children's education is to allow the entire investment grow at an excellent rate. You may want to find great stocks that allow your investments to grow between 15% and 20%. I am soon going to delve into the mechanics of finding such companies."

Sweet Sixty

Don't simply retire from something; have
something to retire to.
Harry Emerson Fosdick

Joe said, "Okay, let's take retirement now. Some people may have children and some may not, but everyone has to retire one day. I read that the average life span is expected to be 90 years due to advancements in medicine and technology."

Bill asked, "What retirement expenses might we have when we are, say, 65? We would have paid off our mortgage and car loans, and our commute to work would be eliminated. Then there are social security and Medicare."

Steve, James' poker friend, replied, "I agree Bill, but even though our life span is 90 years, we wouldn't be able to work until the last day just to make ends meet. Assuming you've paid off your mortgage, car loan, etc., your monthly expenses would average between 70% and 75% of your current monthly expenses. You would need insurance for your home. Even though major expenses like traveling to work, work clothes, etc. would not be required, you would still need to eat, sleep and entertain. And don't forget health-related expenses. Social Security and Medicare definitely do not suffice."

Sam continued, "Thank you, sir. Assuming we retire at age 65 and 75% of our expenses add up to $2,000 as of today, let's find out how much we'll need yearly to meet our day-to-day expenses after we retire." He showed them the following table.

Figure 2.11: Cost of Retirement (Assuming 6% Inflation)

Age	Number of years to retire	Yearly expenses at 65	Total retirement cost (Yearly expenses at 65 * 25 years)
25	40	$360,000	$9 million
30	35	$258,000	$6.5 million
35	30	$182,400	$4.5 million
40	25	$130,800	$3.27 million

Note: Due to advancement in the field of medicine, the average person is expected to live until 90.

"So, the total retirement cost is calculated as annual cost of living at the age of 65 * the number of years of living after retirement. If someone retires at 65 and lives until 90, then he has 25 years of retirement life to lead."

More than 21 million Americans aged 55 or older are a part of the workforce.

Every month, nearly one million senior Americans search for work.

Costs Involved

If you don't set goals for yourself, you are doomed to
work to achieve the goals of someone else
Brian Tracy

Sam said, "Let me ask you to do a fundamental calculation.

"Add up the following figures and decide whether it would be possible to meet your goals if you saved your money in a bank or mutual fund."

Cost of raising a child including college expenses: Half a million dollars per child

Retirement costs (for 20 years): $4.5 million (at least)

Insurance costs (for 20 years): $1 million

"If you want to retire at age 65, you'll need a minimum of six to ten million dollars just to meet your basic expenses.

"Answer me honestly, would you be able to raise six million dollars just by saving in the bank, or would you like to explore how to make six million dollars with your income?"

Bill exclaimed, "Man! This guy with these astronomical figures is sure going to keep the ER in this town busy."

 *Wal-Mart* is one of the largest employers of seniors. More than 22% of Wal-Mart's 1.1 million workers are seniors aged above 55.

More than 3,000 employees of *Wal-Mart* are aged 80 and above.

The Cure for Inflation and Taxes – Stocks

*The measure of success is not whether you have a
tough problem to deal with, but whether it is the same
problem you had last year*
John Foster Dulles

Joe said, "Didn't I warn you? Anyway, let's listen to Sam the Wise."

Sam went on. "Every day, when you work for eight hours, you lose three hours of pay in taxes. In fact, May 3rd is known as tax freedom day. In other words, whatever you earn from January 1st until May 2nd goes to taxes. Everything after that goes to you."

"Similarly, every year an average of 6% increase in prices happens automatically without your knowledge. You pay more for gas, for a gallon of milk, for electricity, for your walkman batteries, etc. This happens no matter how the economy or the stock market is doing. In fact, the better the economy, the higher the inflation. The reason is that money flows more rapidly when the economy is doing well.

"So, every year we lose an average of 10% of our savings from inflation and taxes. Unless your investment earns 10% compounded, you are actually losing your investment value. If you are earning 10%, then you are only breaking even. If you need to make more than 10%, the only solution is to invest in stocks."

Effect of Inflation

It isn't necessary to be rich and famous to be happy.
It's only necessary to be rich.
Alan Alda

Jessica said, "Let's go back to the interest we get investing in banks. What would they be worth in, say, 20 or 30 years?"

Sam agreed. "Let me show you what your investment would be worth, based on the inflation and taxes that we pay on the investment.

"Every year, we lose 6% on inflation and another 2% of our investment to taxes (assuming your tax bracket is around 24%). In total, we lose 8% of our investment every year. Let's compare the net worth of our investment if we earn anything less than 8%."

Figure 2.12: Effect of earning interest less than inflation rate

Amount invested every month ($)	Number of years of regular month-ly Invest-ment	Total amount invested ($)	Interest earn-ed (%)	Actual net worth (Purch-asing power in today's $)
100	20	24,000	2	5,983
200	30	72,000	5	19,026
500	40	240,000	5	31,434
1,000	30	360,000	5	76,104

"Even if your contribution is very high and your bank balance shows $360,000, the net worth would be only $76,104. In other words, if your dream is to buy a Lamborghini after 30 years at a cost of $360,000, you would be definitely wrong. With the amount you saved, you may be able to buy a Corvette, but definitely not a Lamborghini."

Bill said, "Forget it, man! After listening to you, I don't think I can even buy a bicycle after 30 years."

Sam said, "That's because you finally understand the problem. I have the solution too. Invest in the right stocks."

Brazil in the 1990s was experiencing 20% inflation every month. Even though people were earning the same salary, they were getting poorer every day

"Now if you invest in stocks, you could get anywhere between 15% and 20%. You not only beat inflation but also earn money for your investments. See how a 15%-20% return works out for various monthly amounts invested."

Figure 2.13: Effect of earning interest higher than inflation rate

Amount invested every month ($)	Number of years ($)	Total amount invested ($)	Interest earned %	Actual net worth (Purchasing power in today's $)
100	20	24,000	15	30,389
200	30	72,000	20	420,234
500	40	240,000	20	3,447,909
1,000	30	360,000	15	633,088

Steve, who was watching everything unfold, spoke. "The chart proves two things. First, it is not the amount we invest that matters, but it is the number of years we need to wait before we reap the rewards. Second, the interest we earn on our investments matters."

Jessica admitted, "It is very true, and the numbers speak for themselves. $500 invested for 40 years at a 20% return is much higher than $1,000 invested for 30 years at a 15% return."

Sam collected his papers and said, "So would you like your money to work in your favor or against? The choice is yours."

The Gallup Organization found that seven out of ten Americans expect to work part time after they retire.

53% of workers aged 40 and above have saved less than $100,000 for retirement, a far cry from the minimum comfortable retirement savings required.

Who wants to be a Millionaire? – Different Routes, Same Goals

Planning is bringing the future into the present so that you can do something about it now
Alan Lakein

Sam added, "Who doesn't want to be a millionaire? You might want to buy a beach house in Florida that costs a million dollars. You might not have that kind of money today, but you would like to buy one when you are 65 so you can retire peacefully."

"There are different routes to retiring as a millionaire, and we'll explore every one of them. Here let's assume your goal is to retire at 65 as a millionaire in today's dollars."

"Since the inflation rate is 6% and we normally pay around 30% to 33% in taxes, the actual rate of depreciation is 9% a year. Here we have two factors: one is your age, and the other the interest that you earn on your investments.

"We'll find out the monthly contribution required to raise a million dollars in today's value when you reach 65."

Figure 2.14: Monthly investment required to retire with million dollars in today's value at 65

Current age	Investment growth at 2% ($)	Investment growth at 5% ($)	Investment growth at 10% ($)	Investment growth at 15% ($)	Investment growth at 20% ($)
20	64,638	27,899	5,393	863	125
25	49,166	23,662	5,709	1,164	215
30	37,961	20,300	6,074	1,571	371
35	29,896	17,699	6,516	2,127	641
40	20,384	14,619	7,913	4,013	1,932

The United States more than any other country owes its wealth, prosperity and prestige to the efforts of individuals like John Rockefeller, J. Pierpoint Morgan, Andrew Carnegie, Henry Ford and F.W. Woolworth.

Joe said, "Sam, this has been very insightful. You could not have stressed more that stocks are the only way to beat inflation. But I know several people in my family who have invested quite heavily in the stock market. The only sad part is they lost heavily. What do you have to say about that?"

Sam answered, "I am not sure what method they used to choose the specific companies in which they invested. Even in choosing the right companies, specific techniques and methodologies should be adopted."

Joe offered, "Hey, tomorrow we have a dinner get-together at my place. Why don't you guys join us, and we can hear from people who have burned their fingers investing in stocks."

Sam was only too pleased to accept his invitation. He thought maybe he could ask Jessica out during dinner. He was quite sure he had earned some points with her. We'll see!

 One in two Americans invests in stocks. It is for this reason that the U.S. remained powerful after the Civil War.

More than one billion shares are traded in the New York Stock Exchange every day. The U.S. has more public companies than any other country in the world.

Sam's Sprinkles

- Investing in stocks is one way to become wealthy.

- Even though banks retain our principal, it loses its value due to inflation.

- Mutual funds and banks in turn invest our money in stocks.

- To get better returns, it is better to invest directly in stocks.

- The U.S Government provides various methods to get the maximum tax-free returns.

- The average inflation rate is 6%. Even if you have investments in banks, they automatically lose around 9% due to inflation and taxes.

- You need more than four million dollars to retire and live comfortably.

- By investing in stocks, not only is your money growing, you are also helping the companies grow.

- Schemes like Education IRAs and Roth IRAs allow the entire returns to grow tax-free.

- These opportunities are not only for Buffetts and Lynches. They are for common investors like you and me.

- Stocks are not like a lottery or gambling, where luck plays a vital role.

- Warren Buffett is considered to be a wise man and not a lucky man.

- Stock picking is like any other profession. It needs to be understood before you do it.

- Focus only on stocks, because you reap the maximum returns. Other investments are indirectly invested in stocks, giving lower returns.

- Making great returns from stocks is not magic. It is a proven science.

- If you ever doubt whether stocks are risky, just bok at the car you are driving. It is manufactured by a public company.

- You can buy even one share of stocks. In other words, even with a minimum investment, you can become a shareholder.

- You don't need to search far for information. Information about every public company is available on the Internet.

- You can do research in your leisure time. You don't have to spend your entire weekend looking for a great stock.

- It is easy to buy and sell stocks. It takes ten seconds to buy and another ten seconds to sell.

Chapter III

Who is Dollar Wise Penny Foolish?

Blind Followers or Salt Pinchers?

Change before you have to
Jack Welch

Love Thy Money

Teach a parrot the terms "supply and demand" and
you've got an economist
Thomas Carlyle

"Sam! You have a phone call!" his mom called out. Sam was pleasantly surprised to hear the chirpy voice of Jessica, on the phone.

"Morning! Would you like to grab a bagel?" she asked. Sam agreed and said he would meet her in a few minutes at the place she mentioned.

Sam's dad joked, "Well, it looks like Cupid has a station in Wall Street."

Sam and Jessica occupied a cozy corner in the crowded shop. "Sam, I should really thank you for taking the time and effort to educate us about investments."

Sam smiled. She continued, "So, tell me, how is it you are so knowledgeable about stocks?"

Sam took a sip of the coffee. "Thanks Jess. I actually got into the habit of reading quite early. My mother always read to me when I was a child. One of my uncles was an avid investor and he always talked about companies, how they are formed, etc. He also suggested a number of books. He always spoke about Warren Buffett, Lee Iaccocca, Henry Ford, Benjamin Franklin and Peter Lynch. He was a positive influence in my life and because of him, whenever I look at a product, I immediately think of the company that manufactures it. I would also look up information about that particular company. I've done it so much, it has become a habit now.

"I also took several classes to understand certain subjects in depth. In fact, I am happy I have an eager audience now."

Jessica remarked, "It all started as a simple class discussion, right?" Sam nodded in agreement.

Jessica said, "I think I will also have to take some classes to understand how to pick the right companies. Looking at your charts illustrating the past performance of certain good companies, I wish I had invested in them. Some of them are too good to be true."

Sam said, "You don't necessarily have to take courses on accounting or finance. I think we can learn some valuable lessons about investing from everyday decisions we make. Some knowledge of basic arithmetic would be helpful though."

Jessica sighed, "There you go again. If only it were that simple."

They finished their breakfast and were ready to leave.

Sam said, "It is, and I will make a deal with you. You spend the entire day with me, and I will tell you how you can compare your simple decisions with choosing companies."

Jessica agreed, "Absolutely! How about I meet you here after an hour? We can talk, catch a movie, and have lunch. What do you say?"

Sam agreed, "Yes ma'am, I will see you in an hour." Sam was on top of the world. He thought to himself that his financial knowledge was not only compounding his money but also earning a pretty woman's interest.

Grant Me Patience-Now!

You must first have a lot of patience to learn to have patience
Stainslaw J. Lec

Jessica was waiting for Sam. Her cell phone announced Sam's call. He said he was going to be another 15 minutes late. Finally he showed up and apologized profusely.

Jessica smiled, "Sam, that's okay. You called and explained. It's all right."

Sam said, "Jess, thanks for waiting, In fact, you have already learned the first and most important lesson in investing: *Patience!*"

Jessica laughed, "What?"

Sam said, "Let me tell you about an incident in Warren Buffet's life.

"As a youngster, Warren Buffett had an affinity for numbers, impressing his friends by memorizing the population of scores of U.S. cities. At age 11, he bought his first stock, three shares of *Cities Service Preferred* at $38 a share. The price immediately dropped to $27, but then recovered to $40, at which point the young Buffett sold - making a $2 profit, but missing the company's subsequent rise to $200 a share. It was Buffett's first lesson in patience. He learned that investing requires tremendous patience."

Jessica remarked, "Well, I don't have the 'tremendous patience' you speak of, but for a million bucks, I guess it's worth a shot."

Sam laughed. They headed for the local movie theatre.

Sam exclaimed, "Wow! There are so many movies. I am confused about which one to watch. How about we just pick a random movie? I am guessing it should be good, since all of them are screened in a good theatre."

Jessica wondered if that was a loaded question.

Before Jessica answered, they saw Bill and Troy rushing toward them.

"Hey you guys, we didn't expect to see you here. Why don't we watch a movie together?" Bill asked.

Sam reluctantly said, "Sure, pick a movie, anything is fine."

Troy said, "What do you mean, 'Anything is fine'? I have to spend $8 for the ticket and $3 for snacks. I don't want to watch a movie I know I won't like."

Sam asked, "How do you know whether it is a good movie?"

Troy answered, "I always check the movie reviews in the papers or the *TV Guide (GMST)*, read the synopsis of the movie, and I watch it only if I like it."

So it was left to Troy to choose the movie. After the show, Troy said, "You guys should thank me for suggesting this one. It was worth every penny, wasn't it?"

What's In a Name?

> *The ark was built by amateurs, and the Titanic was*
> *built by Professionals*
> Anonymous

Sam said, "Jess, that is lesson number two in choosing good companies. See how Troy thinks and analyzes before choosing a movie to watch, because he does not want to waste ten bucks? Apply the same logic to investing. *Do not choose a stock based just on its name.* A lot of people choose to invest in certain companies in order to fit into a group.

"Most investors at some point felt that *Enron* was a big name and invested in the company. Later, after sustaining heavy losses, they agreed they could not understand *Enron's* complex financial statements. When asked why they invested when they did not understand, they simply said that a company as big as *Enron* would never fail."

The friends walked to a restaurant that had an open café. A Hummer zoomed past them, and Bill could not take his eyes off of it. Jessica asked Bill, "You love that car, don't you? I bet when you have enough money, you'll dash to a *GM* dealer and buy the gleaming yellow chariot, no questions asked."

Bill laughed, "I sure do admire that car, but I would never buy a car that way. I don't think that would be a good decision."

Sam said, "Why not? I am sure if you walk into a dealership, the car salesman would be able to guide you in making the right decision."

Bill said, "It's true that I want to own a great car like a *Hummer (GM)*. On an impulse, I would even go to the dealer to check out the car and get the salesperson's opinion. However I would never buy a car that way. The car salesman is only going to elaborate on the car's positive aspects. I would test drive the car I am interested in, compare it to similar cars in the same category, read *Consumer Reports*, and then make an informed decision."

Sam smiled, "That's the next lesson. Bill has the answer for how not to choose a bad company. Never ever buy a stock on an impulse. Never buy a stock because your friend owns stocks in that company or boasts about it at a party."

Troy asked, "What if it turns out to be a good company?"

Sam answered, "The probability of that happening is very low. Proper analysis is the only way to choose the right companies. Don't you agree that before we buy anything, we need to investigate and analyze thoroughly? When you are prepared to do research before you spend $8 for a movie and $50 a month for a cell phone, why would you buy stocks based on just its name or on an impulse? When you are prepared to test drive every car and read *Consumer Reports* before making a decision on cars, why do you invest in stocks by simply trusting the words of your advisor?"

Troy said, "Point taken. By the way, Lisa finally agreed to go out with me. I want to take her to the best restaurant in town. On one hand, there are excellent restaurants that have been providing consistent gourmet food for the past ten years, and there are some new ones, which seem to be serving good food on some days and really bad food on others. I am torn between the two types."

Jessica said, "I think it is safe for you to choose the one which has always served good food."

Finance Feast

There are two classes of forecasters: Those who don't know--and those who don't know they don't know
Anonymous

Sam said, "Excellent! This is the point I was trying to make all along. Choosing the right stocks is as simple as Bill's choosing a restaurant for an important evening. Would you buy stocks that have consistently performed well or others that go up and down like a seesaw?"

He continued, "We have all the skills and common sense when it comes to day-to-day life. If we just apply them to investing, no one is going to lose. Okay, I think I am going to take off. I will see you guys at Jessica's tonight."

The house had all the trimmings of a party. Music, food, the works! Sam took considerable care to dress for the occasion. He spotted Jessica and his other friends.

Jessica introduced Sam to her parents. Frank, Jessica's father, said, "Nice to meet you, Sam. I have been hearing a lot about you. I would like to have a long chat with you sometime."

Sam answered, "Likewise, sir."

Frank left them to attend to some other guest. Sam seized the moment to compliment Jessica. "You look great, Jess."

Jessica smiled, "Thanks! So do you! By the way, thanks for the movie, lunch and the investing tips. Let me see if I can remember. Have patience when you invest, don't buy stocks based on the name, never buy stocks on an impulse, and always pick companies that give consistent returns."

Sam admitted, "Very impressive!"

Joe came in with a middle-aged couple. He said "Aunt Sylvia, Uncle George, please meet Sam, the Warren Buffet of our town." Sam was starting to get used to this kind of introduction. He shook hands with the couple. Joe went to find his parents and left the three to get acquainted.

"So, son," Uncle George started the conversation, "Joe tells me you have been giving nuggets of financial advice to your friends. Actually, we had invested quite a bit of money in the stock market and lost a hefty sum in the process. I don't think I can quite get over it."

Sam said, "I am very sorry to hear that."

Uncle George continued, "Since I had made a lot of money and wanted it to grow, I thought I would get someone's help. I sought the help of a financial broker to put together my portfolio. I followed every word of his. I bought all the companies he recommended. I don't know what I did wrong, but I have suffered such a loss. It's unimaginable."

A young couple joined them. They introduced themselves as Greg and Kara. Greg said, "I couldn't help overhearing the conversation here. I lost quite a bit in the stock market too. I did not buy stocks based on the name or because a broker asked me to. In fact, I invested in companies recommended by financial magazines and websites.

"I thought they could never go wrong. If I read something good about a company, I bought their stocks. If there was disturbing news about that company, I sold my stocks."

Kara added, "I think I prefer to watch the financial shows on TV and make my decisions based on them. You don't even have to spend a lot of time reading the paper."

Within minutes, several members joined the group. Joe and his friends joined them too.

Joe began, "Sam, you have been giving out financial advice to novices like me. Agreed, we had never thought of investing. What about these people? They seem to have adopted various solid methods to invest. Why did they lose their money?"

Sam introduced himself to the group, "My name is Sam. Joe and I take a class together. Analyzing stocks is my hobby as I am very much interested in making lots of money."

Listen To Everyone, Follow No One

> *90% of people in the stock market simply haven't done enough homework*
> William O'Neil

Someone interrupted, "Who isn't interested in making lots of money?"

The group let out a small laugh. Sam continued, "I have done a good amount of research in the field of investing and have come up with a set of approaches to find good companies.

"Let me ask you all a question. I think some of you are investing based on advice from a financial advisor, some depending heavily on financial articles or papers, a few by watching the financial shows on TV. How many of you have researched the company?

"Have you done any research on the products made by these companies make or the debt they have? Have you read the annual reports and tried to understand those numbers?"

Aunt Sylvia asked, "Why would a financial advisor ask you to invest in a bad company? I am sure he must have researched the companies before suggesting them to us."

Sam said, "I hate to give you disturbing news, but I have to tell you the truth. Stockbrokers do not necessarily need to be highly qualified. Some major firms even hire people who have filed bankruptcy in the past to work as their brokers. You would be shocked to know that a broker from a financial firm used to sell women's clothing. Granted, he might have passed the necessary exams, but you have gone to him thinking that he has solid experience in the area and would dispense very wise ideas."

Costly Mistakes

Wall Street is the only place people ride to in a Rolls Royce to get advice from people who take the subway
Warren Buffett

"Would you get job search tips from an MBA graduate who is out of work for a year? Would you seek retirement advice from a 70-year-old man holding two jobs and struggling to make ends meet?

"In the case of stockbrokers, there is a startling truth that some financial firms give preferential treatment to customers who are already wealthy. Also, I am sure most people who get the help of stockbrokers never really make the effort to ask them the right questions.

"Besides, stockbrokers put the financial interests of their company before your financial interests. It is quite okay to speak to a broker, but you have to do your homework.

"In fact, Peter Lynch has said, *'Stop listening to professionals. Twenty years in this business convinces me that any normal person using their customary three percent of the brain can pick stocks just as well, if not better, than the average Wall Street expert.'*"

Greg said, "I can't understand how financial magazines can be wrong. They have several top ten lists of stocks to buy or a list of worst performing stocks to avoid. You cannot deny the fact that the people who compile these lists do a lot of research on these companies. There are several news clips about what the future holds for certain companies. Don't you think we can rely on them?"

Sam said, "I agree with you. Let me give you an example. Do you know how many drugs are sent to the *FDA* for approval? Anywhere between 63 and 84 per year. How many do you think get approved? Just 25 to 37. I am sure pharmaceutical companies don't send drugs that are not fit for humans. According to a study, an average drug takes 10 to 12 years to develop and costs millions of dollars to the company. Then why does the *FDA* reject most of them?

"Would people be happy if the *FDA* approved all drugs simply because they were created by someone with a Ph.D.?

"Even after a drug goes through several rounds of testing and clinical studies by the company where it was formulated, it could still have some harmful or undesirable side effects. Hence, the *FDA* rejects it.

"Similarly, I agree with you that the stocks listed as top ten in several papers or magazines can be considered. But, like the *FDA*, we should do a solid amount of research and filter out the companies that fail our tests."

Ad-*Vice*

An economist is an expert who will know tomorrow why the things he predicted yesterday didn't happen today

Laurence J. Peter

Sam continued, "All I am telling you is not to rely solely on one form of research. Advisors are not always right or wrong. Investing in stocks is easy but requires effort. Before buying a company's shares, you should always check if the company is financially stable, and if the stock is priced right. It is definitely not rocket science.

"Aunt Sylvia, would you simply trust a car salesman and buy a car based on his recommendation? He is definitely suggesting a good car, but wouldn't you test-drive it and check if it is at the right price before you make your decision? Why not apply the same principle to buying stocks?

"An expert opinion from a financial advisor is no different from a sales pitch by a car salesman. During the dotcom boom, analysts from *Salomon Smith Barney* not only touted the stocks of *Enron* but also made sure their clients bought them. In fact, they were getting rid of their own Enron stocks...by selling them to their own clients!

"Greg, would you buy a car based on *Consumer Reports'* top five ratings and change your car next year because the car ratings fell? Solely relying on famous names, hot news, or tips obtained at a cocktail party are not reliable methods. You can use the newspaper reports or TV shows as a cross-reference for the research you do about the companies you are interested in."

Uncle George asked, "What do you suggest? Is there one proven method to buy stocks?"

Sam answered, "There isn't *one* proven method, but there are quite a few formulas that can be used to choose right companies. In fact, I am writing several papers on this, and I would be happy to show them to you.

"People like Buffett and Lynch are not born millionaires, they are self-made. Buffetts and Lynches don't buy stocks that are not available to us. One thing I can assure you is that you don't have to be a Buffett or Lynch to pick stocks, whose value not only significantly rise in the long term but also never lose their original investment.

"Losing money is definitely not a pleasant experience for anyone. If stocks are the best forms of investment to get great returns and the safest investment vehicle, why do common investors keep losing money? Is it because of bad luck?

"The only sure way to make money in stocks is to understand and invest after analyzing the company's various financial reports that are filed with the *Securities and Exchange Commission (SEC)*. That is why Warren Buffett and Peter Lynch are regarded as great stock pickers. Even Warren Buffett, who is considered as a genius in investing, wouldn't buy stocks without spending sufficient time on research.

"There are approximately 12,000 companies traded in the *New York Stock Exchange* and *NASDAQ*. Not all of the 12,000 are great companies to invest in. If every company were great to invest in, then no one would ever lose money in stocks. There are only a few companies that can produce great returns. But how do we identify them?

"If you are wondering why every company does not produce great returns and show excellent growth, the simple answer is, why doesn't everyone who participates in a marathon complete it? It is not easy to survive the tough competition that is present in a capitalistic country like the U.S. Only a few companies can raise the required money. Only a few companies have the right people who work very hard. Therefore, only a few companies can win the race."

Do the Math

Statistics are like a bikini. What they reveal is suggestive, but what they conceal is vital
Aaron Levenstein

There were lots of murmurs and discussions going on. Some people went to Sam and expressed an interest in reading the papers he was going to write.

Joe said, "I am definitely learning a lot of things. But you are killing us here! We are convinced that stocks are the best form of investment, and learned what we should not do, but how do we pick the right companies? What is the formula, what is the technique?"

Sam laughed, "I am sorry, you guys. This was the non-math part every investor should know. I am going to tell you what those formulae are and how you should shortlist companies.

"In fact, I am going to teach you the techniques and methodologies one by one, and you will do the research and pick the companies."

Jessica said, "Cool! That is perfect. What about the road trip we were planning? Maybe we could just drive to Las Vegas. I have some friends there. We could pitch a tent with them."

Sam said, "How about we leave this Friday afternoon? Sharpen your math skills, because I am going to dive right into 'earnings per share', 'debt', 'cash flow', 'return on equity', etc."

Bill asked, "Why are you suddenly talking in Greek?"

Sam laughed, "Don't worry Bill, I will teach all the concepts one at a time. We will learn to pick companies by each criterion. After I am completely done, you will be able to read financial statements and balance sheets like a pro."

Sam's Sprinkles

• Patience, however difficult it may be, is the first key to investing successfully.

• However convincing the news or report is, it is prudent to do research before investing.

• The broker who is employed by a major firm puts the firm's interest before the investor's interest.

• The purpose of articles published by various financial magazines and websites is only to entertain you.

• News only speaks about what happened yesterday and today; it never foresees what will happen in the long run.

• Warren Buffett, during his most famous annual shareholder's meeting, once said that if a stock is not good to hold for 10 years, then it is not good stock to hold even for 10 minutes. The *Wall Street Journal* runs a regular competition that demonstrates this, pitting expert stock pickers against stocks chosen randomly via the dartboard, and the dartboard often wins.

• The writers who publish articles in financial news journals may tout various stocks, but they do not usually own them.

• It is not possible to become rich based on the recommendations from television and newspaper articles. If becoming a millionaire were as easy as watching television, then 100% of the U.S. population would be millionaires, not just 8%.

• Newspapers and television should be treated as providers of financial entertainment and not as financial advisors.

• Even geniuses like Warren Buffett or Peter Lynch do thorough research before investing their money.

• Every company that filed for bankruptcy or caused shareholders to lose money had numerous early warning signals.

Self-Explorer

- If you have invested in even one company in the past, can you justify your investment choice with five facts?

- Visit any of the financial web sites (http://moneycentral.msn.com, www.fool.com) and confirm if the author of an article that touts particular stocks also owns them.

- Pick a stock that is touted by any analyst or the author of an article. Verify the ratings from various financial websites including http://moneycentral.msn.com, www.zacks.com, www.quicken.com (One-click stock analysis).

Popular Financial Websites

- www.morningstar.com
- www.money.com
- http://moneycentral.msn.com
- http://finance.yahoo.com
- www.zacks.com
- www.thestreet.com
- www.smartmoney.com
- www.nyse.com
- www.nasdaq.com

Chapter IV

Who is Dollar Wise Penny Foolish?

Profit Makers or Promise Makers?

If little kids don't aspire to make money like I did,
what the hell good is this country?
Lee Iacocca

Take *Stock*

When money talks, there are few interruptions
Herbert V.Prochnow

"*Viva Las Vegas...*" Bill was exercising his vocal chords with the famous Elvis number. Joe commented, "I can't believe you are joining us on this trip, especially since it is about understanding stocks and learning to choose good companies."

Bill replied, "Why not! A little work and a little fun doesn't hurt anybody!"

Kathy, Jessica's friend, called her and was quite surprised to learn of Jessica's trip. "Kathy, this was a last minute decision. I didn't mean to ditch you. I will spend time with you after I return." Jessica tried to convince her.

Kathy replied, 'Jess, tell me something. Is it the 'stocks' that is pulling you to go on this trip or is it the other 'S'?"

Jessica laughed and hung up after her parting answer, "*Both*".

Sam announced, "Well, looks like everyone is here. Let's get moving and start the enlightenment process with 'earnings per share'."

Troy replied, "Not so fast! Can you briefly tell us what 'stocks' are? I will drive the first leg of the trip."

Sam began, "Sure. When you buy even one stock of a company, you become a shareholder of the company. In other words, when you buy even a single share of *Home Depot (HD)*, you become a shareholder and owner of *Home Depot.*

"You find that *Home Depot* is a profit making company and realize that it is worth buying their shares. So you go ahead and buy a share of the company. There are 2.3 billion shares available in the market. When you own a single share, you actually own one-2.3 billionth of *Home Depot*. At the same time, if you buy 100 shares of *Dell*, then you own 100/2.6 billion units of *Dell (DELL)*.

"You are entitled to be an owner of a big corporation even without physically stepping into the office. You can elect the board of directors, participate in all the decision-making processes, and most importantly share the profits of the company. The more shares you own, the more profits you could reap. You can even vote on who should be the next CEO of the company, and your vote counts when a merger takes place.

"That is why *Oracle (ORCL)* directly appealed to the shareholders of *PeopleSoft (PSFT)* to approve their merger. If the shareholders had decided to approve the merger of *PeopleSoft* with *Oracle*, then even the CEO of the company could not have changed the decision. Even though Hewlett strongly opposed the merger of *Hewlett Packard* with *Compaq*, the shareholders approved it and now *Hewlett Packard (HPQ)* is successfully merged with *Compaq*. Once a corporation becomes a public company, the shareholders make every major decision.

"So instead of thinking that stocks are risky, think that you own a business and become part of a business without physically having to run the corporation. By buying shares of *Dell* you don't need to physically relocate to Austin, TX, you can still own *Dell*. You don't need to manage the employees, but you are part of *Dell's* success.

"If you want to share the profits of any company, the best way is to own the shares of the company."

Jessica added, "No wonder CEOs are quite wealthy!"

Sam continued, "Right. Why is Larry Ellison the ninth richest man (as of 6/23/03) in the world? Do you think he saved every profit from *Oracle*? Not really. Larry Ellison owns several jets and big mansions in addition to the stocks of *Oracle*. So the more stocks Larry Ellison owns, the more profits he shares. The reason CEOs are rich is not that they are paid very huge salaries, but that they have high ownership rights in the company. Normally a CEO owns around 10% or more of the shares. Of course, this differs from corporation to corporation."

Bill said, "Great! Now that we know a little about stocks, Sam, can you please unlock the first secret of finding the right company?"

Joe added, "Also, I hope you have your laptop. I am so used to seeing your charts and tables. They're like salsa. We need them to eat your chips."

Reap the Profits

I walk slowly, but I never walk backward
Abraham Lincoln

Sam laughed. He said, "Before you invest in a company, it is very important to find out whether the company is running profitably. I'm sure you don't want to invest in companies that are running at a loss and which are not capable of producing profits."

Jessica nodded in agreement.

Sam continued, "Say, there is a mall close to your home. You find two stores in the mall that interest you. How will you know which one is doing good business? Let us assume that these two stores are *'Cookies Plaza'* and *'Sports Equipment Store'*. What information do we need to determine if the stores are running profitably? First, we need the annual sales that each store is making and the total expenses that are involved in running the store.

"Let us compare them in detail now."

Figure 4.1: Net income of two different stores

	Cookies Plaza	**Sports Equipment Store**
Total sales	$53,000	$72,000
Total expenses	$42,000	$55,000
Net profit (Income)	$11,000	$17,000

"So which one of these stores makes more profits?"

Joe answered, "Even Bill can conclude that it is *Sports Equipment Store* that is more successful."

Bill gave Joe a playful smack.

Sam said, "The first rule of investing is: 'The company must generate great profits'. The company should deliver results to its investors who contribute money. A company that cannot produce profits and therefore cannot deliver results is not the right one to choose."

Joe confirmed, "So however big a company is, it is not worth considering if it does not make profits."

Sam said, "Exactly! The companies that don't make profits are like black holes of the universe. In a physical black hole, light waves go in but never come out. Similarly, a company that doesn't generate profits takes in your money but doesn't produce returns.

"There is a risk of losing our investment with companies that don't generate profits. Companies that generate profits not only help us sleep better but will also make our investments grow in the long run."

Joe asked, "Can you boot up your laptop and show us some companies that generated profits and some that did not?"

Sam answered, "You bet! Take a look!

"For the year 2002, let us compare the net profits of a few companies:

Figure 4.2: Net Income of public companies for the year 2002
Note: The number in brackets represents losses
Source: Morningstar, Inc.

Company	Ticker	Net income in millions (For the year 2002)
NVR	NVR	$331.5
Hovnanian Enterprises	HOV	$137.7
Harley Davidson	HDI	$580.2
Lucent	LU	$(11,949.00)
American Airlines	AMR	$(3,511.10)
XM Satellite Radio	XMSR	$(515.90)

"Now if you have to invest, which one would you choose? Would you choose a company that makes profits, so that it can return some share of its profits to you, or a company that doesn't make profits but that hopes to do well in the future?"

Bill asked, "So, if I had invested in *Harley Davidson*, I would have made money and lost quite a bit if I had chosen *Lucent.*"

Sam nodded in agreement. He continued, "See what would have happened if you had invested $10,000 in 1993 in both types of companies."

Figure 4.3: Result of investing in companies, which makes profits

Source: Morningstar, Inc.

Company	Net income in millions (For 2002)	Value of $10,000 invested on July 16, 1993	Net gain (Original investment: $10,000)	Annual growth %
		Period: 10 Years (July 16,1993 – July 16, 2003)		
NVR	$331.5	$106,540	$96,540	60.51
Hovnanian Enterprises	$137.7	$57,836	$47,836	42.04
Harley Davidson	$580.2	$22,362	$12,362	17.46

"The above example clearly shows that a company making profits is able to generate great returns for its shareholders."

Jessica said, "Show us the ones that didn't make profits, please."

Sam showed her the chart.

"Now, let's investigate what would have happened to our investments, if we had invested in companies which were not making money but just taking money from us."

Figure 4.4: Result of investing in companies that doesn't generate profits

Source: Morningstar, Inc.

Company	Net income in millions (For 2002)	Value of $10,000 as of July 16, 2003, invested on July 16,1993	Net gain (Original investment: $10,000)	Annual growth % (Compound interest earned)
		Period: 10 Years (July 16,1993 – July 16, 2003)		
Lucent	$(11,949)	$ 549.00	Loss of $9451	-44.03
American Airlines	$(3,511)	$3,169.00	Loss of $6831	-20.53
XM Satellite Radio	$(515)	$6,782.00	Loss of $3218	-7.47

"Let us compare the same in a graph.

"The graph clearly indicates that companies that were losing the original investments are *Lucent, American Airlines and XM Satellite Radio* whereas *Hovnanian Enterprises, NVR* and *Harley Davidson* provided great returns for the investors. So are you convinced that the stocks that grow in value are the ones that make profits?"

Source: Morningstar, Inc.

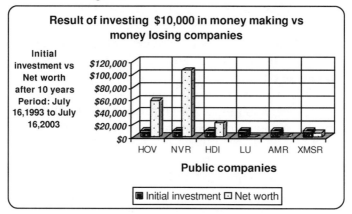

Joe concluded, "So the above example stresses the fact that a company which makes profits is the one which provides great returns to its shareholders."

Sam said, "Well, that is the very first step, but there is more."

Measure Up

> *Common sense is calculation applied to life*
> Henri-Frederic Amiel

They stopped at a rest area. When they were alone, Jessica told Sam about the question her friend Kathy had.

Unable to control his anxiety, Sam asked her, "So which 'S' is it?"

Bill suddenly appeared from nowhere and declared that he would not get into the car without grabbing a bite.

They all walked to the restaurant. Sam was dying to know Jessica's answer. He thought grudgingly, "Somehow this group seems to know when to interrupt an intimate conversation. Anyway, how could they know my feelings for Jessica?"

They sat down to devour the tempting burgers and the freshly made fries.

Bill asked, "So, am I driving now? Sam, don't teach us anything important now, because I won't be able to concentrate on both."

Jessica volunteered, "Well, I can drive. I will have a separate session with Sam to understand the part I missed."

Sam was confused. Did Jessica want to help Bill or was she trying to create a situation to meet him alone? He wished he had some formula to understand Jessica's mind.

Jessica's words shook him from his reverie. She asked, "You seem to be deep in thought."

Sam brushed off the thought. He said, " Okay guys, since we understand that 'measuring profits' is the first step in evaluating a company, let's understand what is meant by 'profits per share'.

"Let's take a hypothetical situation. Let's say Joe runs *'Cookies Plaza'* and Bill runs *'Sports Equipment Store'*. Jessica knows both Joe and Bill very well, and she has loaned each one $1,000 to run their respective shops. Now at the end of the year, both Joe and Bill make a profit of $11,000 and $17,000 respectively. Now, who do you think is making more profits? Who in your opinion would provide more returns for your share of money?"

Jessica answered unhesitatingly, "Why, Bill of course! His profit is $17,000."

Sam said, "Not necessarily. Let me offer another scenario to explain why Bill does not provide more returns for your money. Say Joe and Bill participate in a race. Joe completes a 10-mile race and Bill completes a 12-mile race. Who is the better runner? Is it easy to say? Definitely not! We need one more piece of information, which is how fast each one has completed the race.

"Let us calculate the actual miles they ran per hour. The following table illustrates more details."

Figure 4.5: Calculation of speed in running

	Bill	Joe
Distance	10 miles	12 miles
Time taken to complete the race	57 minutes	80 minutes
Speed	10.52 miles/hour	9 miles/hour

"So after analyzing further, it is very clear that Joe, the CEO of *'Cookies Plaza'*, runs faster than Bill, the CEO of *'Sports Equipment Store'*.

"Similarly, let us understand who runs his shop better. Is it Joe or Bill? How do we get more information on their business efficiency?

"If the efficiency of a runner is measured by miles per hour, then the profitability of a company is measured by profits/share. "

Joe confirmed, "Let me see if I got this. Just as it is not enough to calculate the miles covered but also the time in which the distance was covered, we should not only calculate the profits made by the company but also the number of shares with which that profit was achieved."

Sam exclaimed, "Excellent! Would you like to take it from here, Joe?"

Joe laughed, "Not a chance. I am just a follower of His 'Stocks' Highness!"

Sam continued, "Taking our earlier example, Joe made $11,000 profit with 5,000 shares that he issued at the beginning, whereas Bill made $17,000 profits with 15,000.

"In other words, the profits per share of *'Sports Equipment Store'* and *'Cookies Plaza'* can be calculated as follows."

Figure 4.6: Calculation of profits per share between Joe's and Bill's shop

	Joe's Cookies Plaza	Bill's Sports Equipment
Profits	$11,000	$17,000
Number of shares	5,000	15,000
Profits per share	$2.20	$1.13

"So if you had loaned $1,000 each to both the CEOs, the CEO of *'Cookies Plaza'* would give more returns for your shares, even though you had loaned them equal amounts.

"The profits per share are also known as 'earnings per share' or 'net profit per share' or 'EPS'."

Jessica complimented, "Wow! That was so well explained! I don't think I will ever forget 'earnings per share'."

Joe began, "So, 'earnings per share' of any company should be positive. Now we know what it means. How do we stack up companies that have good earnings per share?"

Sam said, "Actually, I need to explain the importance of 'consistency' and then I will come back to earnings per share."

"Imagine you happen to go to the baseball stadium much before the game begins. You meet Ted Williams, who happens to have run out of cash. He wants to buy a new baseball bat, and since you were one of the very few supporters who came to the stadium early, he asks you to buy the bat for him. He promises that as soon as the game is over, he will share $1/10^{th}$ of the money that he gets from the game with you.

"Now, would you loan the money to Ted Williams?"

Bill answered, "Loan the money? I would have passed out, man!"

Joe said, "Are you kidding? I would loan $10,000 if Ted promised to return $1/10^{th}$ of his game fee."

Sam said, "Lending $10,000 to Ted Williams is no different from investing in a stock that has consistently made profits for at least five years. You know that Ted Williams has consistently performed well, so you don't hesitate to loan him the money. Along the same lines, it is very important for us to look for five-year returns before we loan our money to any company.

"Some companies may have a single profitable year after facing losses for three or more years. That is too risky! If our goal is to make a lot of money, wouldn't we take the proven path, like loaning money to Ted Williams who has promised to return $1/10^{th}$ of his game fee?"

Jessica asked, "But how do we unearth the Ted Williamses of *NYSE* and *NASDAQ*?"

Unearthing the Ted Williamses of NYSE and NASDAQ.

*It is said that one machine
can do the work of fifty ordinary men. No machine
can do the work of one extraordinary man*
Chinese pilgrim

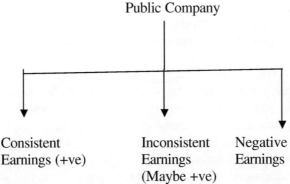

Public Company

Consistent	Inconsistent	Negative
Earnings (+ve)	Earnings	Earnings
	(Maybe +ve)	

Sam began, "A public company can be placed into one of three major categories:

a)   Companies that consistently produce profits and increase profits every year irrespective of the economy, inflation rate, federal rates, etc. The profits of these companies also keep growing every year irrespective of what happens in the world like a war in Iraq, oil exploration in Egypt, etc. These are like Ted Williams, who is capable of hitting against any pitcher.

b)   Companies that may make profitable earnings but not predictable earnings. In other words, a company may be capable of producing profits, but the current year's profits may not be higher than last year's profits. These are like a baseball player who knows how to hit, but you can't depend on him for high scores.

c)   Companies whose earnings are never profitable. In other words, a company that continuously loses its revenues and survives only on the hope that it will make a comeback in the future. These are like rookies who want to shine in the future but keep failing in every championship game."

Bill said, "This makes it very simple. All we have to do is pick companies with consistent 'earnings per share', and BAM! We are millionaires after 10 years."

Sam laughed, "Well, this is the first step. We have to cover more ground, my friend!

"Let me show you some companies that had consistent profits per share and have grown consistently."

Figure 4.7: Earnings per share of some public companies

Source: Morningstar, Inc.

Company	Earnings per share for respective years					
	1997	1998	1999	2000	2001	2002
General Electric	$0.82	$0.93	$1.07	$1.27	$1.41	$1.51
Bed Bath and Beyond	$0.20	$0.26	$0.34	$0.46	$0.59	$0.74
CDW Corpora-tion	$0.59	$0.76	$1.11	$1.79	$1.89	$2.10
Pay Chex	$0.21	$0.28	$0.37	$0.51	$0.68	$0.73
OmniCom Corpora-tion	$1.37	$1.68	$2.01	$2.73	$2.70	$3.44
Kohl's	$0.35	$0.46	$0.59	$0.77	$1.10	$1.45
Target Stores	$0.50	$0.85	$1.02	$1.27	$1.38	$1.51
Apollo Group	$0.19	$0.26	$0.33	$0.41	$0.60	$0.87
Automatic Data Process-ing	$0.86	$0.99	$1.10	$1.31	$1.44	$1.75

"As you can clearly understand from the table Figure 4.7, all these companies have made positive earnings for each share, and the profits have consistently grown even though the economy was not great between the years 2000 and 2003.These companies either explored every avenue to make money, or cut costs so that they could continue to make their shareholders profitable.

"Let me show you this in the form of a graph."

Source: Morningstar, Inc.

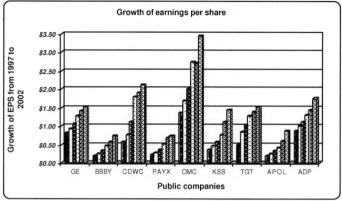

"Since we are loaning our money to these companies, it is our responsibility to find out if we are loaning to profitable companies and whether they can raise profits, even in a poor economy, under any condition.

"Now, shall we find out what would have happened if we had invested in stocks whose EPS are consistently growing?"

Figure 4.8: Result of investing $10,000 in ten years

Source: Morningstar, Inc.

Company	Net worth of our initial investment of $10,000 as of 7/16/2003.	Net profit	Annual growth %
	Period 10 years (7/16/1993 – 7/16/2003)		
Automatic Data Processing	$ 32,355	$ 22,355	12.46
General Electric	$ 40,821	$ 30,821	15.10
Target Stores	$ 77,583	$ 67,583	22.73
Omnicom Corporation	$ 83,470	$ 73,470	23.63
Kohl's Corporation	$127,469	$117,469	28.99
Pay Chex	$128,020	$118,020	29.04
Bed Bath and Beyond	$131,525	$121,525	29.30
CDW Corporation	$343,575	$333,575	42.43
Apollo Group	$452,320	$442,320	46.40

Bill concluded, "So, if we invest in a company that makes consistent profits every year it would return higher potential for our investments."

Sam said, "If you see this in the form of a graph, you will get a better picture." He showed them the graph.

Source: Morningstar, Inc.

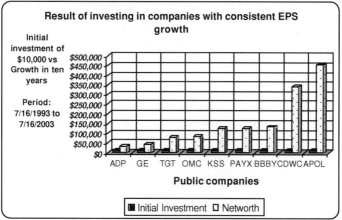

Consistency – The real key behind every success

Consistency is how you build a solid foundation.
Calvin Coolidge

Troy asked, "So are you saying that we would have to check not only the profits, but also the earnings per share of a company for five years?"

Sam said, "Yes. Why do you think Peter Lynch is regarded as the best Mutual Fund manager ever? Why do you think Lance Armstrong is regarded as the best biker ever born in the world? What do you think is the single most important factor for Ted Williams to be considered as the best baseball player ever?

"Peter Lynch has *consistently* beaten the *S&P index* during his tenure as the Mutual Fund manager of *Fidelity's* flagship *Magellan Fund*. He was the manager of the mutual fund for thirteen years and his average annual return was 29.2 percent. These returns were not produced for only one or two years. Instead, Lynch produced these returns for thirteen years consistently. That is the reason the fund had grown from a mere $20 million when he took over in 1977 to $14 billion in 1990.

"In the same way, news was not made when Lance Armstrong won the *Tour de France* for the first time. But when he repeated the feat three consecutive times, especially after recovering from cancer, almost every American citizen was proud of him.

"No one was surprised when Williams received the nation's highest civilian honor, the Presidential Medal of Freedom. Why? Ted Williams's world record of .400 has yet to be broken. Ted Williams achieved this not in just one match, but in almost every game he played for the Boston Red Sox."

Jessica said, "So, it is definitely not sufficient if a company makes good profits for a single year. The company should have a great track record of producing consistent profits."

Consistently Inconsistent

> *It takes less time to do a thing right*
> *than to explain why you did it wrong*
> Henry Wadsworth Longfellow

They reached Jessica's friend's place. She introduced Sam and the others to Charlotte and Chris. They relaxed a bit and got to talk.

Chris asked," What are your plans?"

Bill answered, "Head straight to the casino in a few hours!"

Joe joked, "What! I thought Sam cleansed your mind of gambling and you just learned the first secret to making a cool fortune!"

Chris was intrigued. He asked, "The secret to making a fortune? All I know is that I have invested in stocks, and have made good money out of it!"

Jessica laughed, "Sam! You have met your alter ego!"

Everyone laughed, and Jessica explained to Charlotte and Chris how they had been spending time learning financia l concepts from Sam.

Charlotte complimented, "It's good to see young people like you showing so much interest in understanding vital financial concepts."

Chris said, "That's interesting! So what is the first formula?"

Troy answered, "Consistent earnings per share for at least five years."

Bill joked, "So you were paying attention!"

Chris said, "That is a very vital concept. It is very interesting to note the different strategies used by various companies to maintain their profitability level.

"For example, *Starbucks (SBUX)* clearly knew that it couldn't compete with big players like *Procter and Gamble*, *General Foods*, *Nestle,* etc. So they made coffee kiosks instead of selling coffee beans in retail stores. *StarBucks* not only made huge profits but also made their shareholders very happy.

"*Microsoft* and *Gillette,* in a way, are running a similar business. They provide a low base model and make huge profits on other products. For example, when *Gillette* introduced razor blades, they gave razors for free, but they made their money in shaving cream. Similarly *Microsoft* produced a very low cost operating system but made its money in applications and upgrades."

Over 1.2 billion people use *Gillette* every day.

Charlotte asked, "So that means all the big corporations must maintain consistent earnings, right?"

Chris answered, "Not necessarily. A corporation may not be able to raise profits consistently due to various reasons. For example, *IBM* lost its market share to *Microsoft*. *IBM's* net earnings not only came down, but also the value it added to shareholders didn't rise well."

Jessica asked, "So, how do we find the earnings per share of any company for the past five years?"

Joe answered, "On most websites and in libraries, I guess. It is just that we didn't know what to look for or how to analyze the data."

Bill said, "Going back to my earlier question, can you pull up some information on big companies that did not have consistent earnings per share?"

Sam opened his laptop and showed them a chart.

Figure 4.9: Companies with inconsistent earnings per share

Source: Morningstar, Inc.

Company	Earnings per share ($)				
	1998	1999	2000	2001	2002
Disney Corporat ion	0.89	0.62	0.57	(0.02)	0.60
The Pep Boys	0.80	0.08	0.58	(1.04)	0.68
Circuit City	1.13	1.48	1.60	0.73	0.92
Advanced Micro Devices	(0.36)	(0.30)	2.89	(0.18)	(3.81)
Delta Airlines	6.34	7.20	6.28	(9.99)	(10.44)
American Airlines	7.48	4.17	4.81	(11.43)	(16.22)

Source: Morningstar, Inc.

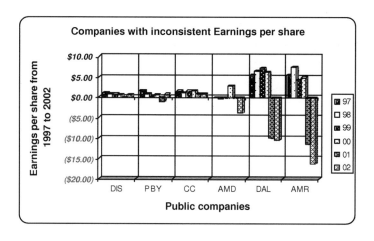

Can Inconsistency Provide Consistent Returns – NOPE!!!

There is only one boss: the customer. And he can fire everybody in the company, from the chairman on down, simply by spending his money somewhere else
Sam Walton

Joe exclaimed, "Whoa! That's scary!"

Bill said, "Well, I agree that some of the large corporations have inconsistent earnings per share, but does that mean they are not worth investing in?"

Troy asked, "Also, I thought that all stocks will perform better in the long run."

Sam said, "No way! A stock will do better only if it is able to return profits to the shareholders. Would shareholders buy stocks of a company that is generating losses? Let me show you what would have happened to your money if you had invested in some of the companies shown in table 4.9."

 To find the earnings per share of a public company, visit www.morningstar.com and key in the ticker symbol. Select the button 'Quote'. You'll be given a snapshot of the company.

Click on financial statements on the left tab and scroll down till you see the row 'Diluted EPS$'.

This row would give the earnings per share of the company for the past 10 years.

Figure 4.10: Result of investing in companies with inconsistent earnings per share

Source: Morningstar, Inc.

Company	Net worth of our initial investment of $10,000 as of 7/16/2003 Invested on: 7/16/1993 ($)	Net profit / loss ($)	Annual compounded growth %
	Period 10 years (July/16/1993 to July/16/2003)		
Delta Airlines	4,730	(5,270)	-7.21
The Pep Boys	6,424	(3,576)	-4.32
American Airlines	6,777	(3,223)	-3.81
Advanced Micro Devices	8,023	(1,977)	-2.17
Circuit City	12,923	2,923	2.59
Disney	16,039	6,039	4.83

Source: Morningstar, Inc.

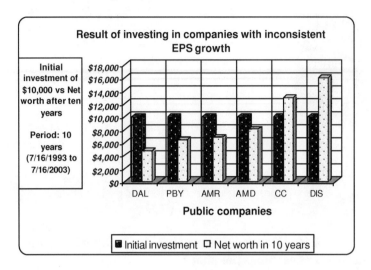

"As you can visualize it here, even though *Disney* is a great company owning everything from theme parks to TV stations, it does not generate consistent profits, and as such it does not generate great returns to shareholders."

Charlotte said, "That's interesting! Well, I have to pick up Madeline, my daughter, from her violin lessons. I will see you all later."

Sam said, "What do you say we go to the strip? You want to join us, Chris?"

Chris replied, "No thanks, carry on! I have some work to do!"

Glitz

Kodak sells film, but they don't
advertise film. They advertise memories
Theodore Parker

Bill said, "I have always wanted to see the *dancing fountain*. Let's go there first."

Sam asked, "Jess, you want to go to the top of the Eiffel Tower? We can watch the fountain from there."

Sam was relieved that the others didn't offer to join him, and that Jessica willingly said yes.

The night was very clear, and the lights that lit up Las Vegas resonated with Sam's mood.

Jessica exclaimed, "This hotel 'Paris' is so romantic !"

Sam pretended not to have heard that and said, "What?"

Her answer was interrupted by the enchanting music played at the fountain.

Once the show was over, they joined the others and headed to *Caesar's Palace*. They had a bite and played for a while, then returned to Chris's home.

Back to Early 90s

> *Your biggest expense is the money you don't make*
> Anon

Chris asked, "So who made a fortune today?"

Joe answered, "Not today, but with Sam's formulas, definitely in the future."

Chris said, "Well, since we are talking about earnings per share, did anyone ask Sam whether a public company that is earning consistently can go bankrupt overnight? Or in other words, if the first rule of investment were applied, do you think the companies that filed for bankruptcy would have passed?"

Bill said, "Yeah! Forgot about that! "

Sam opened his laptop and said, "All right, let's compare the earnings per share of a few companies that went bankrupt and decide whether their earnings per share were consistent."

Figure 4.11: Earnings per share of (in)famous companies

Source: Morningstar, Inc.

Company	Earnings per share ($)				
	1993	1994	1995	1996	1997
Enron	0.63	0.85	0.97	1.08	0.16
World Com	0.28	(0.32)	0.43	(3.71)	0.27
K-Mart	2.06	(2.15)	0.63	(1.25)	(0.45)
ImClone	(0.79)	(0.56)	(0.36)	(0.42)	(0.34)

Source: Morningstar, Inc.

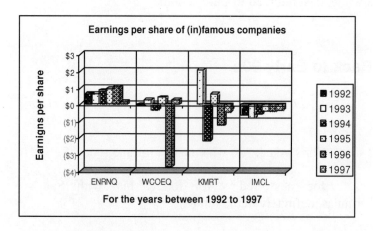

"Can you spot at least one company that made consistent profits but filed for bankruptcy?"

Joe shook his head.

Sam continued, "You can't. Only companies that don't make consistent profits are likely to file for bankruptcy. Isn't this a clear indication that a company doesn't file bankruptcy overnight?"

Chris added, "Unless the company loses profits, it cannot go bankrupt. The warning signs come at least three to four years before the company files for bankruptcy. Remember all these companies filed for bankruptcy only after the year 2000, whereas the warning signs were there as early as the year 1993."

Bill concluded, "So the first rule is that we should invest in companies that have consistent earnings."

The next morning during their drive back, Sam volunteered to drive. Joe asked him, "I have a question. Are there companies that have consistent earnings per share, or in other words, have passed your first formula, but are still not good to invest in?"

Sam stepped on the gas and replied, "Absolutely! You will be inDEBTed to me my friend, when I explain to you the next vital formula."

Sam's Sprinkles

- Any company, be it a Mom and Pop store or *Amazon (AMZN)*, should be able to make profits.

- The company should be weather proof, competition proof, and of course, have a clean financial sheet.

- Invest only in companies that make consistent profits.

- The best way to measure profits is to verify the profits made per share, or in other words, 'earnings per share.'

- A company that earns consistently is not only a safe company to invest in, but also one that will make our money grow.

- No company files for bankruptcy without enough warnings. All the companies that filed for bankruptcy never made consistent earnings and most of them were making losses.

- Any financial website will give historical earnings per share figures.

Self Explorer

- What is a Dow Jones Industrial Average (DOW)? Which companies are part of the DOW?

- Can you the list the earnings per share of the companies that are part of the DOW component?

- What do you think would have happened if you had invested in these companies in 1993 and sold the stocks in 2003?

- What are the relations between earnings and shareholder's value?

True or False

- Only information about public companies is available for us to explore.

- Earnings per share are also known as profits per share.

- No public company ever makes losses.

- A public company, which makes its earnings grow, will also make its shareholders rich.

- A company that files for bankruptcy gives sufficient early warnings.

Chapter V

Who is Dollar Wise, Penny Foolish?

Debt Accumulators or Cash Accumulators?

It is better to measure the company based on what shareholders are getting out of the company and not what companies are getting out of shareholders
Warren Buffett

Knockout Punch

Before borrowing money from a friend, decide which
you need most
American proverb

Bill spotted Sam and Joe talking to someone. He approached them and asked, "Sam, two questions: what are you doing this evening, and when are you going to talk about the next formula?"

Sam said, "Soon, my friend."

Joe turned to Bill and said, "This is Robert. He is an old friend of mine." He added, "Robert is trying to form a 'humor club' here. Interested in joining?"

Bill answered, "Sure. What happens during club meetings?"

Robert replied, "Oh, we choose a particular topic and tell jokes or anecdotes on that topic."

Bill said, "Sounds interesting! Count me in! What is today's topic?"

Robert smiled, "The stock market! Anyway, I have to leave now. I will see you later."

Sam said to the guys, "Let's go to the library. I've asked the others to go as well. I want to lay the groundwork for explaining the next formula."

Once they reached the library, Sam asked, "What comes to your mind when you think of Mike Tyson?"

Joe laughed and said, "Madison Square Garden! Who can forget that incident of Mike Tyson biting Evander Holyfield's ear?"

Sam said, "Let me tell you something about Mike Tyson. You might know that Cus D'Amato brought up Mike Tyson. Cus not only taught him boxing but also gave him shelter and food. Tyson became the heavyweight champion when he was 20."

Bill added, "He must have been really wealthy!"

Sam said, "Definitely! But do you know that this heavyweight champion filed for bankruptcy?"

Joe exclaimed, "I read about that. Shocking!"

Sam said, "Mike Tyson might be the champion in the boxing ring. However, in the financial world, he is also responsible for repaying his loans. Assume his income was around one million dollars per match. His expenses, however, were more than a million dollars every quarter. He would have ultimately filed for bankruptcy. To make a loose comparison, he is like *Enron*.

"I am saying this because, no matter how big a company is, however excellent its product lines are, it is very important for the company to manage its money. If investors focus only on the products and promotions but not on the company's financial health, they might find all their money evaporating. The company might have accumulated a huge debt and, unable to repay the debt, might file for bankruptcy".

Bill quipped, "So even though Tyson was delivering a lot of knockouts, his mounting debt delivered him the ultimate knockout!"

Laugh Your Way to Millions

By the time you can make ends meet, they've moved
the ends
Anon

Joe asked, "How can we avoid investing in public companies that are likely to file for bankruptcy? How do we differentiate between the good ones and the bad ones?"

Sam said, "That is the second formula! Calculating a company's debt. I think I might have to continue this tomorrow, because I have some errands to run. I will meet you guys at the club tonight."

Jessica, who just joined them, asked, "What club?"

Bill explained to her about the humor club, and she decided to become a member herself.

A small group gathered in the local library for the humor club meeting. Robert began, "Welcome, everyone. I would like to thank all the new members for joining. Today's topic is 'The Stock Market'."

Robert continued, "Each person is allowed two minutes to tell a joke! Joe, would you like to begin?"

Joe got up. He said, "Okay, here's a one-liner.

'The market may be bad, but I slept like a baby last night. I woke up every hour and cried.'"

It was Bill's turn. He said, "A mathematician, an accountant and an economist apply for the same job. The interviewer calls in the mathematician and asks, 'What do two plus two equal?' The mathematician replies, 'Four.' The interviewer asks, 'Four, exactly?' The mathematician looks at the interviewer incredulously and says, 'Yes, four, exactly.'

Then the interviewer calls in the accountant and asks the same question 'What do two plus two equal?' The accountant says 'On average, four - give or take ten percent, but on average, four.' Then the interviewer calls in the economist and poses the same question 'What do two plus two equal?' The economist gets up, locks the door, closes the shade, sits down next to the interviewer and says, 'What do you want it to equal?'"

There was a collective laughter. Finally it was Sam's turn. Jessica teased him, "Hey Sam, are you sure you want to tell a joke about the stock market?"

Sam laughed and said, "A minister dies and is waiting in line at the Pearly Gates. Ahead of him is a guy who's dressed in sunglasses, a loud shirt and a leather jacket. Saint Peter addresses this guy, 'Who are you, so I may know whether or not to admit you into the Kingdom of Heaven?' The guy replies, 'I'm Jim Taylor, stockbroker, of *Noo Yawk* City.' Saint Peter consults his list. He smiles and says to the stockbroker, 'Take this silken robe and golden staff and enter the Kingdom of Heaven.' The stockbroker goes into Heaven with his robe and staff, and it's the minister's turn. He stands erect and booms out, 'I am Joseph Snow, pastor of Saint Mary's for the last forty-three years.' Saint Peter consults his list. He says to the minister, 'Take this cotton robe and wooden staff and enter the Kingdom of Heaven.' 'Just a minute,' says the minister. 'That man was a stockbroker-he gets a silken robe and golden staff, but I, a minister, only get a cotton robe and wooden staff. How can this be?' 'Up here, we work by results,' says Saint Peter. 'While you preached, people slept; his clients, they prayed!'"

Robert said, "Good one, Sam!"

They exchanged a few more jokes, and then decided to go to Sam's home.

Debt Free = Worry Free

*If you can solve your problem, then what is the need
of worrying?
If you cannot solve it, then what is the use of
worrying?*
Anonymous

Sam's room looked like something both Peter Lynch
and Aerosmith would be proud of. Jessica asked whether she
could borrow one of his CDs.

Joe asked, "Sam, you started talking about debt last
evening. Can you tell us more about it?"

Sam said, "As always, let me give you a fictitious
example. Jim, a UPS driver, frequently delivered packages to
'Innovative Creatures', a company based in Manhattan
offering solutions from investments to management. He was a
good friend to the senior officer, Christine, and she was quite
knowledgeable about stocks. Since Jim wanted to learn about
stocks, he thought the best way would be to ask Christine
about it.

"Jim asked her an interesting question. 'Why do
companies that are touted by analysts and spoken of well by
the media file for bankruptcy?' Christine, not directly
responding to this, asked Jim an indirect question. She asked
him what debts he had.

"Jim answered that he drove an old Pontiac for
personal travel, and he had paid off the car loan with his
savings. He also said he did not have any debt, because he did
not want to pay a lot of interest."

Sam continued, "Do you know how Jim, earning only
a modest salary, is able to think of investments?"

Jessica answered, "I guess he has no worries, primarily because he has no debt."

Sam said, "Yes! Let us look at the life of the CEO of *'Innovative Creatures.'*

"Rick, the CEO of *'Innovative Creatures,'* runs the business with his wife. He is undoubtedly a smart man, doing reasonably well professionally and leading a very luxurious life. He drives the latest *Bentley* and has two children with an expensive nanny to take care of them. His house is equipped with all the latest gadgets that would give an *Ethan Allen (ETH)* showroom tough competition. Because he always wants to impress his clients, he owns an expensive wardrobe. In addition to all these, he has a huge yacht and memberships in a health club and country club, which he never gets time to visit.

"So, anyone who comes across Rick would think he is very rich and has a lot of money to spend. But no one knows how many bills Rick has to pay every day. He spends the bulk of his time worrying about how to solve his financial crisis.

"Even though Jim, the UPS driver, might not be earning as much as the CEO, he has time to think about his growth. Rick spends most of his time solving his financial crises instead of looking for new business".

Sam concluded, "A company with high debt is not very different from Rick. It places high pressure on the company. Can you imagine what it is like to be the Chief Executive Officer of a company, whose only job is to solve the company's financial crises instead of looking for new growth opportunities? The CEO would not have time to meet his clients. Instead, he would have time to meet only with the banks and institutions that had given his company loans.

"Generally, a company that generates sales, and thus income, should not have too much debt to meet. If it does, most of the income is spent on repaying its loans and interest. And it becomes worse when the interest rates go up. There may not be additional debts, but when the interest rates go up as decided by banks and institutions, the company that borrowed money is liable to pay more interest. On the other hand, a company with little or no debt can use its income for fresh growth opportunities."

Joe added, "I guess high debt also puts psychological pressure on those running the company. They have no other choice but to pay the bankers and lenders. But if the company accrues too much debt and loses business, it is not only likely to file for bankruptcy, but the shareholders would be left with nothing.

"The only solution to a huge debt problem is to file for bankruptcy. So if you need at least a 20% return on your investment, the very first step is to detect companies that are in financial trouble and avoid them."

Jessica said, "So even if a company passes our criteria of consistent earnings per share, we should also check if it has a lot of debt, right?"

Sam said, "Yes. Here is the first assignment. Can anyone here find a company that has consistent earnings but still has a lot of debt?"

Bill said, "Of course! We will give it a shot! That should be interesting."

Sam nodded. He added, "Again, I will show you with examples and numbers how to calculate debt. How about tomorrow?"

Everyone agreed and left. Jessica spoke to Sam, "Tomorrow my folks are having a barbecue. I have asked the other guys to join, too. I would love for you to join us. Even though you have met my folks, I would like them to get to know you better."

Sam was convinced he didn't need any formula to understand Jessica's mind. She was sending out clear signals.

The 'Pits'

Future wealth is purchased with scrutiny of the past
Anonymous

Jessica's father, Frank, was cooking ribs over a 600-degree flame. He saw Sam approaching him.

Sam said, "Hello, Frank. How are you? I bought this new barbecue sauce. Would you like to try it?"

Frank said, "Thanks! I heard about the little 'financial school' you are running!"

Sam laughed, "You are very generous with your compliments."

Frank said, "I have been following the market for some time. But I never quite got the hang of it. I am thinking of enrolling as a student in your school."

Sam reflected that every minute of his effort spent in understanding companies and investments was paying off beyond his dreams. It is one thing to attract the attention of a pretty woman, but it is quite another to win her parents' approval.

Joe took over from Frank and tried to keep the fire under control.

He asked, "Sam, continuing our earlier discussion, tell me, how do you calculate debt?"

Sam began, "Let me explain with an example. Say John and David live in New Jersey. They graduated from college and decided to get into business. New Jersey experienced the worst winter during their final year of college. John therefore decided to open a snow shovel center, so during the winter he could make lots of money renting and selling snow blowers, snowplows, and other snow equipment. On the other hand, David, who is very good at playing pool, opened a pool center.

"Both John and David needed capital to start their businesses. John never saved any money, and so he needed to borrow the entire capital of $500,000 to launch his business. David, who saved all the money right from his school days, had enough cash to start *Pool 'N' Fun*. Let me show you their initial financial statements."

Figure 5.1: Comparison of initial investment between John and David

	Snow Safe	Pool 'n' Fun
Owner	John	David
Initial investment	$500,000	$100,000
Sources of capital	Loans	Own savings

"During 2002, New Jersey experienced a harsh winter with almost twenty inches of snow. Their income sheets for that year look as follows."

Figure 5.2: Income sheet for 2002

	John's Snow Safe ($)	David's Pool 'n' Fun ($)
Annual income	200,000	100,000
Total expenses	160,000	70,000
Net income	40,000	30,000

"Since John was confident of making a lot of money with his investments, he borrowed more money from the banks and wanted to grab every opportunity to become a millionaire. So he borrowed another $250,000 from the banks and bought more equipment for his business. David on the other hand reinvested $30,000 and made his shop look more attractive. He introduced a deli shop in addition to pool tables.

"Another year passed but without heavy snowfall. John, depending on 20 inches of snow every year, blamed the weather and couldn't repay any interest on his loans. Now John's and David's annual income sheet looked as follows."

Figure 5.3: Income sheet for 2003

	John's Snow Safe ($)	David's Pool 'n' Fun ($)
Annual income	70,000	80,000
Total expenses	100,000	60,000
Net Income	(30,000)	20,000

"Why is it that John, the head of *'Snow Safe,'* had more expenses than his total income? Simple. As you are aware, John borrowed $500,000 to begin his business and another $250,000 to expand his operations. When a company borrows money, it is responsible for repaying it, whether the business is doing well or not. Are we not responsible for paying our bills every month? In the same vein, a corporation must pay interest every year and repay its loans, whether they are able to generate income or not.

"Since *'Snow Safe'* borrowed $750,000 but couldn't generate enough income to repay even the interest, it had to file for bankruptcy. Similarly, a public company that is unable to generate enough money to repay loans is definitely going to file for bankruptcy.

"Thus, a very simple way to decide whether a company is doing well or not is to look first at its debt. If it has too much, you would be prudent to avoid investing in it."

Debt Detector

Committing a known mistake is worse than committing an unknown crime
Anonymous

Sam continued, "Let us look at some of the public companies' financial statements for 1997."

Sam showed them the chart and grabbed a glass of lemonade.

Figure 5.4: Financial statements of some companies for 1997
(All figures in millions)

Source: Morningstar, Inc.

	Rite Aid (RAD) ($)	Playtex Products (PYX) ($)	Sinclair Broadcast Group (SBGI) ($)
Cash and cash equivalents	7.0	3.2	139.3
Total debt	2,460	738.2	1,123.6
Accounts payable	601.3	24.5	5.2
Net cash available	(3,054.3)	(759.5)	(989.5)

Pam, Jessica's mother, was visibly shocked to see the figures. "Would you look at that? Do people really invest in companies that have debt as high as that?"

Sam said, "Unfortunately they do! Because they either don't check to see if the company has debts or they just want to make a quick buck.

"See what would happen if someone invested, say, $10,000 in these companies."

Figure 5.5: Growth of $10,000 invested in August 1998 in five years
Source: Morningstar, Inc.

Company	Net cash for 1997 ($ in millions)	Net worth of $10,000 as of August, 2003 invested in Aug, 1998	Net growth %
		($)	
	Period: Five years (August 1998, August,2003)		
Rite Aid	(3,054.3)	1,274	(87)
Playtex Products	(759.5)	5,998	(40)
Sinclair Broadcast Group	(989.5)	6,170	(38)

Source: Morningstar, Inc.

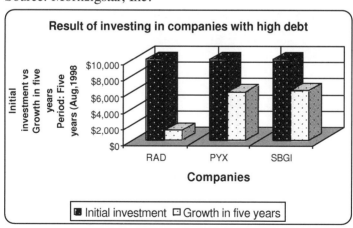

Pam was studying the chart. "Shocking! I suppose all this information is available on the Internet."

Sam said, "Absolutely! If you want, I can show you how to find it."

Pam took Sam to the den and asked her to visit www.morningstar.com on her computer.

He said, "You can type the ticker *RAD* (for the company *Rite Aid*) and click on the button 'Quote'. Now, click on 'Financial Statements' (on the left bar). Do you see the tab '10-Yr Balance Sheet'?"

Pam replied, "Yes."

Sam said, "Click the tab '10-Yr Balance Sheet'. Under the section 'Liabilities and Stockholders' Equity $Mil' you will see 'Short-Term debt' and 'Long-Term debt.' That is the debt I was talking about."

Pam exclaimed, "This is so easy! And it shows figures for 10 years. I am very impressed with your knowledge."

Sam thanked her and they returned to the yard. He said, "Let's look at the financial statements of certain public companies for 1997 that have a satisfactory cash flow."

Figure 5.6: Financial statements of some companies for 1997
(All figures in millions)
Source: Morningstar, Inc.

	Pacific Sunwear of CA (PSUN) ($)	K-Swiss Inc. (KSWS) ($)	Hot Topic (HOTT) ($)
Cash and cash equivalents	10.0	36.1	27.2
Total debt	0.0	0.7	0.0
Accounts payable	6.7	4.4	1.2
Net cash available	3.3	31.0	26.0

"Let us compare the growth of $10,000 invested in these companies as of August 17, 2003."

Figure 5.7: Growth of $10,000 invested in August 1998 in five years
Source: Morningstar, Inc.

Company	Net cash for 1997 ($ in millions)	Net worth of $10,000 as of August, 2003 invested in August, 1998	Net growth %	Annual compounded interest %
Period: Five Years (Aug,1998 - Aug 2003)				
Pacific Sunwear of CA	3.3	35,898	259	29.12
K-Swiss Inc.	31.0	67,890	579	46.67
Hot Topic	26.0	106,735	967	60.57

Source: Morningstar, Inc.

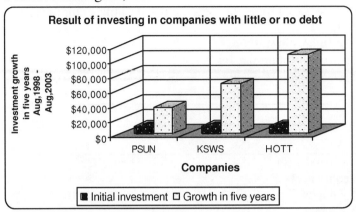

Result of investing in companies with little or no debt

Bill asked, "I can understand the numbers, but can you explain the terms 'accounts payable,' 'cash equivalents,' etc.?"

Joe interrupted, "Let's eat first. I am starved. I am sure you all are too." They spent the rest of the evening eating the ribs, talking and having a good time.

1. Load www.morningstar.com.
2. Type the ticker symbol of the company for which you wish to verify the cash flow and debt. For example, HOTT – for Hot Topic.
3. Click on Quote.
4. Now, click on Financial Statements on the left bar.
5. Also, click on 10-Yr. Balance Sheet on the top bar of Financial Statements.
6. Cash is available under the Assets section.
7. Accounts payable and debt are available under Liabilities and Stock Holder's Equity section.

Can a Company Repay Debts?

He who has cash, wins
Anonymous

Sam said, "Okay, I am going to explain with an example. Say Joe decides to open a shop that specializes in selling clocks and watches. He operates the store successfully and runs it for a year with reasonable profits.

"Joe then wishes to bring in quick profits. He decides the best way to do that is to buy more varieties of clocks and advertise heavily. Since he expects more customers, he wants to make his shop more attractive. So Joe approaches the local *Commerce Bank (CBH)* for a $50,000 loan. *Commerce Bank* approves it, and Joe anticipates more business during Christmas and New Year.

"Joe advertises heavily in the local newspapers, radio stations and TV channels about *'Clock Workz'*, and that pays off too. He gets a decent response from his customer base. However, let us verify whether *'Clock Workz'* is really worth investing in.

"Any business' financial health can be viewed as a triangle. Just as a triangle has three sides, a business has three sides: cash in hand, loans to be repaid, and money to be repaid to its suppliers.

"Joe is responsible for repaying the loan *(Debt)* of $50,000 to *Commerce Bank*. In addition to the loan, he is also responsible for repaying his clock and watch suppliers, which is known as accounts payable.

"So the three sides of the business triangle can be interpreted as follows."

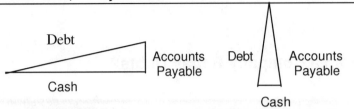

"So which one of these triangles looks more stable?"

Bill said, "I may not be a stock expert, but I do know geometry well enough to know that the triangle with a bigger base of cash would stand by itself."

Sam said, "Using the same concept, let us verify whether Joe's business is stable. Let us look at Joe's financial statement, which has two sides." He took a piece of paper and drew.

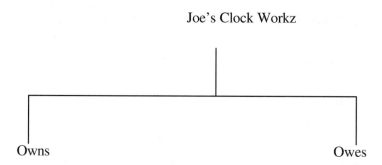

"A company would be stable only if it owns more than what it owes."

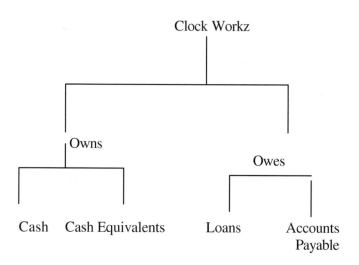

"Now, let us compare the variables in financial statement of 'Clock Workz' and check if it is safe to invest in."

Figure 5.8: Comparison of Clock Workz's cash versus its debt

Clock Workz	Owns ($)	Owes	($)
Cash and equivalents	25,000	Loan from bank	50,000
		Advertising agencies	25,000
		Suppliers	30,000
Cash available	25,000	Total amount to repay	105,000

"Do you think *'Clock Workz'* is in a stable position? Joe is still responsible for repaying the bank, advertising agencies and clock suppliers."

Jessica said, "Makes sense. This company is not safe to invest in. If a company owes more than it owns, then it is *not* a safe company to invest in. On the other hand, if it owns more than it owes, it is safe to invest in."

Sam said, "Yes. But I have to explain something more."

Why Analysts Don't Speak About Debt

If everybody is thinking alike, then somebody isn't thinking
George S. Patton, Jr.

Joe said, "Sam, I don't agree with any of this. Why are you using my name to illustrate bad companies? In fact, if I start a company tomorrow, no one is going to invest in it."

Bill joked, "You are running that risk anyway, buddy!"

Frank laughed, "No wonder these people are always with you. You seem to make child's play out of learning financial concepts. Very impressive! "

Pam complimented too, "You are an adept teacher, Sam!"

Sam thanked her. Troy asked, "But Sam, tell me something, how come analysts never mention debt?"

Sam answered, "It's like this. When the delivery boy drops off a pizza at your house, does he tell you about all the cholesterol it has?"

Troy exclaimed, "Hey! That is business!"

Sam said, "The purpose of every business is to lure consumers and get money from them. That is why a gallon of Coke costs more than a gallon of gas. That is why companies that lend money advertise 0% interest for the first six months. They never advertise the jump to 24% interest after that. Just imagine what would happen if *Best Buy* advertised 24% interest after six months? Would anyone buy a product from them?

"It is our therefore responsibility to do some analysis before investing our hard earned money. Finding the debt of any public company is as easy as browsing *CNN* on the Internet.

"As I was telling Mrs. Calderone, you can visit www.morningstar.com or http://moneycentral.msn.com and type the ticker symbol of a company. You will get all the information you need to make an informed decision."

They thanked the Calderones for inviting them to the barbecue and left.

Bill asked, "Sam, do you mean to say good companies do not have any debt at all?"

In the U.S., total pizza industry sales were approximately $30 billion. In 2001, there were 65,000 pizzerias.

Does the Company Produce Sufficient Income?

Ever wonder why the IRS calls it Form 1040?
Because for every $50 that you earn, you get 10 and
they get 40
Anonymous

Sam said, "Of course they have debt. But you have to understand another vital concept. Take this example. Say, Jessica is very much interested in software development, and she opens a company called *'JC Solutions'*. She uses her savings, and she also borrows money from her dad. Three years pass, and the company has grown and has become famous in our town. You are now contemplating whether investing in Jessica's business is ideal. So how do we measure that?"

Bills aid, "Check if the company has debt."

Sam said, "Yes, but we also need to check whether the business is capable of *repaying* the debt. *'JC Solutions'* has borrowed $250,000 from *American Express (AXP)* to be repaid within the next year, and two million dollars from *Bank One (ONE)* to lease the buildings in which the business is being run. In addition to all these loans, it owes $50,000 to the computer suppliers and advertising agencies.

"Let us calculate the total amount *'JC Solutions'* needs to repay."

Figure 5.9: Total amount to be re paid by 'JC Solutions'

Category	Amount to repay ($)
Loan to be repaid in one year (short term debt)	250,000
Loan to be repaid beyond a year (long term debt)	2,000,000
Accounts payable (to the suppliers etc.)	100,000
Total amount to repay	2,350,000

"Let's look at the business over a three-year period and decide whether it is capable of repaying its debts.

"*'JC Solutions'* generates income from its customers. Its expenses include salaries and commissions to its employees, as well as utility bills. The income it generates after paying all its expenses is known as 'net income.'

"The best way to calculate debt is to find out whether the net income generated is capable of paying both the short-term loans and the long-term loans. The first rule is that the net income should be more than the short-term loans. Even though the repayment period for long-term loans is generally more than a year and may be extended over ten to twenty years, it is safe to invest in a business only if its net income is sufficient to repay its total debt within four years.

"This ensures it is capable of repaying its loans. It also gives an investor confidence in the company's financial future.

"In general, a business' net income fluctuates every year. Therefore, before you invest in a company, you should calculate the previous three years' average income.

"Let us calculate the average net income of *'JC Solutions'* and decide whether it is worth investing in."

Figure 5.10: Net income of 'JC Solutions' between 2000 and 2002

Year	2000 ($)	2001 ($)	2002 ($)
Net income	750,000	875,000	925,000
Average net income between 2000 and 2002		850,000	

"*'JC Solutions'* is responsible for paying its short-term loan and accounts payable in one year. In other words, the net income must be much more than the amount it is responsible for repaying."

Total amount to be repaid in a year's time = short term loans + accounts payable

Joe remarked, "So for *'JC Solutions'*, the total amount to be repaid in a year's time is $350,000, which is much less than the average net income of $850,000."

Sam said, "Yes! Also, let us find out whether its total debt is within four years of its net income."

Total debt of *'JC Solutions'* = $2,350,000

"The number of year's net income required to repay the total debt = $2,350,000 / $850,000, which is 2.76 years. In other words, *'JC Solutions'* can repay all the debt within three years, and thereafter it can run its operations reasonably well."

Sam concluded, "So *'JC Solutions'* is a good company to consider investing in."

Joe exclaimed, "Awesome! Hey, now that we have understood net income and debt, can you show some actual companies with their debt and income?"

Sam said, "Of course. But I need to look at some charts at home. You want to come back to my house?"

After they arrived at Sam's house, Sam offered them sodas and showed them the chart.

"Take a look at the financial statements of these companies and decide whether they can meet their debt within a short time."

Figure 5.11:
Years needed to repay the debt of some public companies as of 1997

Source: Morningstar, Inc.

Company	Lucent Technologies (LU)	Solutia Inc (SOI)	Winn-Dixie Stores (WIN)	Sprint PCS Group (PCS)
Short term debt ($ in millions)	2,538	193	383	348
Long term debt ($ in millions)	1,665	597	54	7,847
Accounts payable ($ in millions)	1,931	221	604	371
Total debt ($ in millions)	6,134	1,011	1,041	8,566
Net income ($ in millions)	541	192	204	(1,123)
Number of years it may take to repay the total debt from net income (Total debt/net income)	11.33	5.26	5.10	Indefinite

"Let us compare our investment growth of $10,000 as of August 2003."

Figure 5.12: Growth of $10,000 invested in August 1998, in five years.

Source: Morningstar, Inc.

Company	Ticker	Is net income higher than (Short term debt + accounts payable)	Years needed to repay the total debt from net income	Net worth in five years ($)	Growth %
Period: Five years (Aug,1998 – Aug,2003)					
Lucent Tech.	LU	No	11.33	700	(93)
Solutia Inc	SOI	No	5.26	1,719	(83)
Winn-Dixie Stores	WIN	No	5.10	3,122	(69)
Sprint PCS	PCS	No	Indefinite	6,475	(35)

Source: Morningstar, Inc.

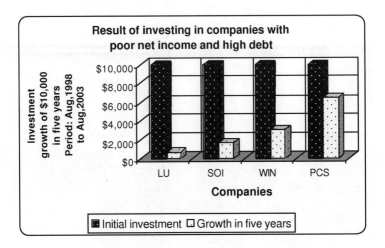

"Now we shall verify the companies whose repayment capability is less than four years and understand their investment growth."

Figure 5.13: Years needed to repay the debt of some public companies as of 1997

Source: Morningstar, Inc.

Company	Concord-EFS (CE)	ITT Educational Services (ESI)	Ansys Inc. (ANSS)	Urban Outfitters (URBN)
Short term debt	$0.5 million	Nil	Nil	Nil
Long term debt	$28.3 million	Nil	Nil	Nil
Accounts payable	Nil	$15.0 million	$0.2 million	$8.7 million
Total debt	$28.8 million	$15.0 million	$0.2 million	$8.7 million
Net income	$42.8 million	$19.1 million	$7.4 million	$13.3 million
Years needed to repay the total debt from net income (Total Debt/Net Income)	0.67 Approximately eight months	0.78 Approximately nine months and 20 days	One day	0.65 Approximately seven and half months

"Let us compare our investment growth of $10,000 as of August 2003."

Figure 5.14: Growth of $10,000 invested in August, 1998 in five years

Source: Morningstar, Inc.

Company	Is Net income higher than (Short term debt + accounts Payable)	Number of years to repay the total debt from net income	Net worth of $10,000 invested in August, 1998 ($)	Growth %
		Period:Five years (Aug, 1998 – Aug, 2003)		
Concord EFS	Yes	0.67 (Less than a year)	21,220	107
ITT Educational Services	Yes	0.78 (9 Months and 20 days)	30,475	205
Ansys Inc.	Yes	One Day	30,950	210
Urban Outfitters	Yes	0.65 (Less than a year)	32,166	222

Source: Morningstar, Inc.

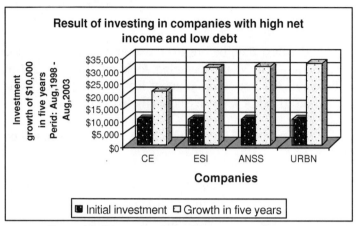

Joe said, "Amazing! So when we analyze a company, we should look for whether its net income is sufficient to pay off its debts."

Bill added, "Also, how many years it would take to pay off its debt. Right, Sam?"

Sam agreed, "Absolutely!"

Bill asked, "So, are we done with the 'debt' part?"

Sam said, "Almost, but I have to cover a few more topics related to debt. Sometime later?" They dispersed.

Sam found Jessica alone, "Jess, I was wondering if you were free for dinner tonight?"

Jessica said, "How about tomorrow, Sam?"

Sam said, "Sure." He didn't want to pry into what plans she had for that night, but she broke his heart when she volunteered: "I am going out with Robert this evening."

Prevent the Unexpected

*I like to do all the talking myself. It saves time, and
prevents arguments*
Oscar Wilde

The next day, before everyone else joined them, Joe
asked Sam, "Why that   hangdog look on your face, Mr.
Millionaire? Are you worried about Robert? Don't be! He is
just a good friend of Jessica. She really likes you!"

Sam began, "How do you know…." His voice trailed
off.

Joe smiled and said. "Well, for starters, I live in the
same house as Jess. I have not heard her utter one sentence in
the past few weeks without mentioning your name."

Sam's heart soared like a company with no debt and
great earnings.

A few minutes later when others joined, Bill asked,
"Sam, do you want to head to the cafeteria? You promised to
explain more about debt."

Sam agreed, and they carried their sodas to an empty
table.

Sam said, "There are two more vital elements
involved in evaluating companies. A company should be
capable of repaying its short-term loans and 'accounts
payable' at any moment. These are known as 'current ratio'
and 'quick ratio'."

Bill asked, "If it is so vital, tell us how to measure it."

Sam said, "Okay, since you are a music fan, let's say
you decide to run a huge music store named *'Music Nirvana.'*
You handpick CDs from your vendors. You borrow money
quite often to keep your store running. Furthermore, you
agree to pay more to your vendors for some rare music
collections.

"You want to improve your store's sales, and so you advertise to the public they can buy your CDs without making a payment for two months. As a result, some of your customers who want to give Christmas gifts do not make payments immediately. Instead, they agree to have their balance charged to their credit cards after two months."

Current Ratio

Intellectuals solve problems; geniuses prevent them
Albert Einstein

"Let us understand the current financial health of *'Music Nirvana.'* We have to check its current assets."

These include the following:
Cash on hand

Items in the store, also known as Inventory to be sold

Amount to be collected from customers who had bought CDs but did not yet make a payment.

Figure 5.15: Current assets of Music Nirvana

Item	Description	Amount ($)
Cash	Cash on hand and short- term investments	65,000
Inventory	Unsold items but readily available for customers to buy	60,000
Accounts receivable	Amount to be collected from customers who already made their purchases	32,000
Current assets	Total current assets	157,000

"Just like current assets, *'Music Nirvana'* is obligated to pay back its current liabilities.

"'Music Nirvana' buys CDs from various vendors, to which it owes $47,000. It also borrowed about $30,000 from *American Express (AXP)*, assuring them he would repay the money within the next six months.

"So *'Music Nirvana'* is liable to pay the following within the next 12 months."

Figure 5.16: Current liabilities of Music Nirvana

Item	Description	Amount
Accounts payable	Amount to be paid to vendors and other creditors	47,000
Short-term liabilities	Amount that needs to be repaid in the next 12 months	30,000
Current liabilities	Total amount to be paid in the next 12 months	$77,000

"How do we determine whether *'Music Nirvana'* is about to hit the iceberg? We can measure it using current ratio. Current ratio measures the value of current assets divided by the current liabilities. In other words, current ratio determines whether the current assets are greater than the current liabilities. If the current ratio is more than 1.00, then the company's current assets are greater than its current liabilities.

"What is the current ratio of *'Music Nirvana'*? Its current assets are $157,000 and current liabilities are $77,000. So the current ratio would be current assets / current liabilities, which is $157,000/$77,000. That equals 2.03.

"This is a clear indication that *'Music Nirvana'* is in sound condition. Consider investing in companies whose current ratio is above two. But that is not all. There is one more ratio you need to calculate."

Joe interrupted, "What amazes me is that all this information is available, but we never bothered to understand it. Anyway, better late than never."

Jessica said, "We have already learned a lot in a short time. And you say there is more? I hope I don't forget everything."

Sam said, "Tell you what! How about we have a little quiz on this? That way, it will be like a revision of the concepts."

Bill groaned, "Oh man!"

Sam said, "Come on, it will be fun! Let me tell you the last formula for now. We will have the quiz tomorrow."

Quick Ratio

I picked companies that could turn a profit even with a monkey running them, and it's a good thing, because at some point that may happen
Peter Lynch

Sam began, "We need to calculate the quick ratio before choosing a company. Now, say Troy runs a small clothing retail store, *'Clothes Busters'*. He stores a huge inventory of summer clothing during February, as the weather forecast predicts a long summer for the year. His financial balance sheet looks as follows."

Figure 5.17: Current assets and liabilities of 'Clothes Busters'

Current Assets

Cash on hand:	$5,000
Inventory:	$200,000
Accounts receivable:	$20,000
Total current assets:	$225,000

Current Liabilities

Accounts payable:	$30,000
Short term loan:	$70,000
Total current liabilities:	$100,000

Bill said, "But the current ratio seems to pass your formula, Sam. Since *'Clothes Busters'* has current assets of $225,000 and current liabilities of $100,000, the current ratio works out to be 2.25."

Sam said, "Yes, but the weather report turned out to be totally incorrect for 2003. 2003 had very few hot days. Troy expected a long summer, but he lost a lot of customers, even though his store was in a good location at the shopping mall. He also faced a money crunch as his suppliers and financial institutions asked him to repay his loans."

Bill asked, "Why is the company facing financial troubles, even though the current ratio looks very healthy?"

Sam said, "Mainly because the current assets are built by *inventory* and *not by cash*.

"The best way to verify a company's actual financial health is to calculate its quick ratio. The quick ratio does not take inventory into account. It is calculated as (current assets – inventory) / current liabilities.

"Let us verify the quick ratio of both *'Clothes Busters'* and *'Music Nirvana'*."

The quick ratio of *'Music Nirvana'* = (Current Assets – Inventory)/ Current Liabilities
($157,000 - $ 60,000) / ($77,000) = 1.25

The quick ratio of *'Clothes Busters'* = (Current Assets – Inventory)/ Current Liabilities

($225,000 - $200,000) / ($100,000) = 0.25

"Even though both stores have high current ratios, *'Clothes Busters'* has a very poor quick ratio. Always invest in a company whose quick ratio is above one.

"This ensures that even if it faces sudden financial problems, it can still run smoothly."

1. Load www.morningstar.com .
2. Type the ticker symbol of the company you wish to verify the cash and debt. For example, LU for Lucent Technologies.
3. Click on Quote.
4. Now, click on Key Ratios on the left bar.
5. Also, click on Financial Health on the top bar of key ratios.
6. Scroll to the last section "Liquidity/ Financial Health."
7. This section describes the Current Ratio and Quick Ratio of the company for the past 10 years.

Companies with Good Current Ratios but Poor Quick Ratios

We are what we repeatedly do. Excellence then, is not an act, but a habit
Aristotle

Joe asked, "Can you show us a list of companies with a reasonably good current ratio but poor quick ratio?"

Sam replied, "Of course. Let me show you the growth of a few companies with reasonably good current ratios but poor quick ratios."

Figure 5.18:
Current ratio and quick ratio of some public companies for 1994 and 1995
Source: Morningstar, Inc.

Company	For 1994		For 1995	
	Current ratio	Quick ratio	Current ratio	Quick ratio
Solutia Inc	NA	NA	1.35	0.56
Winn-Dixie Stores	1.56	0.23	1.41	0.18
Lucent Technologies	1.03	0.58	0.97	0.52

"Let's find out our growth if we invested $50,000 in these companies in 1993."

Figure 5.19:
Result of investing in companies with good current ratio but poor quick ratio

Source: Morningstar, Inc.

Company	$50,000 invested in 1993 as of 2003	
	Net worth ($)	Growth %
Solutia Inc	7,444	(85)
Winn-Dixie Stores	19,065	(62)
Lucent Technologies	24,837	(51)

Source: Morningstar, Inc.

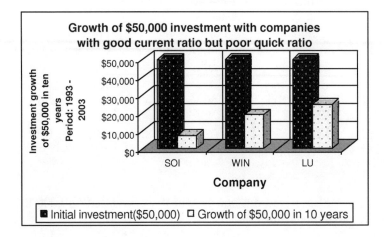

Growth of $50,000 investment with companies with good current ratio but poor quick ratio

Companies with Excellent Current Ratios and Quick Ratios

Money is not the most important thing. Love is.
Fortunately I love money
Jackie Mason

Sam continued, "Here is the growth of some companies with current ratios and quick ratios of at least 1.00."

Figure 5.20:
Current ratio and quick ratio of some public companies for 1994 and 1995

Source: Morningstar, Inc.

Company	For 1994		For 1995	
	Current ratio	Quick ratio	Current ratio	Quick ratio
Ansys Inc.	1.17	1.01	1.12	1.06
Urban Outfitters	5.10	3.76	4.08	2.36
Concord EFS	2.22	2.02	2.07	1.94
ITT Educational Services	1.33	1.49	1.10	1.36

"Let's now confirm our growth if we invested $50,000 in these companies in 1993."

Figure 5.21:
Result of investing in companies with good current ratio and good quick ratio

Source: Morningstar, Inc.

Company	$50,000 invested in 1993 as of 2003	
	Net worth ($)	Growth %
Ansys Inc.	148,838	198
Urban Outfitters	242,151	384
Concord EFS	564,650	1029
ITT Educational Services	1,063,778	2208

Source: Morningstar, Inc.

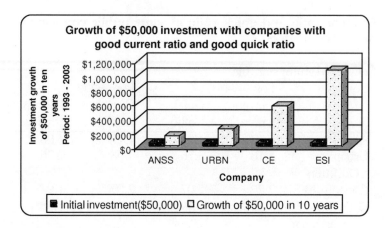

Enron

*Borrow money from
pessimists; they don't expect it back*
Anonymous

Joe said, "That looks impressive. But tell me something. In the beginning of 2001, many books carried articles about *Enron*. The company was ranked #31 in Fortune's fastest growing companies, ranked #22 in Fortune's best companies to work for, and for seven years in a row it was one of Fortune's most innovative companies. The stock price was trading at $80, and then out of the blue, on December 12, 2001, *Enron filed for bankruptcy*!

"How is it the most innovative company for seven years, had to file for bankruptcy so quickly?"

Sam said, '*Enron* was no different from our *'Snow Safe'* we discussed earlier. *Enron* grew, but it grew because of debt and not because of profits.

"A stock that rises too fast has a flip side. A company's revenue might be growing even more than 50%. But it might fall to earth just as fast, and in most cases file for bankruptcy and be de-listed from the stock exchange. The other major reason for a company's lack of growth is that it has too much debt. Any company with a high load of debt will either face a huge financial crisis or file for bankruptcy in the near future."

Jessica asked, "I have a question. Would companies that filed for bankruptcy pass your quick ratio formula?"

Sam said, "Well, that is your assignment: can you find the quick ratios of companies that filed for bankruptcy? Remember, if the quick ratio is less than 1.00, then the company doesn't have sufficient funds to meet its emergency needs."

Before they parted, Sam said he would pick Jessica up the next evening at 7 p.m.

Jessica was already thinking about what to wear.

The next day at the campus, Bill called out, "Sam, before the class begins, let me show you what I came up with. I found the quick ratios of three companies that filed for bankruptcy."

Figure 5.22:
Current ratio and quick ratio in 1994 and 1995 of bankrupt companies

Source: Morningstar, Inc.

Company	For 1994		For 1995	
	Current ratio	Quick ratio	Current ratio	Quick ratio
Enron	0.83	0.32	1.12	0.51
World Com	0.83	0.69	0.33	0.29
K-Mart	1.72	0.08	1.63	0.69

Bill added, "It looks like if people took the quick ratios of these companies into consideration, they would not have invested in them."

Sam said, "That's true. Nice work!"

At the time *WorldCom* filed for bankruptcy, its total debt was $41 billion and it had only $200 million in cash.

Questions for Thought

Questions provide the key to unlocking our unlimited potential
Anthony Robbins

Joe asked, "Sam, you want to check if we were paying attention or not? Bring on the questions!"

Sam nodded and asked, "Okay, *Question 1:* what is the first formula?"

Joe replied, "Consistent earnings per share for the past five years. Oh wait! I forgot. You asked us whether we could find a company that has consistent earnings per share but huge debt."

Sam said, "Yeah! You have one?"

Joe rejoined, "You bet I do! I found a company that has consistent earnings per share but still has high debt. It is *Coca-Cola Bottling Co. (COKE)*. Investing $10,000 around 1998 in *Coca-Cola Bottling* would have become only $9,601 as of June 2003. See *my* chart for a change."

Figure 5.23: Earnings per share of Coca Cola bottling company

Source: Morningstar, Inc.

Company	Ticker	Earnings per share			
		1999	2000	2001	2002
Coca Cola Bottling co.	COKE	$0.37	$0.71	$1.07	$2.56

Joe continued, "Even though *Coca-Cola Bottling Company* has consistent earnings per share, it also has a very high debt. Take a look at this table."

Figure 5.24:
Details from Coca-Cola Bottling Company's income statement and balance sheet

Source: Morningstar, Inc.

Details of Coca-Cola Bottling Company (COKE)	From Income Statement and Balance Sheet			
	1999	2000	2001	2002
Cash availability ($ in millions)	9.1	8.4	16.9	18.2
Net income ($ in millions)	3.2	6.3	9.5	22.8
Accounts payable ($ in millions)	Nil	Nil	28.4	38.3
Short term debt ($ in millions)	38.2	33.5	90.8	13.8
Long term debt ($ in millions)	728.4	684.0	621.1	849.8
Total debt ($ in millions)	766.6	717.5	740.3	901.9
Number of years needed to pay the debt from net income	239	113	77	39.5
Can the company pay its debt from its cash reserves?	No	No	No	No
Can the company pay the debt from its net income in less than four years?	No	No	No	No
Current ratio	0.98	1.11	0.73	1.10
Quick ratio	0.46	0.57	0.41	0.63
Is the current ratio above two and quick ratio above one?	No	No	No	No
Is it a good company to invest?	No			

Sam said, "Excellent! That was really impressive. *Question 2:* What are the three sides of a business triangle, and which one should be highest?"

Jessica said, "I got this one. Debt, cash and accounts payable, and obviously 'cash' should be the highest."

Sam remarked, "Good! *Question 3:* How do you determine whether a company is capable of paying its debt?"

Bill said, "Well! We have to check the number of years' net income required by a company to repay its debts, and it should be capable of repaying its debt in less than four years.

Number of years to repay the total debt = Total debt of the company / Average net income for three years."

Sam said, "Great! *Question 4:* What are the other ratios I told you about, and what should their values be?"

Troy volunteered: "I got this one!" He went on:

Current ratio = Current assets/Current liabilities, and it should be greater than 2.00.
Quick ratio = (Current assets-Inventory)/Current liabilities, and it should be greater than 1.00.

Sam said, "I am very impressed that you guys didn't forget anything. By the way, what are we doing this weekend? I was planning to dive into the next set of formulas."

Bill said, "Just tell us when and where, and we will be there, buddy!"

Self – Explorer

- From the stock screener of http://moneycentral.msn.com, find companies with a quick ratio above 2.00 and current ratio above 1.00.

- Also, from www.morningstar.com, check if the earnings per share of these companies is consistent.

- Now, analyze how many years each of these companies needs to repay its debt and decide whether it is a good company to consider investing in.

- In spite of the recession between 2000 and 2003, a few technology companies did very well in the stock market. Identify these companies and compare their current ratios and quick ratios.

- Visit other financial web sites like www.zacks.com, www.smartmoney.com and understand the format of the financial data presented.

True or False

- Companies with consistent earnings per share will not have any debt.

- Companies that generate high income from total sales are capable of paying their debt very easily.

- Only small companies have high debt, whereas Fortune 500 companies have no debt at all.

- Items in inventory are equivalent to cash.

- Current ratio ignores long-term debt, whereas quick ratio takes long-term-debt into account.

Chapter VI

Who is Dollar Wise, Penny Foolish?

Selfish Investors or Selfless Investors?

Feed an opportunity; starve a problem
Peter F. Drucker

Love Is in the 'Stocks'

He that falls in love with himself will have no rivals
Benjamin Franklin

'Cheesecake Factory' was buzzing with activity on a beautiful Friday night. Sam had booked a table for two in advance. He couldn't take his eyes off Jessica, who looked ravishing that evening.

They were seated in a cozy corner, and the waiter left them with the menus.

Jessica said, "Sam, I think this is the first time I have seen you without your laptop."

Sam said, "I think this is the first time I have dined with a model."

Jessica blushed, "Stop! I thought you never lie."

Sam said, "I am not lying. To tell you the truth, I was bowled over by your looks the minute Joe introduced me to you at that coffeehouse."

Jessica said, "I would have never guessed! I am flattered!" She continued, "Tell me, what are your other interests besides dissecting company reports?"

Sam said, "Well, I like music. I learned to play the guitar and drums. In fact, I wanted to start a band."

Jessica exclaimed, "Wow! I should hear you play sometime. I somehow can't picture the 'stocks-savvy Sam' playing hard rock."

Sam laughed. He said, "Some unbelievable things do happen, you know."

Jessica said, "I love this place. They have great food. How did you choose it?"

Sam answered, "Well, I just wanted to take a very special lady to a very special restaurant."

They enjoyed the rest of their romantic evening, and Sam dropped her off.

The next morning, Sam's mom was talking to Bill, at her home. She asked, "So, what's new, Bill?"

Bill said, "I have learned so much during the past week. I feel like a new person."

Sam's mom told Sam and Bill that she was going out.

Sam said, "Bill, do you have any plans for today and tomorrow?"

Bill asked, "First of all, how was the date last night? You dog! You were flirting right under our noses. Looks like I was paying too much attention to your charts to notice your romance in the corner."

Sam retorted playfully, "What romance? All I have been talking to Jessica about was earnings, debt and profits. You call that romance?"

Bill raised his eyebrows and said, "You tell me! Looks like there is some hidden flirting language. Beats me! Anyway, just kidding! Come to think of it, it will be a marriage of beauty and brains."

Sam chided, "Don't go there!"

Bill said, "How about we go camping tomorrow? I know a great place where we can go biking and camping. I already asked Joe and Troy, and they agreed."

Sam said, "Sounds good!"

They left the next morning. They drove and took their bikes along.

While they were biking along a trail, Joe asked Sam, "So, what is the next formula?"

Sam said, "Return on equity!"

Joe said, "Yeah! Like I know what that means!"

Sam began, "Okay, would you like to work for a company that makes a lot of profits and has no debt?"

Joe said, "Sure! Who wouldn't?"

Sam said, "How about this: would you like to work for a company that does very well but doesn't pay you well?"

Joe shook his head, "No way!"

Sam said, "To put it crudely, if you are considering investing in a company and are convinced it is making enough profits and is free from debt, your first goal is to verify whether it is capable of producing high profits from your investment.

"A couple of decades ago, if you wanted to watch a cartoon, you had to flip between *NBC (GE), ABC (DIS),* and *CBS (VIA),* If you wanted to watch a good movie, again you had a choice only among these three.

"But now, if you want to enjoy a great movie, you have *HBO (TWX), StarZ (L),* and *Show Time (VIA),* to name a few. Similarly, you have tons of choices if you are a sports fan.

"Along the same lines, if you want to own shares of a company, you are not restricted to only a few. The number of public companies in the U.S. alone is more than 12,000 and is still growing. So as an investor, you have a choice to own shares of any of these companies. Since you'll be investing your hard-earned money, it is prudent to find a company that provides great returns for your dollars.

"Once we catch up with the others, I will tell you how to measure profits."

Measuring Profits

One man with courage makes a majority
Andrew Jackson

Troy and Jessica were setting up the camp stove, and Bill was unloading the food.

Sam said, "Once we are done with eating, I will explain 'return on equity'. I didn't bring my laptop, but I have hard copy of the charts."

Jessica said, "Sam, I just want to say I had a nice time last evening!"

Sam replied, "So did I, Jess."

Once they were all ready, Sam said, "I was telling Joe about how important it is to measure profits. Well, let's say that Joe starts a company called *'Joe Pro Soft'*. He needs a couple of million dollars to begin his business. Two hundred people invest $10,000 each, and he opens the new business. He runs his business quite well and completes his projects on time, and thus he is able to get a lot of orders from his clients.

"Even though this information appeals to Joe's investors, they are interested in the profits their shares could make. As a result, they look at Joe's net profits. At the end of the fiscal year, it is $200,000."

Troy said, "The profit looks pretty impressive for a new firm."

Sam said, "Yes, but the investors want to know if the profits are sufficient for their investments. Since $2,000,000 dollars was pooled from investors and *'Joe Pro Soft'* could earn $200,000 per year as profits, the profit each investor realized is calculated as net profits divided by the shareholders' total investment.

"Return on investor's money, or return on equity = Net profit / Shareholder's equity

"For *'Joe Pro Soft'* investors, the return on equity would be = $200,000/$2,000,000 or 10%.

"So as an investor, would you be comfortable with a 10% return on your investments? All shareholders want better returns for their investments."

Joe asked, "Then is the share price directly proportional to return on equity?"

Sam replied, "Yes, the higher the return on equity, the higher the stock price goes up, and thus the greater the profit you as an investor would receive."

Jessica concluded, "So obviously we should expect at least 20% returns on our investments, and it is wise to invest in companies that can produce at least a 20% return on equity."

Sam added, "Also, as investors we want to make sure the company is capable of producing great returns under various economic conditions. So it is always good to measure five years of return on equity and verify that it is capable of producing consistent returns for your money."

Bill said, "Do you have a list of companies that have a good return on equity?"

Sam smiled, "You bet! Take a look. Also, check out the net worth of $100,000, invested in 1998, in companies that produced consistent returns for an investor's money."

1. Load www.morningstar.com
2. Enter the ticker symbol of the company (e.g., HDI for *Harley-Davidson*)
3. Now, click on 'Quote'
4. Click the tab 'Key Ratios'
5. Under the section 'Profitability', the last row shows the 'Return on Equity' for the past ten years.

Figure 6.1: Companies with consistent return on equity

Source: Morningstar, Inc.

Company	Return on equity %				Net worth of $100,000 investment in five years as of September 2003, ($)
	1994	1995	1996	1997	
Rent-A-Center, Inc.	94.15	32.02	16.34	18.62	295,094
Harley-Davidson	27.61	24.11	28.73	23.41	325,128
Bed Bath & Beyond	32.86	32.14	30.41	30.11	348,064
CDW Corp.	32.00	25.16	27.56	29.98	421,333
Apollo Group	355.63	66.91	31.69	32.88	509,408
AAON, Inc.	59.74	16.67	14.24	17.52	513,143
International Game Tech.	31.29	17.22	20.02	24.27	569,845

Source: Morningstar, Inc.

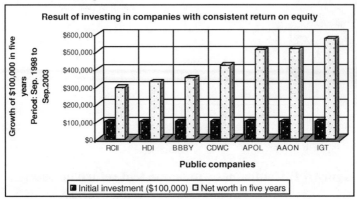

Once Won – Lost Ever

*Success usually comes to those who
are too busy to be looking for it*
Henry David Thoreau

Sam said, "Do you know how many people remember Pete Sampras, and how many remember Michael Chang? No doubt, Michael Chang won his first Grand Slam at the age of 17 years and three months. But in the world of tennis, who will be remembered forever? Would it be Michael Chang or Pete Sampras? Definitely Pete Sampras, "The definition of Champion". Why? He won 14 grand slam titles and not just one. He held the No.1 ranking for 268 weeks during his career. His achievements are not easy for any other individual to repeat. Even though Michael Chang was a good player, a consistent player is remembered forever.

"A great company is no different from Pete Sampras. An average corporation is like a tennis player who wins a Grand Slam at a young age but is not ale to repeat it later. Investing in companies that produce average or inconsistent returns on your investment may either make your investments evaporate or give you an average rate of growth."

Joe said, "A company's share price may go up in the short term, but if it is incapable of producing an excellent return on equity, then naturally the shareholders' value will not go up in the long run. Am I right, Sam?"

Sam said, "Yes! A company with a big name but with a negative return on equity is equivalent to Tiger Woods winning the next chess tournament against Gary Kasparov. However big the name of the company is, the main reason shareholders invest in it is to make profits from their investments. This in turn will make them rich. But if a company's return on equity is negative in the long run, then the shareholders are definitely not going to make money."

Bill concluded, "So the growth rate of a company's stock is directly related to the profits it is able to produce for its shareholders. But if it is unable to produce profits, then it leads to a negative return on equity. Investing in a company with a negative return on equity is like watching a tennis game between Tiger Woods and Pete Sampras and expecting Tiger Woods to win."

Joe asked, "Can we see the companies with inconsistent returns?"

Sam passed the chart to Bill.

Figure 6.2: Companies with average or inconsistent return on equity

Source: Morningstar, Inc.

Company	Return on equity %				Net worth of $100,000 investment in 1998, as of September 2003 ($)
	1994	1995	1996	1997	
Ethan Allen Interiors	14.31	12.20	13.69	20.17	159,738
Washington Mutual	12.28	13.79	4.0	11.98	190,587
Tenet HealthCare Corp.	(27.99)	9.64	15.40	(8.61)	79,867
The Walt Disney Company	21.07	22.76	10.56	11.80	84,438
La-Z-Boy Inc.	13.75	11.80	11.78	12.90	126,143
El Paso Corporation	12.65	12.01	3.00	10.38	27,044

Source: Morningstar, Inc.

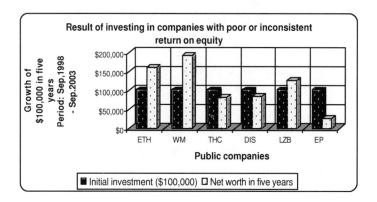

Detective Sherlock Holmes

> *Better to understand a little than to misunderstand*
> *a lot*
> Anonymous

Bill said, "Wow, that was interesting! Hey, can we continue this tomorrow? I feel like taking a walk."

Joe and Troy joined him. Sam and Jessica sat around the fire making s'mores.

Perhaps it was the starry night that induced Sam; or it could have been the campfire. He moved slowly towards Jessica. Neither one knew who made the first move, but soon they were kissing passionately.

That night ended their platonic friendship.

The next morning everyone took turns in churning out a great breakfast.

Bill asked, munching on an egg, "So what next, Sam?"

Sam was still on cloud nine. In this state of mind, he contemplated pronouncing all companies good and skipping off with Jessica. However, he dragged himself back to earth with an effort and sat down to teach the group.

Sam said, "A company with a good return on equity may not be a great company to invest in."

Bill said, "Man! Here we go again! What now?"

Sam laughed, "We have to find out if companies make technical faults to produce a high return on equity."

Troy asked, "Is that possible?"

Jessica said, "It's possible in the sports world! I remember watching the couples' figure skating competition at the 2000 Winter Olympics. Two Russians won the gold medal by the tiniest margin over two Canadians. But after a detailed investigation, it was proven that some of the judges had a deal among themselves to give the gold to the Russians, in spite of a technical fault while performing. So even in a major contest, spotting these mistakes is not impossible."

Sam said, "Actually, the easiest and most straightforward method to find such a possibility is to verify the company's expenses before they calculate their net profits."

Troy asked, "How do you do that?"

Investigation: High Interests

*Physics is like sex. Sure, it may give some practical
results but that's not why we do it*
Dr. Richard P. Feynman

"Say John and Gary are good friends and live in
Virginia. They both make a decent living and bring home
$3,000 every month. They are able to cover their basic
expenses like food, rent/mortgage, utilities, and insurance
for less than $2,000 a month. They are definitely not high
spenders, and they must be really planning well. But let us
play the role of Sherlock Holmes.

"Their monthly financial health looks as follows."

**Figure 6.3: Income and expense statement of John and
Gary**

	John ($)	Gary ($)
Income	3,000	3,000
Essential expenses (Mortgage or rent, utilities etc.)	2,000	1,700
Other expenses	200	300
Net savings per month	800	1,000

"From this table, it may appear Gary is able to
generate more profits (net income) from his total income.
However, we'll explore more about other expenses before
we conclude who is better at finance.

"After his essential expenses, John spends his
additional money eating out, attending Broadway shows,
etc. On the other hand, Gary spends his entire $300 on his
credit card interest .

"So who is better off financially? John or Gary? Wouldn't you agree that John handles finances better than Gary, and he enjoys his life by spending on his own entertainment? On the other hand, Gary hesitates to spend money on his own entertainment, because he has already accumulated a huge credit card debt and is therefore paying interest on his debt every month."

Joe said, "So if you analyze expenses in detail, you can get very different results."

Debt vs. Equity

It is better to debate a question without settling it
than to settle a question without debating it
Joseph Joubert

Sam said, "Yes. You are the CEO of your investments. You are responsible for making sure your investments will certainly return great value for your hard-earned money. So, how do you decide if a company with an excellent return on equity is really good to invest in or not?

"By ensuring it does not have a lot of debt."

Bill asked, "Now what is the major difference between debt and equity? They are both forms of raising capital for a company, right?"

Sam said, "No Bill, debt and equity are like apples and oranges. Even though debt and equity are forms of raising capital for a company, they are completely different.

"For example, *'Barnes & Noble' (BKS)* plans to expand its operations to Asian regions like China and India. It needs millions of dollars to complete this expansion project, and it needs to figure out the best way to raise the required capital.

"So it borrows some part of the required capital from banks and financial institutions, with the assurance that the expansion project is the best thing that can happen to its bookstore business. The bookstore's management team and the banks agree on the interest rate and the number of years within which the loans need to be repaid. This form of raising capital is known as *loan* or *debt.*

"Since *'Barnes & Noble'* received the capital from banks, it is solely responsible for repaying the loan with interest. It needs to repay the principal and also pay interest regularly, no matter how much or how little money it makes.

"Thus, a public company that borrows money is on the hook to pay the interest along with the principal.

"Assume *'Barnes &Noble'* decides to raise part of its capital through banks and the rest by issuing stocks to public shareholders. This is equity. The biggest advantage for *'Barnes & Noble'* is that it does not need to pay any interest on the money it collects from its shareholders, and it also does not need to repay the money it borrows from the public."

Joe concluded, "So you are saying that if you invest in a company with high debt, then the income the company generates goes mostly toward repaying the loan with interest. However, if you invest in a company with little or no debt, it passes its profits on to its shareholders."

Bill asked, "So how do we judge whether a company is doing justice to its shareholders or to its creditors?"

Sam answered, "Simple. It is known as debt/equity ratio."

Debt/Equity Ratio

No one is listening until you make a mistake
Anonymous

Sam said, "I will explain that to you. But I am going for a swim now. Want to join?"

Joe and Jessica stayed back.

Joe teased Jessica, "Someone is glowing! What is happening?"

Jessica blushed, "Nothing! Well, actually thank you so much for introducing me to Sam!"

Joe laughed, "You're welcome! Wow! Come to think of it, we might have a financial advisor in the family."

Jessica warned him with the same words Sam used: "Don't go there!"

At lunch, they sat down to rest. Sam asked, "Care to learn about debt/equity ratio?

"A company with less debt and more equity is always good for its shareholders. A company with a lot of debt and less equity is good only for the banks. Companies that borrow a lot of money are very bad for their shareholders.

"It is best to consider investing in companies with high return on equity and with debt/equity ratio less than 0.30, because they are the ones shareholders benefit from.

"Let us compare different companies with very low and high debt/equity ratios, and we'll calculate how much we would have earned at the end of five years by investing $10,000 in each of them."

1. Load www.morningstar.com
2. Enter the ticker symbol of the company (HDI for *Harley-Davidson*)
3. Now, click on 'Quote'
4. Click the tab 'Key Ratios'
5. Click on the top tab 'Financial Health'
6. Under the section 'Liquidity/Financial Health', for the last row shows the 'debt to equity Ratio' for the past ten years.

Figure 6.4: Companies with low or zero debt to equity ratio
Source: Morningstar, Inc.

Company	Debt to equity ratio between 1994 and 1997				Growth of $10,000 in five years, as of September, 2003	
					Net worth ($)	Annual compounded interest %
	1994	1995	1996	1997	Period: Sep,1998 - Sep. 2003	
Ross Stores	0.15	0.18	0.03	0	35,384	28.75
DR. Horton Inc.	0	0	0	0	38,217	30.75
Electronic Arts	0	0	0	0	42,963	33.85
Thor Industries Inc.	0	0	0.05	0	53,712	39.96
Varian Medical Systems	0.13	0.15	0.13	0.14	64,742	45.29

Source: Morningstar, Inc.

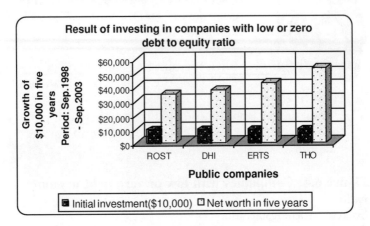

Figure 6.5: Companies with high debt to equity ratio

Source: Morningstar, Inc.

Company	Debt to equity ratio between 1994 and 1997				Growth of $10,000 From June 1998 until June 2003	
	1994	1995	1996	1997	Net worth ($)	Annual com-poun ded inter-est %
Emcore Corpora-tion	NA	1.99	17.21	0.35	8,192	(3.91)
Associated Estates Realty	1.11	1.23	1.38	1.76	7,027	(6.81)
BE Aerospa-ce, Inc.	1.22	1.42	6.33	1.39	2,186	(26.22)
CMS Energy Corporat-ion	2.00	1.79	1.66	1.92	2,217	(26.01)
Continent-al Airlines	13.15	6.16	3.24	2.02	2,516	(24.11)

Source: Morningstar, Inc.

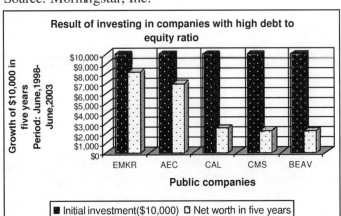

Return on Capital

> *Opportunities multiply as they are seized*
> Sun Tzu

Joe said, "Let me ask you something. Isn't it impossible for companies to function without raising loans? We can't avoid them. What do we do?"

Sam said, "You are right! Even though measuring return on equity is very important, a company with debt is risky to invest in. At the same time, it is very difficult for a public company to raise all the capital it needs without borrowing money.

"So if a company has an excellent return on equity but has outstanding debt, then a better way to measure its financial results is return on capital. If the debt to equity is above zero, we must measure the return on capital before deciding to buy the stock.

"Return on capital measures the profits of the company raised not only with its equity but also with its outstanding loans.

"Return on capital measures whether a company is able to produce sufficient profits from the total investments it collects from everyone. A company with a high return on capital is definitely a good choice, as it is capable of producing profits from the total investment it has acquired."

Bill asked, "Can you explain with your usual example?"

Fishy or Great Returns?

Sam said, "Sure! Say Troy loves fishing and swimming, and he decides to pursue a career in that area. He opens a business called *'Sea by See'* that rents out SCUBA diving equipment, and he does quite well. He realizes his potential and decides to expand his business by buying a couple of glass bottom boats so he can cater to people who are afraid of snorkeling. So, he borrows $100,000 from the local bank as a loan. He needs more money and borrows another $100,000 from his friends who, instead of loaning him the money, become partners by investing in *'Sea by See'*.

"A year passes, and Troy is still interested in expanding his business to include water-skiing and surfing equipment to cater to every tourist's interest. So Troy approaches you to invest $50,000 as a shareholder of *'Sea by See'*. The question is, what would you do?"

Bill joked, "Let me think! Since it is Troy, I would not even bother to calculate return on *anything* and simply say *'No'*."

Sam laughed, "Jokes apart, after the basic calculations, your next step would be to find return on equity and return on capital. For the recent year concluded, Troy's *'Sea by See'* made a $35,000 profit before paying the interest on his loans and a $25,000 net profit after paying the interest.

"So the return on equity would be $25,000/$100,000, which is 25%. The return on equity is very impressive. Since Troy borrowed money in addition to gaining equity, we cannot invest without looking at return on capital.

"Let us calculate the return on capital of *'Sea by See'* for the concluded year. Return on capital is calculated as Net Income Before Interests divided by the Total Capital Invested.

"Troy's net income before interest was $35,000 and total capital invested was $200,000. So is Troy's business really doing well?"

Joe answered, "I guess it is. Dividing profits before interest by total capital invested would be $35,000/$200,000 = 17.5%.

"I think that is an impressive figure for a company."

Sam said, "Right! Return on capital is good for *'Sea by See'*."

Jessica said, "Let me try to sum up the formulas we learned. Before investing our money in a public corporation, we must measure return on equity, debt/equity ratio and return on capital for at least four years."

Sam added, "Also, whenever you compare these ratios, you should also compare them with the Industry and with the S&P 500. This is to ensure that the ratios are better than the average ratio of the 500 companies included in the Standard and Poor index.

"For example, if the S&P 500's average return on equity is 20%, then the ROE of the company we invest in must be relatively higher than 20% and definitely not lower than 20%. This ensures our investments will do better than the average market."

Sam added, "Let me show you some data before we leave. See the comparison of the actual result of investing $10,000 in the following companies whose return on equity and return on capital are good. As it is very important to compare the company's performance with the industry standard and S&P 500, we'll explore the result of investing in companies that have performed higher."

Figure 6.6: Companies with excellent return on equity and return on capital

Source: Morningstar, Inc.

Company	Past five years' average return				Growth of $10,000 in five years
	Comp-any's ROE %	Indust-ry's ROE %	Comp-any's ROC %	Indust-ry's ROC %	Net worth ($)
Period: Five Years (1998 – 2003)					
S&P 500 Index	12.2		5.9		10,088
Oracle Corp.	50.8	14.0	48.5	13.1	25,298
SEI Corp.	53.1	17.0	44.8	13.4	29,323
Utah Medical Products	31.8	12.6	24.6	8.1	41,277
Techne Corpora-tion	17.4	NM	16.2	(3.7)	47,385

Source: Morningstar, Inc.

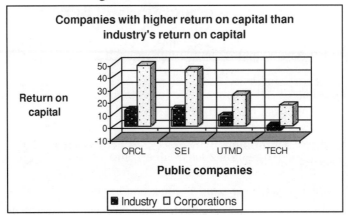

Source: Morningstar, Inc.

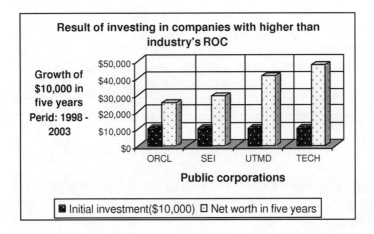

"Also, let us compare some companies that had poor return on capital but good return on equity. Let's see the net result of our investment in such companies."

Figure 6.7: Companies with excellent return on equity but poor return on capital

Source: Morningstar, Inc.

Company	Past five year's average return on equity and average return on capital				Growth of $10,000 in five years.
	Compa ny's ROE %	Industr y's ROE %	Compa ny's ROC %	Industr y's ROC %	Net worth ($)
Period: Five years (1998 – 2003)					
S&P 500 Index	12.2		5.9		10,088
American Business Financial Services	16.0	24.3	2.0	1.5	7,725
Ford Motor Company	13.7	9.0	1.8	2.9	5,535
Pitney Bowes Inc.	44.5	15.3	16.5	5.9	8,517
The Gillette Company	35.3	49.9	21.2	18.2	9,424

Source: Morningstar, Inc.

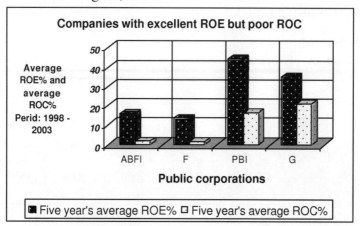

Source: Morningstar, Inc.

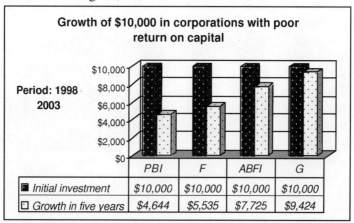

Bankruptcy – A Titanic Disaster!

If bigger was always better, dinosaurs would rule the world
Tom & Marilyn Ross, Authors

All the camping paraphernalia was packed. Troy said, "Oh! I almost forgot! What about companies that filed for bankruptcy? What was their return on equity like?"

Sam said, "Well, the companies that filed for bankruptcy had a clear sign! Their return on equity was either inconsistent or negative.

"Take a look at the return on equity of some of the infamous companies that either filed for bankruptcy or made their shareholder's money worthless."

Figure 6.8: Return on equities of infamous corporations between 1994 and 1997

Source: Morningstar, Inc.

Company	Return on equity %			
	1994	1995	1996	1997
Enron	16.79	17.47	17.15	1.96
WorldCom	(8.65)	11.44	(38.16)	2.78
K-Mart	(15.77)	4.94	(10.11)	(4.24)
Lucent Technologies	NA	(48.56)	11.73	18.00
AOL Time Warner	3.41	(20.41)	8.16	(234.64)

Jessica said, "Well, that was a clear warning bell. Looks like the investors of these companies missed seeing the iceberg, like the captain of the Titanic."

Bill said, "I have never gone on a camping trip like this. I am beginning to think I have multiple personalities. I can't believe I am learning so much on a 'fun trip'."

Joe joked, "Finally it has dawned on you. Anyway, thanks Sam, for sharing your knowledge!"

Sam replied, looking at Jessica, "Always a pleasure!"

Source: Morningstar, Inc.

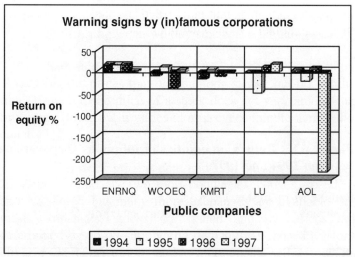

Sam's Sprinkles

My firm conviction is that only by studying the lessons of yesterday, can investors avoid making mistakes tomorrow. In no other area, has history repeated itself as in the stock market
Dana Thomas

• Investments made by shareholders are known as equity.

• A company may borrow from banks and other financial institutions. This type of borrowing is known as Debt.

• A public company with little or no debt is good for shareholders.

• Performance of a company's profit based on investor's contribution is measured by Return on Equity.

• Consider investing only in companies with low debt to equity ratio.

• Total Capital is the total of debt borrowed and shareholder's investment.

• Performance of a company with debt is calculated using Return on Capital.

Self-Explorer

• What are the other instruments besides stocks an investor can use to invest in a company?

• How are stocks different from bonds?

• How is shareholder's equity calculated?

True or False

- A public company has to pay interest for the loans it borrows and not for the equity it collects.

- A public company never pays interest to its shareholders.

- An investor is rewarded not by interest but by the value of shares. In other words, the higher the investment grows, the better the rewards are for the shareholders.

- A company with excellent return on capital may have low return on equity.

- Debt and return on equity are inversely proportional.

Chapter VII

Who is Dollar Wise, Penny Foolish?

Business Moguls or Charity Owners?

The only thing a man can do for eight hours a day is work. He can't eat for eight hours; he can't drink for eight hours; he can't make love for eight hours. The only thing a man can do for eight hours is work

William Faulkner

It's All About Margins

It is not the lofty sails but the unseen wind that moves
the ship
Anonymous

Joe was talking to someone on the phone. "How did the accident happen? How is Sam doing now?"

Jessica interrupted him, "What's going on?"

Joe hung up and told Jessica, "Sam had an accident and is in the hospital. I will fill you in on the way. Let's go."

Pam, their mother, said with genuine concern, "Hope that nice young man is all right."

Bill met Joe and Jessica in the hospital He told them, "Well, apparently his car was hit by a truck. He is okay, but he fractured his right leg and will have to be in a cast for some time."

They went to Sam's room. Sam was awake and smiled when he saw his friends. "Hello guys, thanks for coming."

Jessica asked, "How are you feeling now, Sam? Does your leg hurt badly?"

He replied with a twinkle, "Not much after seeing you, Jess."

Bill joked, "Oh please! Give it a rest! Look around. This is your chance to get the phone numbers of some of the cute nurses here. I saw a couple down the wing!"

Jessica glared at Bill.

Sam said, "I was going to teach you guys all about 'margins' next."

Troy said, "That can wait. Don't worry about it."

Sam said, "Well, it turns out that my accident is perfectly timed. A friend of mine, Diwa, was supposed to join us a week from now. We did a lot of studying together. He is a finance buff. I've asked him to come early, and he will be joining us tomorrow."

Joe said, "Diwa! Sounds like an Indian name."

Sam nodded.

Jessica said, "You know, Indians are very good in mathematics. In fact, they invented the concept of 'zero'."

Sam smiled. A nurse entered and requested them to leave.

Bill looked at her nametag and said, "Hi, Miranda, I have a slight pain in my biceps area. Would you mind taking a look?"

Before the shocked nurse could reply, Joe smiled sheepishly and dragged Bill away from the room.

New Best Friend

Every business is built on friendship
J.C. Penney

Diwa turned out to be a strapping, handsome young man. He hit it off with Sam's friends instantly. They were in Sam's room at the hospital. Diwa asked, "Sam, when are you getting discharged?"

Sam said, "In a week, I suppose. Remember I told you how I taught my friends about the 'stock picking formulas'?"

Diwa nodded.

Sam said, "Well, I have finished 'earnings per share', 'debt' and 'return on equity'. I wanted to talk about different margins, but this 'truck encounter' happened. Would you mind taking over till I get better?"

Diwa replied, "Of course, explaining the different 'margins' shouldn't be a problem. But I am not sure my approach will be as good as yours. I have to rack my brains to explain it using your approach."

Sam teased, "C'mon. We both invented that approach."

Turning to the others, Diwa said, "Okay, can we meet some place tomorrow, and I will go over the concepts with you?"

They agreed, said their goodbyes to Sam and left.

Before Diwa closed the door behind him, he said, "Sam, one of your new friends is extremely cute!"

Before Sam could tell him that he was already seeing her, Diwa left.

Measuring Gross Margin

Great ideas originate in the muscles
Thomas A. Edison

Since it was a bright and sunny day, everyone met at a local park. Diwa had his laptop and was going over some charts.

Bill joked, "Well, we seem to have an Indian clone of Sam here!"

Diwa laughed and began, "You know why Bill Gates dropped out of Harvard?"

Joe laughed, "He definitely didn't drop out to do charity work."

Diwa added, "Of course, he simply knew that developing a software company and making it global would fetch him a lot more money and fame than continuing his education in Harvard. In a way, be it Bill Gates or Michael Dell, everyone is interested in profits.

"So as an investor, how do we measure profit margins before buying stocks?

"Assume you are given enough money to run a car dealership business. As a businessman, what would be your sole motive?"

Bill answered, "Well! I would buy cars from the manufacturer at the lowest price and sell them to the customer at the highest price possible."

Diwa continued, "Now, when you are running a business, you want to maximize your profits. Similarly, when you are investing, you actually own the business. So doesn't it make sense to invest in a company that produces higher profits and margins?"

Jessica answered, "Absolutely!"

Diwa asked, "You guys interested in playing golf? If you are, I will give you examples using golf terminology."

They all nodded.

Diwa began, "Brian, a golf fan, had developed an interest in playing the game. So he made an effort to learn the game by playing miniature golf. During the first few weeks, he not only played well but also competed with his friends.

"Brian made a small bet with his friend Mary. They both agreed to play a round of miniature golf, and whoever won would receive $1,000 from the other person."

Troy interrupted, "$1,000 as prize money in miniature golf is not bad at all."

Diwa continued, "So Brian spent $100 to rent the best golf clubs for his game against Mary. As he had lot of practice, he won the game and earned the $1,000 prize money.

"From this, let's try to calculate Brian's margin. Brian spent $100 to rent the golf clubs, and he won $1,000."

Income   : $1,000
Expenses (Direct)   : $100
Gross profit   : $900

"Gross margin is also known as the gross profit margin, which is calculated by dividing the gross profit by the total income generated.

"Since Brian generated a total income of $1,000 and spent $100 in renting the equipment, his total gross margin would be

Gross margin = $900 / $1,000 = 90%

"Earning a 90% profit margin is very good for any business, be it an individual or a major corporation.

"Let us verify this with actual data.

"Here are some companies with excellent gross margins between 1995 and 1997."

Figure 7.1: Companies with good gross margins

Source: Morningstar, Inc.

Company	Ticker	Gross margin %		
		1995	1996	1997
Biomet	BMET	68.6	67.4	68.0
Factset Research Systems	FDS	100	100	100
Lincare Holdings	LNCR	63.0	63.1	64.0
Mylan Laboratories	MYL	57.2	49.7	41.0
Apache	APA	100	100	100

"The following are some companies with poor gross margins between 1995 and 1997."

Figure 7.2: Companies with poor gross margins

Source: Morningstar, Inc.

Company	Ticker	Gross margin %		
		1995	1996	1997
Administaff	ASF	4.0	4.2	4.2
Cellstar	CLST	13.4	13.5	14.5
Ingram Micro	IM	7.0	6.8	6.5

"Let me ask you this. What is the first and foremost lesson golfers learn before playing in any major tournament?"

Joe said, "Well, I think golfers should be able to identify their ball. If they are unable to do so, then they automatically lose the stroke."

Diwa continued, "Yes! Similarly, an investor should identify whether a company produces sufficient margins from the products or services sold. Investing in a company without knowing its profit margins is like a golfer who doesn't know how to identify his or her ball.

"Even the best golfers practice the stroke before playing. Similarly, however good a company may be, we have to consider its profit margins. Investing in a great company with higher profit margins would be like practicing the swings before playing the actual stroke.

"Don't golfers yell 'Fore!' when they hit the ball, because the ball travels at a high speed? This is a sign indicating 'Hey, hit the deck or you may be in trouble.'

"Well, a company may not yell 'Fore.' But investing in a company with poor margins is no different from not hitting the deck when a golfer yells 'Fore!'"

1.   Load www.morningstar.com
2.   Enter the ticker symbol of the company (e.g., LNCR for *Lincare*)
3.   Click on 'Quote'
4.   Click the tab 'Key Ratios'
5.   Under the 'Profitability' tab, you will see the 'Gross Margin' for the last ten years.

Operating Margin

When your work speaks for itself, don't interrupt
Henry J. Kaiser

Jessica said, "Wow! That was well explained, and I must say you explain things exactly like Sam would."

Bill said, "Diwa, before we go the next formula, let's grab some lunch."

They all agreed and started walking towards the eatery.

Joe asked, "So which part of India are you from, Diwa?"

Diwa replied, "Well, I am from the southern part of India. I was born in the city of Cuddalore."

Jessica asked, "What does that name mean?"

Diwa said, "It means 'a city by the sea'."

Jessica exclaimed, "Wow! So exotic! When did you move to the States?"

Diwa replied, "When I was ten. My dad got a job in the U.S. and we moved. He taught me a lot about the rich Indian culture, and he makes it a point to visit India once a year. Most of my family lives back there."

They reached a restaurant and sat down to eat. Jessica called Sam. The hospital put her through to his room.

Sam temporarily forgot his pain.

Sam asked her, "So, what did you all learn?"

Jessica told him, "First tell me, how is your leg?"

He briefed her on his condition, which was improving.

Jessica said, "We learned about gross margin, and you would be interested in knowing Diwa's nickname, which is 'Sam's Indian clone'."

Sam laughed.

She continued, "He is going to teach us something more after lunch. I will see you tonight. Okay Sam?"

Diwa couldn't help notice Jessica's open show of concern and affection for Sam. He wondered if it could be a little more than just a strong friendship.

They went to an ice cream parlor.

Diwa began, "Since a company spends money on other things besides producing goods, we should look at whether it is capable of producing enough margin after calculating its expenses to run the business.

"If raw material is essential to producing goods, then advertising is essential to selling goods. The cost of raw material is included in calculating gross margin, but advertising costs are not. Since advertising costs are essential only in selling, they come under operating costs.

"In golf parlance, metal woods are not made for distance but for accuracy. Golfers need to know when to use irons and when to use wedges. They get ahead only if they are able to sink the ball in the cup. It is not enough to be able to hit the ball."

Joe interrupted. "Yes, and you should also be able to putt."

Diwa continued, "Along the same lines, gross margin is like metal woods, and operating margin and net margin are like irons and wedges."

Jessica confirmed, "So you are saying that it is not wise to invest in a company by just looking at gross margin. We should also look at operating costs."

Diwa nodded and said, "Yes, it is equally important to look at operating margin and net margin before investing.

"A company with a higher gross margin but a lower operating margin is like a golfer who can hit the ball but can't putt. Looking only at gross margin is like hitting with a nine-iron club. Once you are close to the cup, you should be comfortable using two and one clubs. Golfers should be good at both nine-iron and one-iron clubs. Only then will they be able not only to hit but also to putt before the hole is flagged.

"Similarly, gross margin is important, but operating margin is equally important. By buying shares of a company, you become a business owner of the company. So before buying, you need to understand how much profit the company is able to generate.

"Let's take the same example. Brian was getting ready to play in the state league match. He spent $5,000 to buy the best clubs and hire the best trainer to help him practice. He paid $12,000 for the trainer and spent another $20,000 to use the local country club's facilities. Before entering the competition, Brian spent another $10,000 on accessories like golf shoes, trousers, USGA shirts, etc.

"As Brian was getting ready for the league match, he hired Demy, an experienced caddie. Demy was not only quick in picking golf clubs, she was also a great looking girl. Brian paid $5,000 for her services at the league match.

"Brian won the game for the state, and he not only picked up the trophy but also won the $100,000 prize money. His name appeared in newspapers and local magazines, and he became famous."

Bill remarked, "Sounds very much like a fairy tale!"

Diwa laughed, "Anyway, let's find out Brian's actual operating margin."

Figure 7.3: Brian's financial statement

Description of income and expense	Amount	Remarks
Prize money from the tournament	$100,000	This is treated as total income
Money – spent on clubs	$5,000	Expenses involved in gaining the prize
Trainer	$10,000	money (Cost of
Local country club	$20,000	producing goods)
Accessories	$10,000	
Caddie's salary	$5,000	
Gross profit earned	$50,000	Income - expenses
Gross margin	50%	Gross profit / income

Jessica said, "Yeah! From the table, it looks like Brain made a reasonably good gross margin."

Diwa said, "There were other expenses, too. Brian not only spent money on a trainer, he also spent money on the consulting firm *'Golf Winners,'* who helped him find the best trainer and caddie. They also helped Brian choose the right clubs so he could learn to play like a pro.

"Instead of paying the consulting firm a fixed amount, Brian agreed to share $15,000 if he won the prize money. Since Brian won the tournament, he also distributed gifts to everyone who helped him win, totaling $20,000. So, let us compare the other expenses involved."

Figure 7.4: Calculation of operating margin for Brian

Description of income and expense	Amount	Remarks
Income generated	$100,000	Prize money
Gross profit earned	$50,000	Money earned after spending for the essentials to win the prize money
Money paid to the consulting firm 'Golf Winners'	$15,000	These expenses are not directly involved in winning
Money spent on gifts	$20,000	the tournament, but Brian spent on these after winning the tournament.
Operating profit	$15,000	Profit after expenses
Operating margin	15%	Operating profit margin

Joe looked at the figures and said, "I get it. A company might spend money on advertising, planning, salaries and health benefits for their employees, settlements for lawsuits, etc. All these expenses are not directly involved in producing goods, but they are essential for the company to run their day-to-day operations."

Diwa said, "Exactly, my friend. That is why it is known as operating margin. A company capable of consistently producing 20% or more as operating margin is worth investing in."

Bill said, "So it looks like Brian, the Tiger Woods wannabe, made a killer gross margin, but he made only a reasonable operating margin."

Jessica remarked, "Hmm! Interesting! Thanks Diwa, for teaching us about 'margins'. I am keeping a little book of all the formulas Sam has taught us so far. I have a list of companies in mind, and I am going to see if they pass the formulas or not."

They decided to head to their respective homes and planned on visiting Sam later that evening.

Net Profit Margin

It is your work in life that is the ultimate seduction
Pablo Picasso

The first question Bill asked Sam was, "Did you get any phone numbers?"

Sam said, "Of course! I asked the hot nurses to write their phone numbers on my cast."

Bill quickly turned to see Sam's cast, which of course, was sparkling white and clean.

Bill shook his head. "That was a killer idea. Too bad you didn't use it!"

Sam said, "Diwa, did you teach them about gross, operating and net margins?"

Diwa said, "Oh wait! I forgot about net margin. Shall I explain that now?"

Bill asked, "Here? In the hospital?"

Jessica joked, "Just hearing these terms will make Sam feel better, I think."

Sam laughed, "You can't be more right! Go on, Diwa. I have an interesting assignment for you guys."

Diwa said, "Remember our friend Brian, the golfer? Well, he made profits, but he also had to pay taxes on them. He got the help of *H & R Block (HRB)* to calculate his taxes and his net income." Diwa opened his laptop and showed them a table.

Figure 7.5: Calculation of net profit margin for Brian

Description	Amount	Remarks
Total income	$100,000	Total income generated
Gross profit	$50,000	Money earned after essential expenses
Operating profit	$15,000	Profit after paying all the operating expenses
Taxes	$4,500	Taxes paid to the government
Net income	$10,500	Net profit after paying for all the expenses
Net profit margin	10.5%	Net profit margin

"Even though Brian made a huge gross profit of 50%, his net profits were only 10.5%."

Joe exclaimed, "Whoa! He had a good gross margin, reasonable operating margin but a paltry net margin."

Diwa said, "Yes! A company with a huge gross margin but poor net margin is like someone making a huge salary but saving very little. Always consider companies that have a net margin of at least 15%.

"Now, if you are running a corporation, it is not enough if you make a considerable gross margin. At the end of the day, as a business, you would certainly like to have a sufficient amount of money as profits."

Joe concluded, "So a business that cannot make a sufficient net margin will suffer in the long run, because it is unable to generate income for its future expenses. Right, Diwa?"

Diwa answered, "Yes. I think I covered all the margins, and here are the charts you can refer to."

Sam said, "Yes, you can read these charts when you find time. But I have an interesting assignment for you guys. Trust me, you will love doing it."

1. Load www.morningstar.com
2. Enter the ticker symbol of the company (e.g., LNCR for *Lincare*)
3. Click on 'Quote'
4. Click the tab 'Key Ratios'
5. Under the 'Profitability' tab, you will see the Operating Margin for the last ten years.
6. Also, under the 'Profitability' section, you will see the Net Margin for the last ten years.

Figure 7.6: Companies with excellent gross margin, operating margin and net margin

Source: Morningstar, Inc.

Company	1995			1996		
	Gross margin %	Opera-ting margin %	Net margin %	Gross margin %	Operat-ing margin %	Net margin %
Biomet	68.6	26.3	17.51	67.4	25.7	17.59
Factset Research Systems	100	22.4	13.65	100	24.0	14.59
Mylan Laboratori es	57.2	34.8	30.51	49.7	25.5	26.05
Strayer Education	100	16.2	18.46	100	35.5	31.79

Figure 7.7: Growth of $10,000 in companies with good gross, operating and net margins

Source: Morningstar, Inc.

Company	Growth of $10,000 invested in 1998 as of 2003 - in five years		
	Net worth ($)	Growth %	Average compound ed annual interest %
Biomet	20,757	108	15.72
Factset Research Systems	21,042	107	16.04
Mylan Laboratories	19,185	92	13.91
Strayer Education	32,639	226	29.69

Source: Morningstar, Inc.

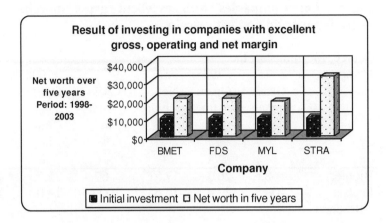

Figure 7.8: Companies with excellent gross margin, but low operating margin and poor net margin

Source: Morningstar, Inc.

Company	Margin during 1995			Margin during 1996		
	Gross %	Operating %	Net %	Gross %	Operating %	Net %
Datawatch	80.5	4.9	4.93	84.9	3.8	3.76
Epicor Software	64.6	(10.3)	(10.17)	50.2	(81.1)	(81.21)
Segue Software	86.1	(2.5)	(2.7)	86.7	(0.8)	(3.77)
Mannatech	46.3	(0.6)	7.30	43.7	9.5	8.30
MicroStrategy	74.8	0.8	0.51	76.7	(10.1)	(10.53)

Figure 7.9: Investment Growth of $10,000 in companies with poor margins

Source: Morningstar, Inc.

Company	Growth of $10,000 invested in 1998 as of 2003 - in five years		
	Net Worth ($)	Growth %	Average annual compounded interest %
Datawatch	9,163	(8)	(1.73)
Epicor Software	10,256	3	0.50
Segue Software	1,284	(87)	(33.67)
Mannatech	10,170	2	0.33
MicroStrategy	3,537	(65)	(18.76)

Source: Morningstar, Inc.

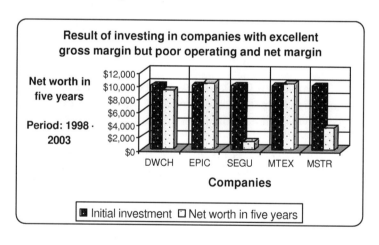

You are the CEO

Success isn't a result of spontaneous combustion.
You must set yourself on fire
Arnold H. Glasow

Bill said, "Sam, I think we are going to take off now. Is that okay?"

Sam laughed, "Not so fast! Here goes.

"It is 10:00 AM, and each of you has received a call from the head of the recruiting firm *'CEO Hunters'*. The caller, Mr. Smith, is giving you an option of becoming the CEO of one of three major corporations, namely *General Motors (GM)*, *Hot Topic (HOTT)* and *Paychex (PAYX)*. Let's say Joe and Jessica are given a joint offer from *GM*, Bill is given an offer to head *Hot Topic* and Troy is given *PayChex*.

"The recruiter also says you will be paid one million dollars as a base salary plus 10% of the company's profits.

"Now, as a CEO, you would be interested in picking up the offer from the company that makes the maximum profits, so you will earn the most amount of money.

"An investor is no different from a CEO, except for the title. As an investor, it is your responsibility to invest in a company that generates maximum profits.

"So, I want each of you to find out whether the company you are asked to head is making sufficient profits.

"I think by the time I am discharged you will have your answers, right?"

Joe said, "Piece of cake! Diwa, if you don't mind, will you join us?"

They all laughed.

Diwa said, "Sorry guys, I am actually flying back in two days."

They said their goodbyes and left.

Joe answered the phone at his home. He said, "Hey Diwa, have you changed your mind about helping me?"

Diwa laughed, "Actually, I was hoping to talk to Jessica, if she is around."

Joe said, "Sure. Hold on a minute."

Diwa asked Jessica, "Hey Jess, I was wondering if you have any plans tonight."

Jessica hesitated because she knew where this was going.

Diwa asked, "Can we have dinner and catch a movie? If that is okay with you?"

She said, "Well, this is awkward, but I am already seeing someone."

Diwa masked his disappointment and said, "Oh! That's fine. Not a problem. I will see you the next time I am in town."

The next morning he went to the hospital to see Sam.

Sam said, "Hey man, thanks for coming here."

Diwa said, "Not a problem. I had some work here anyway. Glad to be of help. By the way, I asked Jessica out last night."

Sam hesitatingly asked, "And...?"

Diwa said, "Well, she said is already seeing someone. Lucky guy! Okay, I have to go now. I will see you later. Get well soon."

Sam felt very relieved after hearing about Jessica's refusal to go out with Diwa.

The 'Three Margins'

Wisdom is the reward you get for a lifetime of listening when you'd have preferred to talk
Doug Larson

When Sam was discharged, he met his friends at school.

Joe said, "Good to see you, man!"

Bill said, "Welcome back!"

Sam replied, "Thanks! So, are you ready with the assignment?"

Jessica smiled, "You bet! We did our research individually, but we will present the solution together. Is that okay?"

Sam smiled, "Yes ma'am! Let's meet after school at my place. We can go over it then."

Troy said, "Sam, we are taking you out to an Ethiopian restaurant tonight to celebrate your discharge."

Sam was overwhelmed. "Wow! Thanks! Ethiopian? What an interesting choice of restaurants!"

Bill smiled, "Troy wants to revive his African connections!"

They all laughed and agreed to meet at the Ethiopian restaurant 'Makeda.'

Troy asked them, "Which dining room do you prefer? One of the two dining rooms has colorful basket-weave tables called *mossobs*, where you sit on handsome rosewood stools, share a communal plate and dine in customary Ethiopian fashion. The other dining room has a more Western setting."

They all decided to go with the former.

Jessica began after helping herself to the exotic appetizers, "Can I start?

"*General Motors (GM)*, as we all know, makes cars like Saturn, Chevy, and Hummer. Based on the requirements from dealers all over the world, they manufacture cars by buying raw materials like iron, glass, tires, etc. They buy these from various vendors, including *General Electric (GE)*, *Delphi Automobiles (DPH)* and *Goodyear (GT)*.

"After buying the raw materials, GM uses the labor in their plants to produce the actual cars, which they then ship to the dealers. They collect money from the dealers for the cars they ship.

"GM's business model is as follows."

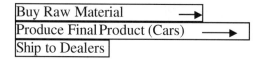

"So, GM's main source of income is from its dealers. The money it collects in one year from its dealers is known as 'Total Income' or 'Sale of Goods'."

Bill interrupted, "Similarly, *Hot Topic (HOTT)*, a major manufacturer of fashion dresses, is influenced by music trends. They sell fashion clothes through their nationwide stores and online channels. When a customer picks up an item, the corporation makes money.

"So, the money it collects during one year from its stores and online purchases is known as 'Gross Income' or 'Net Sales'."

Jessica said, "We have made a table showing the total income in 2002 for all three companies."

Figure 7.10: Total income of GM, Hot Topic and PayChex for 2002

Source: Morningstar, Inc.

Company	Ticker	Industry	Total income for the year 2002 ($ in millions)
General Motors	GM	Automobiles	186,763
Hot Topic	HOTT	Textile	443
PayChex	PAYX	Data Processing	1,099

Sam said, "The above data reflects the total income the businesses generated. But as investors, we are concerned not only about revenues but also the expenses involved. Only then will we be able to decide whether the businesses are really making good profits."

Joe said, "Yes! So *General Motors* has to pay its raw material vendors. Similarly, *Hot Topic* has to pay its garment vendors.

"The money companies pay for raw materials is known as 'Cost of Goods Sold'. This is the most important expense involved in any business. Right, Sam?"

Sam nodded.

Joe continued, "So, let us explore the expenses involved for these three companies and understand the profits each of them made."

Figure 7.11: Gross profit of GM, Hot Topic, and PayChex for 2002
(All figures are in Millions)

Source: Morningstar, Inc.

	General Motors (GM)	Hot Topic (HOTT)	PayChex (PAYX)
Total income for the year 2002	$186,763	$443	$1,099
Cost of goods sold	$144,550	$273	$257
Gross profit	$33,410	$170	$841

"But how do we know which one runs its business most efficiently? In other words, if it earns $100, what is its Gross Profit? This is calculated using gross margin; that is

$$\frac{Gross\ Profit}{Total\ Income} * 100$$

"Let us explore the gross margin of these three major corporations."

Figure 7.12: Gross margin of GM, Hot Topic, and PayChex for 2002

Source: Morningstar, Inc.

	General Motors (GM)	Hot Topic (HOTT)	PayChex (PAYX)
Total income for the year 2002 (In Millions)	$186,763	$443.250	$1099.1
Cost of goods sold (In Millions)	$144,550	$273.13	$257.7
Gross profit (In Millions)	$33,410	$170.11	$841.4
Gross margin	22.6%	38.4%	76.6%

Troy was very pleased. "Check out the gross margin of my company, *'PayChex'*."

The waiter took their orders.

Joe continued, "But is it possible to run a business by just paying vendors? Definitely not. In addition to paying its raw material vendors, *General Motors* has to pay its own employees. It also needs to launch a new advertising campaign to lure customers, so it has to run TV and radio commercials, newspaper ads, billboards, etc. Such day-to-day expenses are known as operating expenses or 'Selling, General, Administrative Expenses.'"

Bill added, "Similarly, *Hot Topic* has to pay its employees and introduce new fashion designs every now and then, according to the current music trends. It must also spend heavily on advertising and marketing. Even though these expenses are not directly related to manufacturing fashion dresses, they are essential, because shoppers would never know about them if they did not advertise.

"Companies like *GM* and *Hot Topic* also have to pay for their utilities. In fact, *General Motors'* utility bills must be very high because of the huge operational costs involved in running its factories."

Troy said, "On the other hand, *PayChex's* utility bills must be very minimal, because it is a service-oriented industry and not a manufacturing industry.

"So, let us understand the actual expenses involved in operating the business, over and above the cost of producing the goods. The remaining money after covering all the day-to-day operating expenses is known as 'Operating Profit'."

Figure 7.13: Operating profit of GM, Hot Topic, and PayChex for 2002

Source: Morningstar, Inc.

	General Motors (GM)	Hot Topic (HOTT)	PayChex (PAYX)
Total income for 2002 (In millions)	$186,763.00	$443.00	$1,099
Cost of goods sold (In millions)	$144,550.00	$273.00	$257.00
Gross profit (In millions)	$42,213.00	$170.00	$841.00
Gross margin	22.6%	38.4%	76.6%
Operating expenses (In millions)	$30,988.00	$115.00	$440.00
Operating profit (In millions)	$11,225.00	$54.00	$401.00

Jessica added, "How do we decide whether the company is maintaining sufficient profits? Again, it is not enough for it to generate a huge income. Income without sufficient profits is like having a huge car that doesn't get good mileage.

"As an investor, you would be an owner of the business, so you would like to make sure it makes sufficient profits.

"Now, how do we measure a corporation's operating profit margin? It is very simple. Operating profit margin, also known as operating margin, is as follows."

Operating margin = (Operating Profits / Revenues) * 100

Figure 7.14: Calculation of operating margin
Source: Morningstar, Inc.

	General Motors (GM)	Hot Topic (HOTT)	PayChex (PAYX)
Total income for the year 2002 (In millions)	$186,763.00	$443	$1099.00
Cost of goods sold (In millions)	$144,550.00	$273.00	$257.00
Gross profit (In millions)	$42,213.00	$170.00	$841.00
Gross margin	22.6%	38.4%	76.6%
Operating expenses (In millions)	$30,988.00	$115.00	$440.00
Operating profit (In millions)	$11,225.00	$54.00	$401.00
Operating margin	6.0%	12.3%	36.5%

Troy remarked, "Ha! Ha! My company is still in the lead!"

Bill said, "It's not a race, Troy."

Troy retorted, "If it were, I would be clearly in the lead."

Sam praised them. "Wow, you guys are fantastic! How about we eat and then continue?"

They had a sumptuous Ethiopian feast.

Sam said, "Thanks for visiting me every day at the hospital."

Bill teased, "C'mon! Admit it. You were more impressed with our assignment results than our visits to the hospital."

Sam laughed, "Both, my friend."

Joe added, "Your friend Diwa was quite a help. He used the same approach you use to teach us how to calculate margins."

Sam said, "Yep! He is something! Joe, can you pass me the dessert menu, please?"

Joe joked, "Someone has had too much hospital food!"

Jessica said, "Okay, let's find out how these companies stand with regard to net margin. Whenever a company earns a profit, it has to pay taxes.

"But there is a difference. The difference between an individual and a company is that an individual has to pay taxes on his gross, and he's allowed to spend only what he earns after taxes. Someone making $40,000 would have to pay taxes on the entire $40,000, even before buying a cup of coffee. So even though he gets $40,000 on paper, he would receive about $27,000 per year, with the IRS collecting the rest in taxes."

Troy continued, "Right. On the other hand, a corporation pays taxes on its earnings after expenses. A company making billions of dollars in revenues will not pay taxes on the entire amount. It will pay taxes only on the income it generates after all its expenses.

"So before we decide who is more profitable on the basis of total revenues, we should take taxes into account.

"The revenue generated after expenses, including taxes and interest to the debtors, is known as 'Net Revenue' or 'Net Income,' which is equivalent to earnings.

"Let us find out which one of the companies is profitable on the whole and which company generates maximum profits."

Figure 7.15: Net income for 2002
Source: Morningstar, Inc.

Description	General Motors (GM)	Hot Topic (HOTT)	PayChex (PAYX)
Total income for 2002 (In millions)	$186,763	$443	$1099
Cost of goods sold (In millions)	$144,550	$273	$257
Gross profit (In millions)	$42,213	$170	$841
Gross margin	22.6%	38.4%	76.6%
Operating expenses (In millions)	$30,988	$115	$440
Operating profit (In millions)	$11,225	$54	$401
Operating margin	6.0%	12.3%	36.5%
Interest paid or collected (In millions)	($9145.00)	$1	$30
Income before taxes (In millions)	$2,080	$55	$431
Tax rate	23.5%	37.7%	30.50%
Taxes (In millions)	$533	$21	$138
Net income after taxes (Actual profit) (In millions)	$1,689	$34	$293

"As you can see, the taxes are paid only on the income earned after expenses. Even though *General Motors* earned $186,763 million as revenues, it earned only $2,080 million after expenses. Therefore, it pays taxes only on $2,080 million and not the entire $186,763 million.

"Even if a company generates good revenues, it is very important for it to make sufficient profits."

Sam asked, "So which of these companies is the most profitable and makes sufficient returns for its shareholder's investment?"

"Troy said, "Let us find out from the net profit margin, which is calculated as follows."

Net profit margin = (Net Income / Revenues) * 100

"Let us calculate the net profit margin for these companies."

Figure 7.16: Net profit margin for 2002

Source: Morningstar, Inc.

	General Motors (GM)	Hot Topic (HOTT)	PayChex (PAYX)
Total income for 2002 (In millions)	$186,763	$443	$1099
Net Income after taxes (Actual profit) (In millions)	$1689	$34	$293
Net profit margin	0.90%	7.81%	26.7%

Joe asked, "How come *PayChex* is able to generate more profits from the revenues it collects compared with *General Motors* and *Hot Topic*?"

Troy answered, "*PayChex* is purely a data processing company that doesn't have to depend on individual customers. It contacts small and medium businesses directly, without spending too much money on maintaining shops in malls, and so on.

"On the other hand, *General Motors* spends a lot of money on both manufacturing cars and advertising. In addition, it has to target individual customers. It has to cut into much of its profits to compete with Japanese companies. Even though it makes huge sales, its net revenues are less than 1%."

Sam said, "Good work, folks. I am very impressed."

Bankruptcy with Warning Signs

Joe said, "We also have one more special chart for you."

Sam asked, "What is it?"

Jessica said, "We have compiled a list containing the margins of companies that went bankrupt."

Sam exclaimed, "Awesome! Show me the chart."

Figure 7.17: Bankrupt companies' margin details between 1995 and 1997

Source: Morningstar, Inc.

Company	Margin in 1995			Margin in 1996		
	Gross %	Operating %	Net %	Gross %	Operating %	Net %
Enron	13.5	6.7	5.48	10.5	5.2	4.27
World Com	45.3	18.6	6.44	45.2	(41.1)	(49.37)
K-Mart	24.3	1.8	0.86	22.1	(1.2)	(1.65)
ImClone	100	(1463)	(1205)	100	(2,473)	(2670)

Sam congratulated them on their efforts.

Bill asked, "So, what is the next formula, and when are we going to discuss it?"

Sam said, "Well, I have some catching up to do. Maybe in two or three days."

Bill looked at Jessica and Sam. He winked and said, "I understand!"

Sam's Sprinkles

- An investor is no different from an owner of a corporation. It is very important for an investor to invest only in companies with a high profit margin.

- Every corporation makes money by selling either products or services. The total income generated per year is known as Gross Income.

- The cost involved in producing goods is known as Cost of Goods.

- Gross Profit is calculated by subtracting cost of goods sold from gross income.

- Gross margin is calculated by dividing the Gross Profit by Gross Income.

- Consider investing only in companies with a gross margin of at least 40%.

- In addition to spending money to produce goods, a company has to spend money on advertising, employees' salaries, and other day-to-day operations. These are known as Operating Expenses.

- Money earned after deducting operating expenses is known as Operating Profit.

- Operating Margin is calculated by dividing the operating profit by gross revenues.

- A well-managed corporation generates at least a 20% operating margin.

- A corporation also has to pay taxes and interest on loans. Deducting these expenses from operating profit produces Net Profit. Net profit is equivalent to cash available after all expenses.

- Net Margin is calculated by dividing net profits by gross revenues.

- A good company should produce at least a 15% net margin.

Self Explorer

- Use the stock screener tool from http://moneycentral.msn.com to identify companies with at least a 20% net margin.

- Add the debt to equity ratio of less than 0.20% and short list the companies even further.

- What is an ADR? How is it different from U.S.-based companies?

- Visit the website of at least two of your favorite companies and download their annual reports. How much of the annual report can you actually understand?

- What is the difference between a balance sheet and an income sheet?

Chapter VIII

Who is Dollar Wise, Penny Foolish?

Bill Pay- From Investments or Paycheck?

Even if you are on the right track, you'll get run over
if you just sit there
Will Rogers

Bed, Breakfast and Beyond

It's easy to meet expenses- everywhere we go, there
they are
Anonymous

Sam asked, "What is this?" He was opening a small gift from Joe, Bill, and Troy.

Sam exclaimed, "Wow! It's a gift coupon for two at *Martha's Bed and Breakfast*. C'mon guys, you didn't have to do this."

Joe said, "You totally deserve it, Sam!"

Sam said, "Thanks! Gee! I wonder who I am going to take with me."

Bill laughed, "Yeah, right!"

Sam and Jessica decided to spend the weekend at the bed and breakfast.

'*Martha's Bed and Breakfast*' was an elegant 19th century inn. The innkeeper, Mr. Denny Collins, greeted them, "Hello, Welcome to Martha's. Let me show you the rooms."

He took them round the Martha's and showed them the facilities, which were quite impressive.

Sam and Jessica then went to their room. Jessica exclaimed, "Such a beautiful place. It's so romantic!"

Sam hugged her passionately and said, "I missed you so much, Jess."

She replied softly, "Me too, Sam."

That evening, they rented out bicycles and went for a short ride. They took a break near a brook and sat down for a while. Sam said, "The brook looks beautiful. I think I feel that way because you are here with me, Jess."

Jessica blushed and said lightly, "I thought your strength was in finance. Looks like someone is a poet, too."

Sam said, "Well, I always wanted to meet a woman who is good-looking, intelligent and has a lot of common sense. I am so glad I found all that in you."

Jessica smiled and said, "Thanks. You are not so bad yourself."

Sam was shocked, "What?"

Jessica, "Should I say, 'perfect'?"

Sam laughed and said, "You go for the extremes, don't you?"

They headed back to the inn and met Denny and his wife Martha, after whom the inn was named. They decided to chat with them for a little while.

Jessica told Denny and Martha what brought them there.

Denny said, "So you're a finance whiz, huh? You are so young, it's quite amazing."

Sam laughed, "Not a whiz! I just happen to be interested in finance and understand how companies operate."

Denny said, "I know you two have come here to take a break. But would you be able to spare some time and explain something to me? I have invested in stocks, and I have a few questions about certain things."

Sam replied, "Absolutely! Is that okay, Jess?"

She smiled and nodded.

Pay Your Bills

*The best thing about the future is that it comes only
one day at a time*
Abraham Lincoln

Jessica and Sam had a sumptuous breakfast the next morning. Mrs. Collins had prepared a delicious spread of French toast, buttered Danish pastries and freshly brewed coffee.

Sam declared, "Oh! What a meal! I can't breathe. You want to go for a walk, Jess?"

She said yes, and they went for a lovely walk in the rustic woods. Sam asked her, "Are you sure you are okay with my spending time with Denny and Martha explaining financial stuff?"

Jessica said, "Let me remind you about something, Sam. I lost my heart to you during one of your financial lectures, not sure which one."

Sam joked, "Oh, good! I will give more and more lectures in the future."

When they came back, Dennis waved to them, "Hello kids, having a good time?"

Mrs. Collins complained, "Sending out these bills takes forever!"

Dennis said, "You know what makes a human superior to others? Human capacity is unlimited. Humans invented everything from the wheel to satellites. We have discovered many countries to live in. We have produced goods that can make our lives better, more productive.

"Even small things we cannot live without are marvelous inventions. Like masking tape and clear cellophane tape invented by Richard G. Drew.

"Earle Dickson, a cotton buyer at *Johnson & Johnson*, invented and perfected the BAND-AID® in 1920, making a small, sterile adhesive bandage for home use. Dickson invented the BAND-AID® for his wife, who had many kitchen accidents and needed an easy-to-use wound dressing. *Johnson & Johnson* rewarded Dickson by making him a vice-president of the company.

"We have invented planes, trains, and automobiles to make our world smaller. But there is one product that can never, ever be made."

Sam asked, "What is that?"

Dennis said, "A solution for our day-to-day expenses, or in other words, a solution to paying our bills."

They all laughed.

He continued, "We work hard to earn money, and the IRS takes its share even before we get our paycheck. With the remaining money, we have to take care of our mortgage or rent, bills, gas, entertainment, etc. No doubt, some of us have to live paycheck to paycheck."

Sam said, "Well, 'money' is an interesting word. Unlike other assets, your money doesn't always stay with you, even if it is millions of dollars. You lock your house and go on a week's vacation to Florida. When you come back after a week, the house is still there with all the furniture in place.

"You go to shop in the mall. You park your car in the mall at 11:00 AM, and after a day of shopping you return to the parking lot around 8:00 PM. You still find your Corvette in its place with the same license plate number.

"But what about money? You deposit a $100 bill in *Commerce Bank (CBH)* in the morning and after a day you withdraw $100 from an ATM. Do you get the same bill and serial number from the ATM? Definitely not!

"Unlike other assets, money doesn't stay with us. Instead, it rotates. The more cash flow you can generate, the better.

"Therefore, I have a solution for paying your bills."

Martha was curious. "What is that?"

Sam replied, "Well, it is possible to pay bills out of your investments without losing the value of the investments. It is known as dividends."

Dennis said, "Right! I know. I have invested in stocks, and I think I get dividends. But I don't understand it very well."

Sam said, "I can explain it to you. How about around five-ish today?"

Martha said, "Oh! That would be so nice of you. Let's have tea together."

Sam said, "Mrs. Collins, you are such a good cook. We will most definitely come back to enjoy your tea."

Sam and Jessica visited the local attractions and had a wonderful time.

Sam said to Jessica, "Jess, I know we already spoke about this earlier, but I hope you don't mind my spending some time with the couple at the inn."

Jessica said, "Sam, I know it is one thing you love to do. Go ahead, no problem. We have been having a great time ever since we left home."

Sam said, "You know, there is something else I am crazy about."

Jessica laughed and shook her head, "I find that hard to believe!"

Sam said softly, "You! I am crazy about you, Jess."

Jessica blushed and didn't say anything.

Dividends

I know at last what distinguishes
man from animals; financial worries
Romain Rolland

They went back at five o'clock for the tea Mrs. Collins promised.

Sam started, "Well, you know that *Starbucks (SBUX)* started as a coffee shop way back in 1971 at Seattle's Pike Place Market. *Starbucks* slowly expanded into a chain of coffee shops in espresso bars and fine restaurants. Expanding from one coffee shop to thousands of stores was possible for two reasons. First, they initially took out a loan from the bank (Debt), and at the same time, they borrowed money from shareholders (Equity). Second, once they started making profits, instead of borrowing for expansion, they made use of their profits to branch into various countries like China.

"Now, *Starbucks* is an established company, and they are making sufficient profits every year to meet their growth. They are expanding rapidly in many countries, including China and other Asian countries. They use every dollar of profit from their U.S. stores to cater to their Asian expansion.

"*McDonald's* Corporation *(MCD)* is different from *Starbucks*. *McDonald's* is an established chain of fast food restaurants. They also initially borrowed both from shareholders and from banks. But now, they are an established corporation and don't use their entire profits for expansion. Instead, they return a portion of their profits to shareholders like us. It is a way of thanking their shareholders.

"For example, as of October 2003, *Starbucks* made a profit of $0.65 per share (Earnings per Share) and *McDonald's* made a profit of $0.76 per share. *Starbucks* is using all their profits for expansion, whereas *McDonald's* gives back $0.40 for every share invested. This sharing of profits is known as a Dividend.

"Assuming you bought 100,000 shares of *McDonald's*, your original investment would not only grow but would fetch you $40,000 every year in dividends.

"Both *Starbucks* and *McDonald's* return value to their investors. *Starbucks* expands into new horizons, and naturally their share price keeps rising, thus returning profits to their investors.

"However, *McDonald's* investors profit both from the increase in the share price and from the dividends *McDonald's* pays to their shareholders."

Martha said, "Hmm! This is interesting. Why don't you eat something and then continue, son?"

Sam said, "Sure. How can I resist?"

He helped himself to some scones with fresh lemon curd.

He continued, "From an investor's point of view, a public company can be categorized into two divisions: They are…"

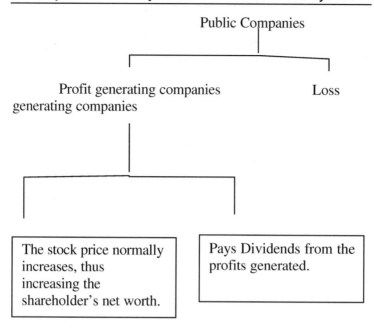

Dennis asked, "So how does a company that pays dividends differ from a company that does not?"

Sam said, "Assume you are going on a road trip from Los Angeles to San Francisco. You may have sufficient cash to buy eats and drinks on the way. If you feel thirsty, you might stop at a nearby gas station for a bottle of Coke and pay a couple of dollars. When you feel hungry, you may stop at a *Pizza Hut* for a pepperoni pizza and pay around twenty dollars. But after about ten hours, you'll reach San Francisco.

"There is another possibility. You may not have sufficient cash, or you may not want to spend on eating out. Instead, you may pack some food for the trip.

"An investor choosing a company to invest in is no different from a person planning for a road trip. Investors who need regular cash should consider investing in a company that pays sufficient dividends to meet their needs.

"However, if their ultimate goal is to earn lots of money and they are not really interested in intermediate benefits, then they do not need to invest in a company that pays regular dividends."

Dennis said, "Well, that is an interesting angle."

Sam continued, "Let me give you another example.

"What is the difference between the business models of *Sony Pictures*, which produces movies, and *Blockbuster Videos*, which rents movies?

"*Sony Pictures* is known for producing movies like *Once Upon a Time in Mexico* and *Bad Boys II*. But their business model is definitely a lot different from *Blockbuster Video*. *Sony Pictures* initially invests all of its dollars in producing a movie by paying for everything from actors and actresses to the equipment and advertising.

"On the other hand, *Blockbuster* is a video rental company. It collects rental charges from the moment it buys the video. Unlike *Sony Pictures*, *Blockbuster* doesn't have to wait many months before making money. *Sony Pictures* has to wait until the movie is fully produced and screened in theatres.

"The two types of investors I referred to earlier are analogous to either *Sony Pictures* or *Blockbuster Video*. If you are an investor whose only aim is to make long-term profits, then identifying a company with great potential is the only thing that matters. However, investors who are looking for regular returns from their investments should invest only in companies that pay dividends."

Dennis said, "Thank you so much, Sam. Now I have a better idea of what these dividends are about."

They finished their tea and said goodbye.

Driving Home the Point

*In a great romance, each person plays a part the
other really likes*
Elizabeth Ashley

The next morning, Jessica said, "I don't feel like going back."

Sam said, "I agree! It was awfully nice of the guys to give us a gift like this."

Jessica said, "Yes. I must say that I enjoyed every minute of it."

Sam winked and said, "Anytime, my dear."

When they were driving back, Jessica asked, "I have a question, Sam. What is the difference between banks paying interest and public companies paying dividends?"

Sam shook his head in mock disapproval, "You always go back to comparing with banks, don't you?"

Jessica laughed.

Sam said, "Anyway, when you invest money in banks, it earns interest and nothing else. When you invest $10,000 in bank, the bank may regularly pay 3% interest every year. As an investor, if you use the interest for meeting your expenses like paying bills, etc., then you would never ever see the growth of your original investments. In other words, earning interest is the only way you can profit from investing in banks.

"On the other hand, investing in public companies that pay dividends not only fetches you a regular income, but it also increases your original investment exponentially. Investing $10,000 in a public company like *McDonald's* pays regular interest in the form of dividends, and also expands your initial investment of $10,000.

"The difference between investing in a bank and in stocks is the same as the difference between running a family-owned burger shop and running a *McDonald's*.

"Investing in a bank is no different from running a family-owned burger shop and not expanding at all. You get your Return on Investment by regularly cashing in to meet your expenses, but your growth is limited. The only benefit of running such a shop is that you can make ends meet, but you don't really become rich."

Before Sam dropped off Jessica, he said, "Jess, I had a wonderful weekend. You are amazing."

Jessica kissed Sam passionately and did not want to let go.

Sam said, "Hmm! That was nice."

He told her he would meet her and the guys at their favorite haunt, the coffeehouse.

Return of the Titans

There is no security on this earth, only opportunity
Gen. Douglas MacArthur

When Bill saw Sam and Jessica, he commented, "Needless to say, you had a great time."

Sam said, "Absolutely! Thanks once again for the gift."

Joe said, "I am sure you didn't start explaining the next formula."

Jessica smiled and said, "Well, I have news for you guys. I learned something!"

Bill joked, "What! You could not stay away from finance even during a romantic getaway! Jessica, please take my advice. Stop going out with this guy."

They all laughed. Sam said, "Well, it's not really a formula. But let me explain."

Sam explained to the group what he had told the couple at the bed and breakfast.

Joe asked, "Hey, what about if a company pays dividends, but you don't want to take them out?"

Sam said, "Dividends are like seeds from a tree. A seed planted will grow into a big tree in the long term. But a seed consumed loses its value and purpose immediately.

"Similarly, we can either make use of the dividends for meeting our expenses or re-invest them for buying additional shares.

"Assuming you have earned $1,000 from your investment at *McDonald's*, you may either withdraw it for meeting your expenses, or you may buy additional shares of *McDonald's*. Buying additional shares helps you in many ways:

a)   The additional shares will pay more dividends in the future.
b)   The additional shares will grow."

Bill said, "So the invested shares can produce additional money for us in the long run."

Sam said, "Yes, take a look at this chart. It illustrates the difference between using and re-investing dividends."

Figure 8.1: Result of investing in companies paying dividends and cashing them out

Source: Morningstar, Inc.

Company	Investment of $100,000 in 1993 in ten years Period: 1993 - 2003			
	Net worth in 2003 $	Total dividends earned from 1993 to 2003 $	Sum of dividends and investment's growth $	Average dividends earned per year $
General Electric	344,508	48,970.25	393,478.26	4,897.02
McDonald's Corporation	180,912	12,210.52	193,122.80	1,221.05
Pfizer	598,260	48,347.82	646,608.69	4,834.78
Phillip Morris	286,677	75,134.84	361,812.29	7,513.48
Citi Corp	733,909	35,807.99	769,717.54	3,580.80

"Let us analyze the same set of companies, with all the dividends re-invested."

Figure 8.2: Result of investing in companies paying dividends and reinvesting them

Source: Morningstar, Inc.

Company	Ticker	Net worth of $100,000 invested in 1993 after ten years (Dividends reinvested in buying additional shares) ($)
General Electric	GE	421,507
McDonald's Corporation	MCD	196,524
Pfizer	PFE	694,011
Phillip Morris	MO	470,767
Citi Corp	C	908,913

Source: Morningstar,Inc.

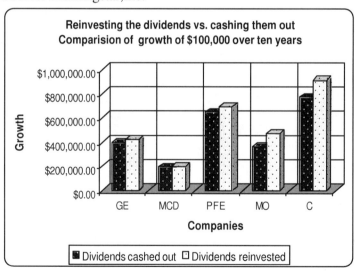

Jessica asked, "I agree that one might need a certain amount of money from her investments, but what can you infer from companies that pay huge dividends?"

Troy said, "Yes! How do we measure whether a company's dividends are reasonable?"

Sam said, "First of all, if a company shares most of its profits with its shareholders, it is indicative of limited growth."

Joe was shocked. "Really? Can you name some companies that belong to this category?"

Figure 8.3: Companies paying high dividends but experiencing very little growth

Source: Morningstar, Inc.

Company	Ticker	Investment of $100,000 in 1998 in five years Period: 1998 - 2003		
		Net worth ($)	Total dividends earned ($)	Average dividends earned per year ($)
Fab Industries Inc.	FIT	24,511	57,441	11,488
Scor	SCO	4,381	14,685	2,937
Corrections Corporation of America	CXW	13,731	22,146	4,429

Figure 8.4: Effect of investing in companies paying high dividends by reinvesting them

Source: Morningstar, Inc.

Company	Ticker	Net worth of $100,000 invested in 1998 after five years (Dividends reinvested in buying additional shares) ($)
Fab Industries Inc.	FIT	93,899
Scor	SCO	8,992
Corrections Corporation of America	CXW	37,509

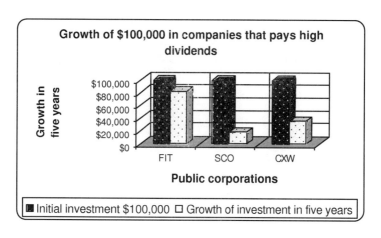

Joe asked, "So, how do we measure the amount of dividends being paid out?"

Sam said, "The best way is to find out the dividend yield and payout ratio."

1. Load www.morningstar.com
2. Enter the ticker symbol of the company (GE for *General Electric*).
3. Click on 'Quote'
4. Click the 'Financial Statements' tab
5. In the financial statements, click on '5-Yr Restated'
6. The financial statement of the company for the past five years is shown.
7. In the five-year financial statement, the Dividends paid out are detailed in the row 'Dividends per Share'.

Dividend Yield

"Dividend Yield measures the percentage of dividends paid out to investors based on the current stock price. A higher dividend yield indicates the company pays too much dividends. A company with a reasonable dividend yield indicates it is not only growing, but it also shares some of its profits.

"Dividend yield = (Dividends paid / Current share price) * 100

"It is good to invest in companies with a dividend yield less than 30%. Let me show you some companies with reasonable dividend yields."

Figure 8.5: Some companies with reasonable dividends and good growth

Source: Morningstar, Inc.

Company	Investment of $100,000 in 1998 in five years			
	Period: 1998 - 2003			
	Net worth $	Total divide- nds earned $	Average divide- nds earned per year $	Dividend yield as of 2003 %
Factset Research Systems	201,652	2,526	505	0.60
Liz Claiborne	218,187	7,287	1,457	0.60
United Mobile Homes	163,499	36,782	7,356	5.30

Figure 8.6:
Reinvesting dividends in companies offering reasonable dividends and good growth

Source: Morningstar, Inc.

Company	Ticker	Net worth of $100,000 invested in 1998 (Dividends reinvested in buying additional shares) $
		Period: 1998 - 2003
Factset Research Systems.	FDS	206,782
Liz Claiborne	LIZ	228,813
United Mobile Homes	UMH	231,744

Source: Morningstar, Inc.

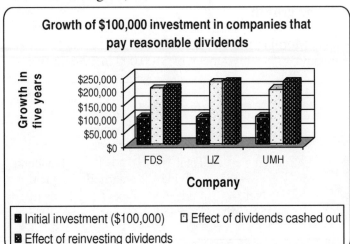

Growth of $100,000 investment in companies that pay reasonable dividends

Payout Ratio

Sam said, "Actually, even dividend yield is not a true picture of the profits being shared. A truer picture is payout ratio. Payout ratio is calculated as total dividends paid compared to the income earned by the company."

Payout ratio = Dividends / Net income
In other words,

Payout ratio = Dividends paid per share / Earnings per share

"A high payout ratio indicates that the company has slow growth, whereas no payout ratio indicates that the company has very high growth. It is good to invest in companies with a payout ratio of less than 25%.

"The following is a comparison among companies with high and low payout ratios, and the result of investing in these companies."

Figure 8.7:
Effect of investing in companies with reasonable payout ratio by reinvesting dividends

Source: Morningstar, Inc.

Company	Payout ratio for 2003 %	Net worth of $100,000 Invested in 1998 (Dividends reinvested in buying additional shares) ($)	Annual growth % (Compounded)
		Period: 1998 - 2003	
Applebee's International Incorporation	3	395,949	14.75
Cardinal Health	3	553,039	18.65
Engineered Support Systems	2	6,498,457	51.80

Source: Morningstar, Inc.

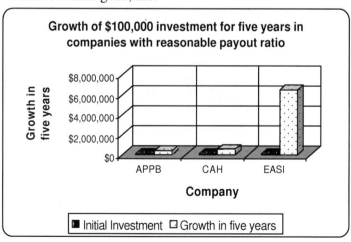

Figure 8.8:
Effect of investing in companies with higher payout ratio by reinvesting dividends

Source: Morningstar, Inc.

Company	Payout ratio for 2003 %	Net worth of $100,000 invested in 1998 (Dividends reinvested in buying additional shares)($)	Annual growth % (Compounded)
		Period: 1998 - 2003	
Amcor Limited	67	156,367	4.57
Psychemedics Corp.	75	61,428	(4.75)
Worthington Corp.	74	98,672	(0.13)

Source: Morningstar, Inc.

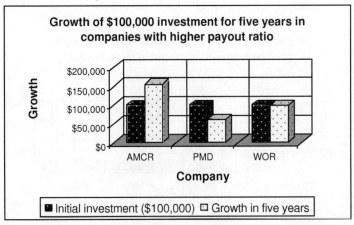

Bill said, "Neat! I could really use those dividends."

Sam said, "Yep! Okay, the next topic is very interesting and probably one of the most important topics, too."

Joe said, "Cool! What is it about?"

Sam replied after a pause, "Cash flow!"

Sam's Sprinkles

• Mature companies pay dividends from the profits they earn.

• Companies that are still growing may not pay dividends, because they need to reinvest for expansion.

• Buying additional stocks with the money earned from dividends is known as reinvesting.

• An investor can either cash out the dividends or reinvest them.

• The appreciation of money invested in a bank is limited to the bank's interest rate.

• An investment with reasonable dividend-paying stocks not only generates regular dividends but also appreciates in value in the long run.

• Investing in a company's stock that pays high dividends may run the potential risk of slow growth in its stock price.

• Dividend yield and payout ratio are two measures of verifying whether a company pays low or high dividends.

• Dividend yield is measured by dividing the stock's price by the dividends paid out. The higher the ratio, the higher the number of dividends the company pays out.

• To combine the advantages of having regular income and higher growth in a stock's price, it would be wise to invest in a company whose dividend yield is less than 30%

- Another method to verify whether a company is paying high dividends is to look at the payout ratio. Payout ratio is calculated by dividing the stock's price by dividends paid out. Higher the dividends paid, higher the payout ratio.

- To achieve both regular income and high growth potential, invest in companies whose payout ratio is less than 25%.

- Dividends are normally paid every quarter, although this may vary among companies.

True or False

- Technology companies generally don't pay dividends.

- A company's dividends are always at a fixed percentage just like the bank's interest.

- An investor can always negotiate for higher dividends.

- Payout ratio is a better measure of deciding whether a company is paying higher dividends than dividend yield.

- Dividend yield changes every day, whereas payout ratio remains constant for the quarter.

Self-Explorer

- What is ex-dividend date?

- Who decides the amount of dividends to be paid out to investors?

- List five companies from the Dow components that consistently pay dividends.

- List five public companies that have never paid dividends but are generating sufficient profits.

- What is an earnings yield?

Chapter IX

Who is Dollar Wise, Penny Foolish?

Money Gainers or Money Drainers?

That some achieve great success, is proof to all that
others can achieve it as well
Abraham Lincoln

New York Lotto

The ladder of success is never crowded at the top
Napoleon Hill

James greeted Sam, "Morning, son."

Sam smiled and said, "Morning, dad."

James asked, "You remember my friend Philip Basehart?"

Sam said, "Yes I do."

James continued, "Well, he is visiting us this evening with his daughter. Will you at home this evening?"

Sam answered, "Yes, dad. I will be here."

Sam called and informed his friends.

That evening, James and his wife welcomed their friend. "Hello Philip! Good to see you. Monica dear, how are you?"

Monica said, "Doing fine. Thank you."

Sam said, "Good to see you again, Monica."

They settled down to some excellent wine.

Philip said, "Sam, what are you up to these days?"

James answered for Sam, "Well, he has been unofficially named the 'Financial Advisor of the town'."

Philip was surprised. "Impressive! Actually, I do remember you were always asking me questions about companies."

Monica said, "I am taking a course on 'Stock Analysis'. I would love to get some tips from you, Sam, if that is all right."

Sam's mom said, "I think that is like asking a child if he wouldn't mind taking a trip to Disneyland."

They all laughed.

They talked a while longer and then had dinner.

Once they were finished, Philip asked Sam, "Sam, how do you go about explaining financial concepts?"

Sam said, "Well, Monica asked me some questions on cash flow. To explain that concept, I would use a fictitious example.

"Rick, an employee at a small firm, suddenly turned in his resignation letter. He had won five million dollars in the New York Lotto, and he decided to run his own show rather than work for someone else."

Lotto is like any other business. Its main purpose is to make money. In the year 2002, more than $40 billion dollars in revenues were collected from the lottery business.

"Rick was very happy about winning the lottery, and he celebrated that night with his family and friends. During dinner, he revealed his plans to start a 'computer mouse' business. Since his wife Dana was very good at designing computer hardware, he wanted to start a great business developing an interactive mouse with digital technology, including a calendar and alarm. The concept was very interesting and creative. With encouragement from friends and relatives, he and his wife developed an excellent computer mouse and named it *'DigiMouse'*, as it could handle much more than just moving the cursor."

The computer mouse was designed and developed by Doug Engelbart and built by Bill English at Xerox Parc (Palo Alto Research Center).

As of September 2003, 500 million mice were produced since its invention. If laid from end to end without cords, they would circle the earth 1.6 times.

Mouse Hunt

A ship in harbor is safe -- but that is not what ships are for
John A. Shedd

"*'DigiMouse'* was a great start by Rick and Dana. Not facing any financial issues and not wanting to assume any debt, Dana researched the latest digital technology, and Rick started planning to market the product. They didn't have to wait too long before they got a great business order from *Dell*. They turned in their first order to *Dell*, who requested a few changes. Dana, awake day and night, built the best mouse she could."

Monica interrupted, "Wow, this is interesting."

Sam said, "Thanks, Continuing with the example, *Dell* requested *'DigiMouse'* to come up with one million computer mice in the next two months. Dana and Rick expanded their business in a big way, leasing new buildings and hiring new employees. They celebrated the confirmation of a ten billion dollar deal from *Dell*. They worked out the most efficient process they could to produce the *'DigiMouse'*. Producing one mouse cost almost $5, and since they had five million dollars, they agreed to fulfill the entire order in less than a month.

"*Dell* was also happy to receive the shipment from *'DigiMouse'*, and the entire process went pretty smoothly. Rick's accountant called him to confirm that he had finished preparing the draft of the income sheet *'DigiMouse'* was responsible for filing with the IRS.

"At work the next day, even before going for his cup of coffee, Rick checked his voice mail. It was a very urgent call from the manager of the local *Fleet Bank*.

"The caller said, 'Hello Rick, this is Tim Glova, manager at *Fleet Bank*. I'm really sorry to say that I had to return your check for $20,000, because there is no cash left in your account.

"Rick was shocked to hear this message. He rushed to the accountant's office and found him ready with his income sheet. Rick was completely confused. The income sheet looked perfect, and the thought of the bank not clearing his check agonized him."

Philip asked, "What did the income sheet show?"

Sam booted his laptop and showed them a table.

Figure 9.1: Income Sheet of "DigiMouse"

	Description	Amount
Income	Total revenue generated	$10 millions
Cost of sales	Total cost involved in producing the mice	$5 millions
Gross income	Profit less cost of goods	$5 millions
Gross margin	Profit% just taking only cost of goods sold into account	50%
SGA	Sales, general and administrative expenses	$1 million
Operating income	Profit after deducting SGA from Gross Income	$4 millions
Operating margin	Actual profit in running the business	40%
Taxes	Taxes to be paid to IRS	$1 million
Net income	Actual income for DigiMouse	$3 millions
Net profit	Net profit after deducting all expenses	30%

Monica said, "But there is absolutely nothing wrong with the income statement. Why would a small check of $20,000 bounce?"

Cash Chaos

Profits are an opinion, Cash is a fact
Anonymous

Sam resumed, "The income statement looks great. But did you know it is made of accrual entries?"

"What is that?" asked Philip.

Sam said, "The income statement and balance sheet are prepared with accrual entries. *'DigiMouse'* made a sale for $10 million, but that doesn't mean *'DigiMouse'* collected it. In other words, *'Digimouse'* sent the shipment to *Dell* and they agreed to pay the money, but *'Digimouse'* had not received it yet.

"*'DigiMouse'* did the entire work without collecting any revenue from *Dell*, but the income sheet did not reflect that."

Cash Flow

Experience - a comb life gives you after you lose hair
Judith Stern

"The money Rick won in the lottery was used to set up the factory and to pay for initial expenses. When *'DigiMouse'* grabbed the order from *Dell*, it used its entire savings to set up the factory and to fulfill the order. Even though it was a big break for a startup company, poor cash management put Rick and Dana in a situation where they didn't have money to pay even salaries and rent.

"Cash is like the air we breathe. Unless we miss it, we don't realize the importance of it. We can see the true reflection of a company's cash management only in the cash flow statement, and not in the income sheet or balance sheet."

James asked, "Does this happen with public companies?"

Sam said, "Of course, all companies across the U.S. commonly use the accrual system to reflect sales made instead of actual income produced. But an investor could be fooled as easily as Rick and Dana if they focus only on the income statement and balance sheet. An investor should look not only at the income statement and the balance sheet, but also at the cash flow statement.

"This is how I explain the concepts, sir."

Philip said, "Very insightful. I would like to chat more with you, but it is getting late. We have to get going. We are in town for a couple of days. Let's meet when time permits."

They said their goodbyes and left.

The next morning, Sam met Jessica and the guys for breakfast.

Jessica said, "It is quite unlike you not to show up and to cancel plans with us."

Sam replied, "I am sorry. We had guests at home. My father's friend and his daughter, Monica."

Jessica asked, "Daughter?"

Bill teased, "Uh oh!"

Jessica retorted, "C'mon!"

Sam said, "Interestingly, we got into the topic of finance. Monica is doing a paper on 'Stock Analysis' and I gave them a brief overview of cash flow."

Bill added, "Needless to say, you must have charmed the woman."

Sam laughed and briefed them about cash flow with the same *'DigiMouse'* example.

He continued, "Let's say that as a proud owner of a latest *BMW 5 series*, you are driving across a highway in Central Nevada. You are at the peak of your happiness as you pass every other car with ease. But after a few hours, the car comes to a sudden halt. How come? Especially when it is a *BMW*?

"Be it a *BMW* or a *Honda*, the most important component of a car is fuel. A *BMW* can enhance your driving experience, but neither a *BMW* nor a *Honda* can run without fuel. Ignoring the fuel level will only put you in a most difficult situation. Ignoring cash flow is like ignoring a *BMW's* fuel level.

"An investor should look at a company's income statement and balance sheet to understand its performance, including profit margins, return on equity, etc.

"On the other hand, however big a company may be, an investor must check its cash flow statement. It is like screening donors' blood before accepting their donation. The blood bank wants to make sure they are free from AIDS and other diseases before accepting their blood.

"A company should constantly generate cash, and only the cash flow statement will show a true reflection of cash holding."

Joe asked, "Jess, are you with us? You seem to be lost!"

Jessica said, "No! I am listening."

Sam looked at Jessica and hesitantly continued, "Both the income sheet and balance sheet reflect accrual, and many companies fix their previous year's income sheets, stating they couldn't generate sales as expected in the current year. However, no company will manipulate its cash flow statement, as it reflects the current level of cash flow."

Troy asked, "So, what is cash flow?"

Sam answered, "Cash flow indicates the cash a company received vs. the cash it spent.

$$\text{Cash flow} = \text{Cash Received} - \text{Cash Spent}"$$

Joe said, "So, if cash flow is positive, the company is receiving more cash than it is spending, whereas if it is negative, the company is spending more money than it is receiving."

Cash is Ultimate in Business

In God we trust; all others must pay cash
Anonymous

Bill said, "So you are saying that cash is ultimate in business. Having too little cash can literally kill a business, whether it is *Enron* or a mom and pop store."

Sam said, "Yes. When it is time to pay its employees, how can a company survive if it doesn't have enough cash? In our earlier *'DigiMouse'* example, can Rick ask the landlord to take a mouse worth $20,000 instead of rent? Can Rick give his employees a mouse instead of pay for a couple of months?

"A company could manufacture candies, candles, or refrigerators. But its essence is cash.

"Even though sales are important, a company with a great product can easily make a huge market share if it offers great discounts. But just because a company has a huge market share, it doesn't mean it is very profitable. High sales growth does not necessarily mean a high amount of cash. The cash generated may not necessarily be proportionate to sales.

"A company out of cash will end up filing for bankruptcy. Cash is the energy of a company. A company should be capable of producing cash along with its resources."

Sam's cell phone rang. He said, "Hello Monica!" He excused himself and left the table.

Jessica did her best to mask a tinge of jealously.

Sam rejoined the group a few minutes later. He said he would meet them tomorrow.

Sam said, "Jess, I am really sorry. I promised Monica I would help her out. I hope that is okay with you."

Jessica said, "Why would you ask me if it is okay with me when you already promised her? I will see you tomorrow."

Sam felt confused for the first time in his life.

Monica was chatting with his mom when he entered his home.

Monica called out, "Hey, Sam."

Sam said, "Monica, sorry I am late. You want to grab a sandwich before we begin discussing 'cash flow'?"

She agreed and they went for a bite.

Sam began, "Cash is like fuel for a car, but with one difference. If an automobile runs short on gas, its driver stops at a gas station and refills the fuel. However, cash is a self-producing fuel. A company spends money to produce a product, and the product in turn generates cash for the company. The only thing an investor should verify is whether the cash spent in manufacturing a product is much less than the cash earned in selling the product.

"The only reason a company goes bankrupt and causes its investors to lose their savings is that it has handled its cash flow badly. A company doesn't need a huge investment to make a huge income, but it should be capable of handling cash well."

Monica asked, "So, the only reason people want to invest their money in a company is they trust the company will use their cash wisely and provide better returns for them. If it handles its cash poorly, the ultimate losers are the investors, because the stock price will tumble once the news breaks that it is incapable of handling its cash."

Handle with Cash

Happiness is a positive cash flow
Fred Adler

"I have always wondered how a big company survives in spite of hectic competition. How did a company like *Hewlett Packard*, which was started in a garage, become the world's most admired company? *Hewlett Packard's (HPQ)* laser printers are everywhere in the corporate world. How was it possible for *Microsoft (MSFT)* to beat *IBM (IBM)* and *Apple (AAPL)* so successfully?"

Sam said, "It all depends on how the company manages its cash. A company with a good product is only the beginning of a success story. A company with good products and excellent marketing has a success rate of only 50%. Companies like *Microsoft*, *GE*, and *Coke* have one thing in common. They build great products, market exceptionally well and manage their cash very well."

They finished their lunch and started to walk. Monica dutifully took notes.

Monica asked, "What is the secret of cash management? How can an investor understand a successful company's cash management? How did *Microsoft* succeed in managing its cash while *Enron* failed? Is *Microsoft* a bigger company than what *Enron* was?"

Sam said, "Not really. The only difference between *Enron* and *Microsoft* is that *Enron* didn't learn to manage its cash, whereas *Microsoft* manages its cash very well."

Monica smiled, "Yeah I guess. Actually there was a discussion in our class on who the best CEO of the 20th century was."

Sam asked with a lot of curiosity, "Interesting. Who was it?"

Monica replied, "Roberto Goizueta, the CEO of *Coca-Cola Company (KO),* not only built a great brand, but also managed to gain a large market share in spite of hectic competition from *Pepsi (PEP)*. He had a great product to sell and an excellent marketing team, and the only thing he had to do was to sell *Coke* without running into any cash problems.

"When Goizueta inherited *Coca-Cola Company*, it was a good company but not the best. *Pepsi's* competition was fierce. He had to make *Coke* the leading brand by promoting it aggressively, but at the same time, he wanted to make sure he had sufficient cash to manage the company."

Sam said, "Excellent! Do you know how he achieved this? Simply by spending less money than the company made to manufacture and market the product. This would not only ensure the company functioned smoothly without financial problems, but also enable the company to focus on its products rather than on its cash flow."

They reached the hotel where Monica was staying. Sam said, "Mon, can I ask you a favor?"

Monica said, "Sure. What is it?"

Sam said, "I told you that I am teaching a group of my friends, right? Do you mind if we meet up with my friends? That way, I can explain this topic in more detail to everyone at the same time."

Monica replied, "Absolutely! C'mon Sam, you are doing us all a favor. Tell me where we are meeting."

Sam said, "Thanks, Mon. Actually, we are going to Troy's apartment. I will pick you up at seven. Is that okay?"

Monica smiled, "Absolutely. Thanks again, Sam."

Strongest Link

The importance of money flows from it being a link
between the present and the future
John Maynard Keynes

Sam called Troy and asked permission to invite Monica for their evening meet.

Troy said, "Sam, do you know the Japanese word 'hara-kiri'?

Sam laughed, "Of course. Don't worry; there is no 'suicide' here."

Troy said, "Whatever, my friend! I have no problems inviting Monica to my place."

Sam thanked him and hung up. He called Jessica, but just got her voice mail. He left her a message and went home.

Later that evening, Sam and Monica rang Troy's doorbell.

On seeing Monica, Bill exclaimed, "Have mercy!"

Jessica shot him a look.

Bill complained, "What! I'm not supposed to say anything now?"

Sam introduced Monica to the group and had a chat with Jessica in another room.

Sam said, "Jess, you know for a fact that I am crazy about you. I am sorry I had to cut you guys off. Monica is just my father's friend's daughter."

Jessica said, "Sam, I am sorry too!"

Sam smiled, "That's okay Jess. In fact, I like it that you are possessive of me."

Jessica gave him a playful smack, and Sam just grabbed her and kissed her.

Feeling much better, they joined the group in the other room.

Sam said, "Okay, ready go back to cash flow? Let me start with an example. Steve, who was a vibrant character in *Fed-Ex (FDX)* Corporation, wanted to start a business. He saved almost $100,000 and wanted to start a small coffee shop in downtown Memphis, Tennessee, where he worked for almost a decade serving the neighboring cities. He eventually consulted a senior financial guru, Richard, for advice on managing his shop. Richard gave Steve only one piece of advice to help him succeed in his business. He said, 'Steve, spend whatever you want. But make sure whatever you spend doesn't amount to more than 50% of your net profits. Even if it takes time to grow, make sure you don't spend too much on expansion and run out of cash in the end.'

"Steve took Richard's advice. He discovered he had $100,000, but as per Richard's advice, he started a small shop with an investment of $50,000. Since he was very well known in his circles, people started visiting his shop quite regularly. His coffee shop, *'Columbia Coffee Circle,'* became quite popular in the downtown area of Memphis.

"A year passed, and Steve sought Richard's help once again. He wanted to expand his shop. Richard looked at Steve's financial statement and was quite impressed with his progress. His first year's income statement looked like this."

Figure 9.2: Financial statement of Steve's business

Total sales	$200,000
Cost of goods sold	$25,000
Gross profit	$175,000
SG&A expenses (Selling, General and Administrative)	$40,000
Operating profit	$135,000
Taxes	$35,000
Net profit	$100,000

Monica said, "Looks good. Steve has made a profit of $100,000 with an initial investment of $50,000, and that too in one year."

Sam continued, "Richard recommended that Steve expand his business to include breakfast and lunch, so his customers could buy food in addition to coffee. Steve took Richard's advice, remembering to spend only 50% of his net income on expansion. He spent another $50,000 on expanding *'Columbia Coffee Circle'* to serve breakfast and lunch. His cash flow statement then looked like this:

Figure 9.3: Cash flow statement for Steve's business

Net profits	$100,000
Capital expenses	$50,000
Free cash flow	$50,000

"Net Profit is how much *'Columbia Coffee Circle'* actually made from its operations, and Capital Expenses is how much was spent in expanding the business. Since *'Columbia Coffee Circle'* changed from a coffee shop to selling breakfast and lunch, Steve had to buy new equipment for baking bagels and muffins. The expenses involved in expansion are known as 'Capital Expenses'. The money left after paying for the expansion is known as 'Free Cash Flow'.

"Steve's second year was also successful, and his profits jumped from $100,000 in the first year to almost one million dollars in the second year. He once again consulted Richard, looking for ideas on how to expand his business from a small coffee shop to a bigger enterprise. Richard was again impressed with Steve's million-dollar business, and he offered to help Steve buy the businesses adjacent to *'Columbia Coffee Circle'*.

"Since customers might also like to browse through books during breakfast and lunch, Richard suggested buying a small newspaper shop that specialized in selling good books and newspapers. The newspaper shop owner offered to sell his shop as he was planning on retiring anyway. So Richard offered to complete the transaction on Steve's behalf.

"Again with the golden rule of spending only within 50% of his profits, Steve expanded his business and bought the newspaper store. His cash flow for the current year looked as follows."

Figure 9.4: Cash flow statement of Steve's business

Net profits	$1,000,000
Capital expenses	$100,000
Purchase of newspaper store	$400,000
Free cash flow	$500,000

Joe said, "So even though he started very small, he was able to expand successfully. He limited his expansion within his profits, and as a result he always had enough cash for emergencies. On the other hand, *'DigiMouse'* was left with no cash, in spite of starting a business with five million dollars."

Sam said, "Exactly! You know what, my friend? That is the key difference between *Microsoft* and *Enron*."

Joe declared, "I am hungry. Shall we order a pizza?"

Monica said, "Or we could make something here and eat."

Bill laughed, "Good one, Mon!"

Monica said, "What! I don't mind preparing something. I love to cook."

Bill approached her and said solemnly, "Marry me, Mon!"

They all laughed.

GM vs. Coke

Don't ask the barber whether you need a haircut
Daniel S. Greenberg

While they were waiting for their pizzas, Jessica asked, "Sam, how does cash management vary among different companies?"

Sam said, "Well, let's take *General Motors (GM)* and the *Coca-Cola Company (KO)*. They are equally big, and are both Fortune 500 companies. *General Motors* runs a global business in car manufacturing and owns several brands of cars including Saturn, Corvette, etc.

"*Coca-Cola* is the leading manufacturer of soft drinks. Its closest competitor, *Pepsi*, is far behind *Coke* in revenues.

"Even though *General Motors* is excellent in car manufacturing, it is very poor in managing its cash. That is why a person who invested $50,000 in *General Motors* in 1993 would have ended up with only $70,000 in 2003, despite waiting 10 years.

"On the other hand, *Coca-Cola* built a great business not only in brand building but also in managing its cash. That is one of the key reasons it provides great returns to its shareholders. An investor who invested $50,000 in *Coke in 1993* would have ended up with $127,240 as of November 2003."

Joe said, "Okay. You have to stop right there and show that in the form of charts."

Sam smiled and said, "With pleasure. Let's take a look at the cash flow statements of *GM* and *Coca-Cola*."

Figure 9.5: Cash flow comparison between GM and Coca-Cola (All values are in millions)

Source: Morningstar, Inc.

Title	Description	1993		1994		1995	
		GM	KO	GM	KO	GM	KO
Net profits ($)	Net profits made	2,465	2,176	4,900	2,554	6,800	2,986
Capital expenses ($)	Dollars spent on expanding existing business	6,470	800	7,225	878	10,077	937
Purchase of businesses ($)	Dollars spent on buying fresh businesses	232	0	246	0	616	0
Total dollars spent ($)	Dollars spent on expansion of business	6,702	800	7,441	878	10,693	937
Is amount spent on expansion lesser than net profits?		No	Yes	No	Yes	No	Yes

Jessica said, "Interesting! Looks like every year, *Coca-Cola (KO)* spent much less than its net profits for expansion, whereas *General Motors (GM)* spent much more than its total profits."

Sam said, "Yes. How did *GM* manage its expansion when it spent more than its profits? Since *GM* had to expand to beat its competition and couldn't generate sufficient profits, it had to borrow more money from lenders. Consequently, it had to pay more in interest.

"However, *Coca-Cola* not only expanded to the international market but also spent much less than its net profits for its expansion. Therefore, it was able to repay the debt it borrowed earlier and was freer from debt than *General Motors*.

"That is why, even though *Coca-Cola* had a long-tem debt of $1.5 billion, it was able to reduce its debt to $800 million by 2000, due to its excellent cash management strategy.

"Now, let us compare this with the cash management strategy of *General Motors*. In 1993, *General Motors* had $70 billion in long-term debt. Besides, it had to expand its business to meet its customers' needs as well as to survive, so it borrowed more money from the banks. It ended up with $150 billion in long-term debt in 2000.

"*Coca-Cola* reduced its debt by 50%, whereas *General Motors* increased its debt by 100%. So, which one is better in managing its cash?"

Bill answered, "Naturally, *Coca-Cola* was the better company when it came to managing its cash."

Warren Buffett holds 8.1% of Coke's shares.

As of November 2003, the market value of *Coca Cola Company* is $115 billion, which means Buffett owns almost $9.5 billion of *Coca Cola Company*.

Troy concluded, "So, the first thing we should look for is whether the company we invest in is capable of handling our money well. That can be easily determined by looking at the company's cash flow statement."

While they were eating, Sam said, "Since we covered a lot of formulas, I have an idea. How about we have a quiz? You guys can spilt into teams, and I will ask you questions on the formulae."

Joe said, "Sounds like fun. I'm game."

Sam said, "Team A can be Jessica and Monica. Team B will be Joe and Troy. Bill will join…"

Joe answered, "Join us, Bill."

Monica said, "Or Bill can be in our team."

Bill smiled and said, "Always a pleasure, ladies."

Sam said, "That's settled, then."

Quiz Time

A prudent question is one half of wisdom
Sir Francis Bacon

Sam said, "I will ask both teams the same question. Whoever comes up with the answer first gets 10 points."

Bill said, "Bring 'em on, my friend."

Sam said, "Okay, first question. Tell me the earnings per share of *'Best Buy'*.

They started browsing frantic ally on their laptops.

Joe said to Troy, "Go to www.morningstar.com and type *Best Buy*. There you go. See the financial statements. Now where is it again?"

Troy said, "Scroll all the way down, man. See the diluted EPS$. That is it. Okay, Sam, we have the answer."

Joe said, "It was $0.17 in 1994, $0.22 in 1005, $0.18 in 1996, $0.01 in 1997, and $0.35 in 1998."

Sam said, "Excellent. Ten points for Joe's team."

Bill said, "We are getting the next one, all right ladies?"

Sam said, "What was the debt for the company *Johnson and Johnson* in 2002?"

Jessica said, "I definitely know how to find this one. Type the name *'Johnson and Johnson'*."

Monica said, "Oh good. We got the ticker *(JNJ)*. Click it, Bill."

Bill said, "Whatever you say, Mon. I go to 'Financial Statements', then 10yr Balance Sheet. I see under the section 'Liabilities and Stockholders' 'Equity $Mil', 'short-term debt' and 'long-term debt'."

Monica said, "Ok Sam, we got this one. Short-term debt for *JNJ* in 2002 was $2,117 million and long-term debt was $2,022 million."

Sam said, "Excellent work. Now it's a tie. Let's try rapid-fire questions. What is Return on Capital?"

Jessica said, "Return on capital measures the profits of a company raised not only with its equity but also with the loans it must repay."

Sam, said, "Good. Next question. How is return on equity calculated?"

Bill said, "Oh! I know this. Return on equity = Net profit / Shareholder's equity."

Sam explained, "Impressive, Bill. How is gross profit margin measured?"

Joe said, "It is calculated by dividing the gross profit by the total income generated."

Sam said, "How is operating margin calculated?"

Troy said, "Easy. Operating margin is (Operating profits / Revenues) * 100."

Sam asked, "What is dividend yield?"

Monica said, "I know this one. Dividend yield measures the percentage of dividends paid out to the investors based on the current stock price."

Sam said, "Good work, guys. I guess all of you are winners."

Joe said, "So we can get out there and invest like there is no tomorrow?"

Sam laughed and said, "Not so fast. I have a few more concepts to cover."

Monica said, "I have an idea. Sam, how would you like to be on radio and take listeners' calls?"

Sam was stunned. "What! Are you kidding?"

Monica said, "No! One of my good friends is a radio talk show host. I could call him and ask. In fact, the radio show is also aired on TV."

Bill declared, "That would be excellent!"

Sam said, "I am flattered. Actually, I was going to talk about accounting scandals and how to detect them."

Jessica said, "I think that is something everyone would love to know about."

Monica said, "I will call him tomorrow and see how fast this can be arranged."

Bill said, "Girl! You are something. Seriously, marry me!"

Everyone laughed again.

Bill looked hurt. "Is no one going to take me seriously at all?"

Sam's Sprinkles

• Income statement and balance sheet entries consist of accrual entries.

• An accrual-based accounting system reports income and expenses at the time the sale or purchase is made, not when the money is paid. For example, a company might place an order for one million dollars, and it will report the expense as income, even though it has not yet received it.

• An alternative to accrual-based accounting is cash-based accounting. Cash-based accounting reports income and expenses at the time of payment. Under cash-based accounting, a company might make a 10 million dollar sale, but it will not report it until it receives the money. However, most public companies use only accrual-based accounting.

• The true reflection of cash movement can be seen in a cash flow statement.

• Capital expenses reflect the money spent on expanding the business, such as constructing new factories or adding new showrooms.

• Capital expenses for a business will be shown only in its cash flow statement. The net profit a company makes must be higher than its capital expenses. Otherwise, the company has to borrow heavily for expansion.

• A company might spend money to buy other businesses. This is also reflected in a cash flow statement.

- The money available after spending for expansion and buying other businesses is known as free cash flow. An investor must look at the free cash flow statements for at least three to five years. The company's free cash flow must be positive throughout this period.

- High net profits do not necessarily mean high free cash flow. A company may have high net profits but can still have negative free cash flow. This means it spends too much money for expansion.

True or False

- A company's accounting system can be understood from its income statement.

- By looking at the expense sheet (income statement), one can determine the money spent for expansion.

- A healthy percentage of net profits reflects a high free cash flow.

- Capital expenses are deducted from net profits to calculate free cash flow.

- Money spent on business expansion is deducted before calculating net profits.

Self-Explorer

• Identify companies with positive net profits and free cash flow. Determine the performance of these companies during the past ten years.

• Identify companies that either went bankrupt or lost a lot of money during the dot com crash. Check their cash flow statements during the years 1998, 1999 and 2000.

• How do you calculate the percentage of money spent for expansion from net profits?

• What is the NASDAQ-100?

• What is an exchange-traded fund, and how does it differ from mutual funds?

Chapter X

Who is Dollar Wise, Penny Foolish?

Detectives or Brooders?

If a person with money and a person with experience
meet, then the person with experience gets the money
and person with money gets the experience
Anonymous

Accounting Scams- Only Enron?

Success is a lousy teacher. It seduces smart people
into thinking they can't lose
Bill Gates

Monica called Jessica on her cell phone, "Hey Jess, got a minute?"

Jessica said, "Sure. What's up?"

Monica said, "Well, remember I told you that my friend is in the radio business? He is a talk show host in a radio station dedicated to youngsters. I got a one-hour slot for Sam this weekend. This radio program is also broadcast live on TV."

Jessica exclaimed, "Wow! That's fantastic. Did you tell him yet?"

Monica said, "No! I figured he must be with you, and I called you."

Jessica laughed and said, "Not for 24 hours a day."

Monica said she would call Sam and hung up.

That Saturday Sam, accompanied by Monica, Jessica, and the guys, went to the radio station 55.5 Ultra Lite FM. There they met Eric Bennett.

Eric said, "Sam, this is going to be a question and answer session. Most of the listeners are in our age group. You have half an hour to get ready."

Sam sat with Eric in the telecast room.

After the commercials, Eric began, "Hello, folks! This is Eric Bennett, and welcome to the show. We have a guest this afternoon for our question time. He is Sam Cohen. Sam is a finance expert. Welcome, Sam."

Sam smiled and said, "Thank you, Eric."

Eric said, "Since finance is such a wide subject, would you like to tell the listeners any particular area they can ask questions about?"

Sam said, "How about accounting scandals."

Eric said, 'Excellent! I have a couple of questions myself on that subject."

They laughed.

The phone rang. Eric said, "That's our first caller. Hello?"

"Hi! My name is David. I have a question for Sam. There is this company, *Bausch & Lomb (BOL)*, which inappropriately recorded supplies to distributors as sales in 1993 through an aggressive marketing plan. They supplied all their distributors with contact lenses and sunglasses. Even before collecting money from their distributors, they recorded this as sales. Once the public came to know about this, their shares went down.

"Similarly, *California Micro Devices (CAMD)*, a chipmaker, disclosed that it was writing off half of its accounts receivable due to product returns. Their shares plunged about 40%.

"Also, *Cendant Corporation (CD)*, which used to be a high-flying company, lost more than 47% in the market owing to improper accounting.

"*Bre-X Minerals Limited (BXMNF)* reported a significant gold find in the jungles of Indonesia. Wall Street was excited, and many public announcements were made about this. The company's share prices went up in no time. After a few weeks, when the geologist committed suicide by jumping from a helicopter, the news came out that they actually added gold to the test samples. As a result they filed for bankruptcy a few months later.

"The victims of such accounting scandals are none other than investors like us. How do we, as common investors, detect these practices and avoid such land mines?"

Joe, who was watching Sam through the glass window outside the recording room, said to his friends, "Sam's earlier methods would have identified risky companies, but once we identify a company that meets all our criteria, we need to see if it has been involved in an accounting scandal. Let's see what Sam has to say."

Accounting Scandals – Why Do They Happen?

A man begins cutting his wisdom teeth the first time
he bites off more than he can chew
Herb Caen

Sam said, "Quite a few of us invest in stocks based on the image a company has in the public eye. A public company's image depends entirely on the earnings it produces every quarter. Investors, especially momentum investors, will beat up a company that fails to meet its earnings, but a public company that produces consistent earnings goes up in the market.

"What if a company is unable to make money, but doesn't want its share price to go down? One way is for it to manipulate its accounting. Let me give an example.

"John, who works as a tax consultant, was deeply attracted to his colleague Sandra. He bought a small condo in Denver, Colorado. He was out of cash, but he still wanted to impress her. He bought a brand new convertible car, and he filled his house with a fabulous couch, bed and entertainment center.

"How was it possible for John to do all these when he didn't have money? He maxed out his credit cards, took out an equity loan, and borrowed money from some of his friends.

"He did all these things to impress Sandra so she would date him. She initially refused to go out with him, but later on she accepted a dinner invitation at his place. She was impressed with his new condo and his stylish BMW. They fell in love and got married. After a few days of marriage, when he reached his credit card limit, he couldn't fulfill even simple wishes like buying his wife a rose.

"This caused small arguments to break out between them, and later on it developed into a huge fight.

"Sandra asked John why he never informed her about his debt. He simply said, 'If I had told you about all of my problems, you wouldn't have fallen for me'.

"Now, we are in Sandra's shoes. Some public companies are like John. As investors, we need to find out if his assets are real or not.

"Why did he fake his wealth? Only then could he have asked Sandra to marry him. If he showed himself to be dirt poor, do you think Sandra would have been attracted to him?

"Similarly, only when a company projects a good image and excellent earnings will investors buy more shares. But once the scandals are out in public, then naturally investors will no longer want to hang on to their shares.

Instead, they will sell their stocks, and naturally the stock prices will come down.

"Like John, who borrowed from credit cards and friends to project a false image to Sandra, a company does everything it can to hide its problems. The moment its problems come out in the open, naturally its share price comes down.

"As investors, we should check whether a company's reported accounting is real. That makes our investment decisions much easier."

Eric said, "Interesting! You are saying a company may not be completely honest with its financial statements. As investors, we have to be cautious."

Sam said, "Yes. Every brokerage firm makes money when investors buy and sell stocks. They are for-profit organizations, and they cannot survive by always telling the truth."

Eric said, "We have the next caller. Hello?"

The caller said, "Hi, My name is Henry. I just want to make a comment. I remember the case against *California Micro Devices*. Around that time, Mr. Henke had been appointed CFO. Only later, when the company ran into huge trouble and was involved in a scam, did investors realize he never majored in finance and took only one course in accounting with a D grade. Isn't that odd?

"A person who had invested $10,000 with *California Micro Devices* in 2000 would have lost all his money in the next two years. The accounting scams its management team performed came to the limelight, and everyone started selling their stocks.

"When complications set in, companies are tempted to manipulate figures."

Sam said, "That's a good point, Henry. There are good companies that are not involved in any scams and still produce excellent earnings. Creating and running such a company is like winning a marathon race. Not everyone can be a winner. Only one can win.

"When a company fails to produce consistent earnings or fails to increase its earnings, it will lose many advantages it had gained over the years. First, its stock price will crash. After that, its credit rating will come down, and then it will be extremely difficult for it to continue its business.

"To avoid such complications, a company might find it easier to manipulate its earnings rather than accepting them. Sometimes, the auditing firm may not reveal all the problems with the books, because it needs the company's money to stay in business. If it blows the whistle, it will no longer get any business from the company. It would rather continue getting business instead of losing it."

Eric said, "Yes even the auditing firm *Arthur Andersen* saw evidence of improper accounting with *Waste Management (WMI)*, but chose not to push the client. Even though the auditors knew the company was cooking its books, they decided not to force the client to open up with its financial statements."

Sam said, "You are right. During the 1993 audit of *Waste Management, Arthur Andersen* found that their client inflated its earnings by almost 12%. If they forced their client to restate its earnings, the client would not only lose its share price, but it would never get business from *Waste Management* again. So, the auditors agreed to work with *Waste Management* to inflate its earnings and give a great impression. Since none of *Waste Management's* investors knew it was manipulating its earnings, it continued with its deceptive practices for several years with *Arthur Anderson's* help.

"The sad part is that the ultimate losers were the investors. If investors assume a company's financial reports are accurate and do not investigate any further, they will end up losing all the money they invested."

"The *SEC (Securities and Exchange Commission)* is like the police. Even though the police force's duty is to capture every thief, it is very difficult to do. As a result, we install alarms in our homes to prevent thieves from entering. Similarly, an investor needs to be cautious before investing in a particular company.

"As investors, we have to understand the difference between great companies and ordinary ones. Since we are interested in investing our hard-earned money, it is important for us to invest in the best companies that exist in the market."

Earnings and Sales

I know at last what distinguishes
man from animals; financial worries
Romain Rolland

Eric pressed the commercials button and said, "Sam, you are doing a good job. I am sure more calls will be pouring in."

Sam said, "Thanks. Since this program is also telecast on TV, can I show some charts to explain certain concepts?"

Eric said, "Sure. Okay, we are on in 60 seconds."

Once they were back on the air, the next caller said, "Hello! I am Tim. I have a question, Sam. When a company projects good earnings, how do we know if their earnings are real or not?"

Sam said, "Good question. Earnings are calculated from the gross sales after deducting all expenses. The main source of earnings for any company is from its sales. But can a company without consistent sales produce consistent earnings? Yes."

Manipulative Methods

Failure is success if we learn from it
Malcolm S. Forbes

"You don't have to be a Sherlock Holmes to find out whether a company's earnings are real. By learning a few fundamental things, anyone can find out the methods it uses to manipulate its earnings. Let me give an example.

"Steve learned the art of making gourmet pizzas. He started a restaurant called *'Anytime Pizza.'* Sales were strong during the first few years. But his customers became health-conscious and slowly avoided pizza. He had $150,000 in earnings for 1999, but made only $130,000 in 2000. However, his earnings per share were growing. How?"

Scandal 1: Hide Expenses

"The CEO of *'Anytime Pizza,'* in a conspiracy with his auditors, decided to hide a few expenses.

"The company settled a $25,000 lawsuit in the first year when a new employee added meat to a vegetarian pizza. During the second year, they invested in a new store near a strip mall, but sales were not up to their expected level. As a result, they closed the store and incurred a huge loss of $50,000. Since the store did not make sufficient money in the second year, they decided to hide the store closing expenses. Instead, they showed excellent earnings by showing very little expenses for the second year. This made the shareholders believe *'Anytime Pizza'* was still a great company to invest in.

"Here is a table that shows the actual income statement of *'Anytime Pizza'* for 1999 through 2002."

Figure 10.1: Anytime Pizza's actual income statement

	2000	2001	2002
Income ($)	130,000	180,000	110,000
Essential expenses ($)	70,000	100,000	40,000
Hidden expenses ($) (Law Suits, Store closing, etc.)	50,000	40,000	50,000
Total expenses ($)	120,000	140,000	90,000
Actual net profits ($)	10,000	40,000	20,000

"Steve and his auditors decided to hide all their expenses such as lawsuits, store closing, etc., to project a great image with the public. Since investors are mainly interested in the earnings per share, the company came up with a different income statement as shown here."

Figure 10.2: Anytime Pizza's income statement as shown to investors

	2000	2001	2002
Income ($)	130,000	180,000	110,000
Essential expenses ($)	70,000	100,000	20,000
Net profits ($)	60,000	80,000	90,000
Earnings per share ($) (Number of shares issued: 10,000)	6	8	9

Eric said, "Whoa! An investor looking at the earnings per share row would assume the company was consistently making profits, but it had actually hidden quite a lot of expenses."

Companies Involved in Scams

A lie gets halfway around the world before the truth has a chance to get its pants on
Sir Winston Churchill

Eric greeted the next caller. "Hello. Who is this?"

The caller said, "My name is John. I have made some observations regarding a few companies. *JDS Uniphase Corporation* excluded the charges related to the merger that took place in 2000. It not only showed the company's expenses were less than they really were, but also showed its earnings were more than they actually were. If they had shown these expenses, their growth would have slowed down.

"*3Com Corporation*, during the first quarter of 2001, completely hid their realignment. If they had showed these expenses, their share price would have gone down.

"*Toys 'R' Us Inc.* had major losses from www.toysrus.com during the second quarter of 2000. Instead of accepting their losses, *Toys 'R' Us* decided to hide these expenses and projected a great year in earnings.

"*Venator Group Inc.*, during the second quarter of 2000, had to close quite a few stores, causing heavy losses. But instead of showing its losses, the company decided to hide them, showing instead that their revenue was good.

"Who can forget AOL's sudden growth but finally ending up on the verge of bankruptcy? *AOL*, now part of *Time Warner (TWX)*, spent a lot of money on marketing its Internet service. But instead of expensing these marketing costs, they simply changed their method of expensing and hid them. When these accounting frauds were revealed to the public, their stocks became worthless. *AOL's* share price of $75 around December 1999 was literally worthless around December 2002.

"When so many companies are involved in such scams, how can an investor detect whether a company is manipulating its expenses?"

The Source for Earnings is Sales

The difference between 'involvement' and 'commitment' is like an egg-and-ham breakfast: the chicken was 'involved' - the pig was committed
Anonymous

Sam said, "A company that produces consistent earnings should have consistent sales, too."

Eric said, "Let me ask you this. If a company has consistent earnings and sales, does that mean it will not practice any deceptive accounting?"

"Not necessarily.

"This reminds me of something. We play blackjack either in Las Vegas or in Atlantic City, and we think beating the dealer depends on luck, because the dealer is controlling the cards.

"This may be true for you and me, but not for six M.I.T. students who mastered the art of beating the dealer. In the novel *Bringing Down the House*, author Ben Mezrich describes a true story of how six M.I.T. students made millions of dollars playing blackjack.

"They adopted new methods the dealers themselves hadn't experienced before. Even though they followed all the rules of the game, they never really gambled. Nevertheless, they made tons of money with their skills.

"In the same way, a company can still play within the rules of the game when it can't hide all its expenses. The easiest way for them to show more earnings is to increase their sales without actually selling."

Eric was shocked. "What!" he exclaimed.

GAAP

Sam said, "Companies in the U.S. follow what is known as GAAP. GAAP stands for Generally Accepted Accounting Principles. These are the standards and generally accepted accounting principles followed by almost every company in the U.S.

"GAAP are the rules a company is expected to follow. There is plenty of room for a company to exploit the loopholes and make an investor believe it is really doing very well."

Sales Management

In theory, there is no difference between theory and practice. But, in practice, there is
Jan L.A. van de Snepscheut

"In fact, the testimony of *California Micro Device's* chairman's in his criminal trial was shocking. The company booked bogus sales for fake products they did not even manufacture. An even more shocking factor is that the team from *Coopers & Lybrand*, which was auditing this firm at that time, gave the chipmaker's books a clean bill of health.

"When a company finds it difficult to promote its product or service and cannot admit it to the public, it manipulates its sales.

"Under the rule of GAAP, if a company has made a sale but has not yet collected the money from its customer, it can still be included in the yearly sales."

Eric exclaimed, "Oh! Is that right? Can you explain that some more, Sam?"

Sam said, "Sure. Take an example. Mark, who is excellent at assembling computers, started his own manufacturing company *'Mark Systems'*. He had the idea of asking customers to come to his shop and choose the products they needed for their computers. It was like making your own pizza by choosing the ingredients yourself.

"Customers who came to *'Mark Systems'* liked the idea and responded well. Mark opened more stores across the country.

"His company became very popular in a short period of time, and he started extending credit to his customers. They bought the computers and paid the company on a monthly basis over a period of 6 to 24 months.

"How did Mark account for this under GAAP?

"Let us assume Mark sold ten computers to *American Express (AXP)*. They were billed $100,000, but they decided to use the store's credit facility. The company's income statement would include the $100,000 as part of sales and would be considered as part of the current year's income.

"However, *'Mark Systems'* hadn't collected the money yet, even though a sale was made. How can we, as investors, find out that customers were billed but had not yet paid? In addition to looking at the income statement, we should look at the 'Accounts Receivable' value under the balance sheet. This would indicate how much money was yet to be collected.

"Since *American Express* hadn't paid *Mark Systems* yet, the $100,000 would show under 'Accounts receivable'. This indicates a sale of $100,000 was made, but the company hadn't yet received it as income."

Eric asked, "Can you please explain the drawbacks of this?"

Accounts Receivable

All truth passes through three stages. First, it is ridiculed. Second, it is violently opposed. Third, it is accepted as being self-evident
Arthur Schopenhauer

Sam said, "Sure. Since *American Express* hasn't paid *'Mark Systems'*, they can delay the payment as much as possible. If the company were depending on its income for expansion and a customer delays his payments, its expansion would be seriously affected. In the end, the shareholders would get hurt.

"If credit is a great flexibility for a customer, it may be a great way of cooking earnings for a company.

"*'Mark Systems'*, which was very successful in its initial stages, was hurt by the economy in 2002. Customers were no longer spending a lot of money on computers and accessories.

"Instead of accepting low sales figures, the company decided to employ a unique selling technique. Instead of selling computers to consumers, they gave away a brand new computer with the latest technology as a free trial to whoever was referred to them by existing customers. The customers were given a choice of keeping the system as long as they wanted and paying for it only if they liked it.

"New customers liked this flexibility a lot, and many systems were sold, even during the recession period. For all practical purposes, the company didn't actually make a single sale. Instead, they donated the computers. But due to the loophole in the accounting system, *'Mark Systems'* reported millions of dollars in sales.

"Investors were stunned. Every investor loved this company because they were able to generate sales even during poor economic conditions, and naturally its share price went up.

"After a couple of months, the company started sending bills to its customers, but more than 75% refused to pay and started filing law suits.

"Finally, *'Mark Systems'* not only made a huge loss, but also had to file for bankruptcy because more than million dollars from its customers were left outstanding."

Eric said, "Shocking! At least we know that 'Accounts Receivable' should be kept in mind."

"Absolutely!"

They got another call. "Hi! My name is Mary. It was interesting and a little bit shocking to learn about companies manipulating sales and earnings. But how do we determine from 'Accounts Receivable' whether the company is good to invest in? I would really love to know."

Sam said, "Well, as I was saying, even though *'Mark Systems'* entered these transactions as sales, they did not collect revenues, and the total amount of the sales would be recorded as accounts receivable."

Scandal 2: Accounts Receivable More than 10%

If you never change your mind, why have one?
Edward De Bono

"We should not only check a company's income but also the amount to be collected as accounts receivables and how long it takes the company to collect the money.

"If a company's accounts receivables are more than 10% of the total sales, it is a clear warning sign it is into some scheme to generate income. No corporation pays a bill the instant it arrives. It takes anywhere between 45 and 60 days for pending bills to clear. But if a company's accounts receivables are not cleared within 60 days, there is a clear indication it is unable to collect revenues from its customers on time.

"What is the use for a company to generate heavy sales if it cannot collect revenues from its customers? It is no better than a non-profit company, and the best thing an investor can do is to avoid it."

Valentine's Day

The first duty of love is to listen
Paul Tillich

Eric said, "For those who just joined 55.5 Ultra Lite FM, we have Sam Cohen, a student with a brain for finance. He is talking to us about accounting scandals and how to detect them. You can call the station to pose any question to him. Looks like we have the next caller standing by. Hello?

The caller said, "Hi! My name is Michelle. I was listening to your program and got quite scared listening to the story about how a woman got attracted to a man because of his fancy car and condos. My boyfriend sends me flowers every other day, and he is very romantic, but how do I make sure he is sincere?"

Eric said, "I think some listeners got confused as to what kind of an advisor our dear friend Sam is."

They both laughed.

Sam said, "Actually, Valentine's Day is the busiest day for *1-800-Flowers.com (FLWS)*. The number of roses and gifts delivered by florists on Valentine's Day outnumbers every other holiday's cut flower sales. Women love to receive flowers from *1-800-Flowers*, but would they invest in it?"

Eric said, "I think Michelle wanted to know whether the flowers came from a person who is not only affectionate, but also rich?

"What is the best way to figure out if someone is really earning tons of money or actually running on credit cards to survive?"

Sam laughed and said, "The best and easiest way to figure that out is to find out his tax bracket. If someone were really earning a lot of money, then his or her tax bracket would be 35% or more.

"Even though women love to receive flowers from *1-800-Flowers*, as investors we should not only get enticed by the company's products but also measure its stability. If a company doesn't generate income to pay taxes, how can it provide returns to its shareholders?"

Eric remarked, "Good point."

Sam said, "Thanks. Even corporations like *Microsoft* and *1-800-Flowers* have to pay taxes on their total profits earned after expenses. But the key difference between *Microsoft* and *1-800-Flowers* is that *Microsoft* does pay taxes, and an investor can safely assume it is generating some profits out of its sales.

"As a woman, you love to receive flowers from *1-800-Flowers.com*, but as an investor you might be more comfortable avoiding it. The simple and straightforward reason is that *1-800-Flowers.com* hasn't paid a single dollar in taxes from its inception, and its income tax ratio through 2002 was 0%."

Eric said, "That is a good thing to know, Sam. We will be right back after these messages."

Bill said to Jessica, "I think it is safe for you to assume you are never going to get flowers from *1-800-Flowers.com*."

Jessica quipped, "He didn't say he wouldn't buy flowers from them. He just said he wouldn't invest in them."

Monica said, "Touché."

Scandal 3: Very Little or No Taxes

People who complain about taxes can be divided into two classes: men and women.
Anonymous

After the break, Eric said, "We are back. As Sam was saying, a company is no different from a common man. Just as you and I must pay taxes, a company also must pay taxes. But the key difference is that a company needs to pay taxes only if it makes profits after all its expenses, but common investors to pay taxes on every dollar of income they earn. Right, Sam?"

Sam said, "Yes, a company can continue to run its businesses forever, without paying taxes, as long as it is not making profits. You can assume a company generates good profits if it pays over 35% in taxes. . However, it may have consistent earnings and sales, but if it is not paying taxes, say at least 30%, then it is either into an accounting scam or has no money to pay taxes.

"That is why, even though there are search engines like *www.ask.com* run by *Ask Jeeves(ASKJ)*, everyone is eagerly waiting for *www.google.com's* IPO. Simple reason: *'Ask Jeeves'* has never paid taxes. Even though it is quite popular with users, investors had better avoid companies that haven't generated enough profits to pay taxes."

Primal Fear

The road to success is dotted
with many tempting parking places
Anonymous

Eric said, "Hello! Yes, Mark. What is your question?"

Mark said, "Remember the movie *Primal Fear?* Who would have thought Edward Norton was playing the roles of both Roy and Aaron? Richard Gere not only wanted to become popular by taking the case against a Chicago cleric but also wanted to help the innocent boy. When Richard Gere was fully convinced it was not Aaron but Roy who actually killed the cleric, every one including the judge thought the boy should be freed.

"But a few minutes before the end, when Richard Gere realized Roy didn't really exist and it was Aaron's ploy to introduce Roy, everyone was shocked.

"The movie was a class apart for Edward Norton's brilliant acting, and he was able to switch between the two roles quite easily. Any ardent movie fan wouldn't believe it was his maiden appearance on the big screen.

"Sam, if I understood you right, I think a big company is no different from Edward Norton in the movie, when things go wrong. A big company may try to find accounting loopholes and try to play a good role, but in the background it might really be playing a very evil one. Richard Gere might not have had clues to Edward Norton's dual identity because he was a lawyer and not a detective. It might have been impossible even as a viewer to have come to the conclusion that Roy didn't really exist and it was Aaron who murdered the cleric.

"But analyzing a company is far different from detecting the real motive behind a killer's mind. If analyzing the killer's mind requires lateral thinking, then analyzing whether a company is practicing bad accounting requires lot of common sense."

They laughed, and Sam said, "Wow! Mark. That was some comparison!"

Mark said, "Thanks. Uh, are there any other ways of detecting accounting scandals?"

Car (Un) Sold

The greatest mistake you can make in life is to be continually fearing you will make one
Elbert Hubbard

Sam said, "Okay, let me mention another way to find out if a company is manipulating its accounts. Say for example, Jones, who is passionate about cars, opened a dealership. He was very aggressive in pushing cars, and it took everyone by a huge surprise when he was able to sell more cars than any other dealer on Long Island. He entered the arena of selling cars in a big way. He opened offices and dealerships along the entire east coast in the name *'Cars R Jones'* and took his company public, as he needed millions of dollars to expand his offices.

"He took the risk of buying cars from the manufacturer with a huge down payment, assuming his sales team was also as effective as he was. He ordered thousands of cars and kept them in the dealership's parking lot.

"Of course, customers did visit his shop and bought cars. But sales were not as high as he projected. Eventually the year-end came, and it was time to announce his earnings to the public. The company had to project an excellent sale value to retain its investors.

"Even though they did not sell to the end customer, they created an image that they sold every car in their inventory. They created an impression that they made a huge profit in sales.

"Investors also believed the earnings report and bought the stock. Days passed, and as new models of the cars were introduced, *'Cars R Jones'* was left behind in buying them, as they practically ran out of cash to run the business. After a huge loss, they had to file for bankruptcy. This is a common problem for a company that overproduces but cannot find a buyer for its product. By overproducing a product, it creates an image there is a heavy demand for it, but by not being able to sell it, the production costs go to waste. In the end, it has no choice but to sell its goods at lower than the production cost."

Scandal 4: Inventory More than 20% of Sales

> *Reality is merely an illusion,*
> *albeit a very persistent one*
> Albert Einstein

Bill commented, "I think Sam is going to send a lot of people to the hospital with all this shocking news."

Joe joked, "It is a pity you are not one of them."

Eric asked, "Oh man! How can an investor find if a company is showing goods in inventory as a projection of goods sold?"

Sam said, "When cars are not sold, they remain as inventory. If an inventory level keeps rising, then it is a warning sign the company is unable to sell.

"The only reason a company increases its inventory level is to project a great deal of income to the public. They hope to clear their inventory in the long run. But when they fail, naturally the company's money is locked, and it has no funds to run its business.

"When a company runs out of cash, then naturally it has no other choice but to file for bankruptcy. The ultimate loss is to none other than the shareholders. As a shareholder, you are better off avoiding companies whose inventory level is more than 20% of their sales, and companies that take more than 60 days to clear their inventory."

Companies Involved in Scams

> *Going to work for a large company is like*
> *getting on a train. Are you going sixty miles an hour*
> *or is the train going sixty miles an hour and you're*
> *just sitting still?*
> J. Paul Getty

Eric spoke to the next caller. "Hello, Karen. What is your question?"

Karen said, "Thank you guys for explaining a lot of financial realities. Well, I just wanted to know if could you give me some names of companies that showed abnormally high inventories?"

Sam said, "Sure, *Craig Consumer Electronics, Inc.* increased its inventory levels on the grounds of customer needs, but actually ended up storing all its items in its inventory without making a lot of sales. If investors had checked the inventory level, they could have avoided investing in this company.

"*Health Management Inc.* overstated inventories to meet earnings expectations during 2000. This not only created a false impression that its customers needed its products, but it also resulted in high inventory levels.

"*Lucent Technologies (LU),* a spin-off from *AT & T (T),* is a primary lesson for investors who failed to look at inventory levels. When it produced great earnings, investors wanted to buy its stock, and the price went to $81 around November 1999. However, as of November 2002 it was trading at less than a dollar. In other words, if someone invested $10,000 in Lucent around November 1999, it became worthless in a couple of years. The main reason was that the company produced massive amounts of equipment; assuming customers would buy every product they produced. Unfortunately, no one was willing to buy outdated equipment. Eventually, the company ended up having a huge inventory without any buyers.

"The share price of *Cisco (CSCO)* was climbing to $80 during November 2000, and analysts were betting that the share price would touch around $150. People invested all their savings without checking its inventory levels. *Cisco* took steps to buy components from its suppliers, even before it had confirmed orders from its customers. During December 2000, the company failed to get any more orders from its customers, and its revenue fell drastically. Since it couldn't sell its products, it naturally lost a sizeable portion of its revenue by writing off its inventory. This was reflected in the share price, which was trading at $10 in November 2002."

Scandal 5: Inventory Clearance Days are More Than 60

> *When a company president is ready to buy lunch, it's time to sell the stock. When he has something really good, you can't get him on the phone*
> Anonymous

Karen said, "Whoa! That was a lot of names."

Sam laughed, "Yes. The number of days it takes on average for an item to be cleared from the shelf must be less than 60 days. If inventory takes longer than 60 days to clear, the company must be having difficulties selling its products and would be facing huge difficulties to generate cash.

"Not only would a company be facing difficulties in generating cash, it would also devise all sorts of methods to project high earnings in spite of not clearing its inventory. This means an investor is better of avoiding such a company, which has difficulties in moving its products to its customers.

"For example, as a reader, you might have picked up a book either from *Borders (BGP)* or from *Barnes and Noble (BKS)*. But who is really doing very well as a business? Both *Borders* and *Barnes and Noble* sell books. In fact, you would find almost the same books at the same price in both stores. But how do we determine which store is really doing well?

"The main purpose of *Barnes and Noble* and *Borders* is to sell books. Both order books from publishers and sell them to end customers like us. When a book or music CD arrives in the store, it is put on the shelf, with additional copies being kept in inventory. Whenever the inventory runs low, the store orders additional copies from the publisher. This provides customers the flexibility to buy the book whenever they want it.

"Be it a store like *Borders* or a business like *'Cars R Jones'*, its main purpose should be to clear its inventory as early as possible. Even though inventories are good to meet the customers' needs, it is equally bad if the inventory is not sold or takes a longer time to clear."

Eric said, "We have about 15 minutes. Let's see who the next caller is. Hello? Yes, who is this?"

The caller said, "Hello! My name is Jim. I was listening to this program as I was driving home with my son. I have a question to ask Sam. Are there any other underhanded ways companies use to project great earnings?"

Sam said, "Yes sir. Let me give you an example."

Non-Operating Profits

Whenever you see a successful business, someone
made a courageous decision
Peter Drucker

"Jason, a big time entrepreneur, started renting cars and trucks in and around Chicago. Since he knew the art of buying old cars and trucks at a low price and modifying them to meet his customers' requirements, he did a great business at first.

"He expanded his operations of *'Renterprise'* not only to Chicago, but also to nearby areas like Columbus and Cleveland and requested shareholders to join with him. The shareholders were skeptical about his business, but they looked at his financial statement and liked what they saw, since renting cars and trucks is a never-ending business in the U.S.

"Even though he was good at servicing old cars and trucks, his repairs started showing their true colors after a while. The vehicles kept breaking down, and customers faced too many difficulties driving them.

"*Renterprise* started spending money on servicing its cars and trucks by replacing the transmissions, engines, etc. This was a big expense for *Renterprise*, and it dented its earnings per share figure.

"In addition to repairing some of his inventory, he ordered the sale of very old trucks and cars. Even though each of them fetched very little money, selling them fetched almost $500,000. That was a major income boost, especially since business was bad.

"*Renterprise's* income statement looked as follows."

Figure 10.3: Renterprise's income statement

Details	Amount ($)	Remarks
Sales	100,000	Total income from renting trucks and cars
Cost of goods sold	20,000	Primary cost involved in renting trucks and cars
Gross income	80,000	Income after spending for cost of goods sold
Sales, general and admin expenses	60,000	General expenses to run the business
Operating income	20,000	Income after deducting essential expenses
Taxes	3,000	Income taxes paid to IRS
Discontinued operations	**500,000**	**Sale of old equipment**
Net income	517,000	Net Income
Total shares	100,000	Number of shares
Earnings per share	5.17	Earnings per share

"As you may notice, by selling its old trucks and cars, *Renterprise* made $500,000. However, something like that is not likely to happen every year. This is another common practice some companies employ to project great earnings.

"Even though it is legal, it creates an impression the company made huge profits. In reality, it may not be able to create profits every year by selling its equipment or land, and it would create a huge dent in the coming years."

Scandal 6: Non-Operating Income More than 20% of Sales

"Manipulating earnings by producing very high income from discontinued operations is not magic. It is a clear way of stating that a company has not produced sufficient sales this year, and to show positive earnings, it had to sell its assets to generate income.

"If a company produces more than 20% of its income from discontinued operations or anything other than sales, you would be wise to avoid investing in it. It cannot run its business solely by selling its assets. Instead, it should generate new business from its operations."

David Copperfield sold more tickets in a week than Lion King and every other show on Broadway.

David Copperfield made more than one billion dollars in one decade.

Practical Examples of Non-Operating Income

Dawn comes slowly, but dusk is rapid
Alice B Toklas

Eric asked, "Can you give some examples of companies that manipulated its revenues?"

Sam said, "In 1999, *Bankers Trust* participated in a scheme to convert unclaimed funds in the bank's custody to *Bankers Trust* reserve and income accounts to meet the bank's revenue.

"When *Boston Chicken (BOST)* was being hailed as the next *McDonald's*, it inflated revenues by selling shares in the company's *Einstein/Noah Bagel* subsidiary. This resulted in almost $38.1 million additional revenue during 1996, thereby boosting its EPS. Investors loved the company without really noticing such scams. Alas, *Boston Chicken* filed for bankruptcy, and its stock is not traded on *NASDAQ* anymore."

Eric said, "I think we are almost towards the end of the hour. I would like to thank Sam on behalf of all the listeners and everyone here at *Ultra Lite FM*, including myself. We are certainly going to be more cautious before we invest. Thanks for sharing such a wealth of information. It was a great pleasure to have you here, Sam."

Sam said, "Likewise, Eric. Thanks, everyone."

Eric pushed the commercials button and stepped outside with Sam.

Bill, Joe and the girls rushed towards him.

Monica said, "Great show, Sam."

Sam said, "Thanks, Monica. I owe this to you."

Monica said, "You are very welcome. I guess we all learned lot of things about accounting scandals and how to avoid them."

Eric suggested, "Sam, I guess you should leave your address and phone number. After the show, I am sure some people would like to get in touch with you. Also, I would like to discuss the possibilities for you to do more shows here."

Sam said, "Eric, I really appreciate the offer. But I think this will be my last couple of months in LA. I am thinking of moving to the east coast."

Eric said, "Well, that's your decision. But the slot is always open for you."

Monica said, "It was really nice knowing you guys. Let's stay in touch. I am flying out tomorrow."

Bill said, "Oh! Mon! Don't break my heart."

They all laughed.

When Sam and Jessica were alone after everyone left, Jessica exploded and said, "You didn't tell me you were moving to the east coast. What about us?"

Sam said, "I was going to tell you, Jess."

Jessica was seething with anger and said, "You are just like the companies you mentioned back in that radio show. Your charm and niceness was just an act, and now you throw this bombshell."

Sam said, "Jess, I love you a lot. But I need to think about my career, too."

Jessica was in tears and she said, "I am sorry. I can't be with you right now. I have to go."

Sam's Sprinkles

- To attract customers, a company might tweak its accounting to project good earnings.

- To hide its financial problems, a company might make changes in its accounting books. Before investing, an investor should not just look at the books but should check whether the books are cooked.

- A company with consistent earnings but inconsistent sales should be avoided.

- GAAP stands for Generally Accepted Accounting Principles.

- Accounts Receivables refer to a sale that was made but the customer has not yet made a payment.

- To project good earnings, a company might create non-existent sales. To avoid such companies, check its accounts receivables. If its accounts receivables are more than 10% of its sales, you should avoid it.

- Like individuals, even corporations have to pay taxes. However, the key difference is that individuals pay taxes on their income, whereas corporations pay taxes on their profits.

- A corporation that doesn't pay taxes is a clear indication that its earnings are not profitable. An investor should avoid investing in such companies.

- In order to project excellent sales, a company might manufacture products but not necessarily sell them. As a result, it may end up with a high inventory it may not be able to sell in the future. Wise investors look at the inventory level before investing their money.

- If a company's inventory levels are above 20% of its sales, you should avoid it.

- A company should not only be able to deliver good products, it should also clear its inventory as early as possible. A company that takes a long time to clear its inventory is not a great company for investors.

- Avoid investing in a company that takes more than 60 days to clear its inventory.

- Non-operating profits are irregular income for a company. To project high earnings, a company might attempt to produce high non-operating profits.

- Avoid investing in a company whose non-operating profits are more than 20% of its sales.

- Always look at the balance sheet, income statement and cash flow statement before investing in any company. Rankings by various firms and websites should not be an investor's sole decisive factor.

True or False

- As auditors evaluate a company's annual and quarterly reports, they do not discover any accounting scams.

- An investor can simply trust the financial books of a company, because the SEC approves it.

- A company cannot increase its earnings without an appropriate increase in sales.

- Inventory levels are not included in sales.

- Non-operating profits are like regular sales, so i is perfectly fine to obtain a major source of income from them.

Self-Explorer

- What is the role of auditing firms? Order the annual and quarterly reports of some of your favorite companies and verify the auditing firm involved.

- Understand the role of a Chairman, CEO and Directors for a company.

- Find out how a CEO is elected.

- Calculate the following for *Wal-Mart* and *Target*, and decide which company operates more efficiently:

  - How soon is their inventory cleared?
  - What is the credit period extended to their customers?
  - What is the average time it takes for them to pay their suppliers?

- How do S&P's ratings differ from Moody's? What is the net effect when either S&P's or Moody's ratings go up or down?

Chapter XI

Who is Dollar Wise, Penny Foolish?

Bargain Hunters or Antique Collectors?

Society does not go down because of the activities of criminals, but because of the inactivity of the good people
Swami Vivekananda

Solution to Every Problem

*What we anticipate seldom occurs: but what
we least expect generally happens*
Benjamin Disraeli

Bill opened his door to see Sam standing outside. He said, "Hey man! Come on in. What's going on?"

Sam entered and said, "I have good news. I have an interview with an investment firm."

Bill said, "Fantastic. Good for you, man."

Sam said, "The job is in New York."

Bill said, "Oh! That was why you were talking about going to the east coast. By the way, have you taught us all there is to know about picking a good stock?"

Sam said, "Well, just a couple more things."

Bill said, "Then, have a nice flight."

Sam made a face. Bill laughed, "Just kidding, man. I am happy for you, but we will miss you a lot."

Sam said, "Jessica is very upset about this. I am not sure how to handle this now. This is a great career opportunity, for sure."

The entrance of a young boy and Bill's mom interrupted them. Bill introduced his mother and brother to Sam.

Bill's brother, Eliot, said, "What are you guys talking about?"

Bill hesitatingly said, "Uh, about the 'Stock exchange'."

Eliot asked, "What do they exchange?"

Bill's mother told Sam, "I never understood anything about the stock market. Bill tells me you have taught him a lot."

Sam thanked her.

Bill said, "Eliot, I think you are too young to understand that, and now is not a good time."

Sam said, "That's okay. Well, let me put it in a way he will understand. Eliot, when you go to a supermarket like *Wal-Mart* or *Target*, what do you do?"

Eliot said, "I buy stuff. Different kinds of things."

Sam said, "Do you know who puts those items there? They are called manufacturers. You and anyone else who buys stuff from these stores are called buyers. Isn't it cool you can buy everything from one shop?"

Eliot nodded.

Sam said, "Stores like *Target (TGT)* and *BJ's wholesale (BJ)* buy directly from the manufacturer and specialize in selling to people just like you, Eliot.

"A stock exchange is no different from a supermarket, except that you can buy and sell stocks."

Bill asked Eliot, "Did you understand?"

Eliot said, "Part of it. Okay, I gotta go. See you later."

Bill's mom asked, "Hmm! That was interesting. What is the benefit of the stock exchanges, Sam?"

Sam said, "A stock exchange is beneficial both to corporations and to investors. Now, to buy any stock, you don't have to visit every corporation and look for sellers. Similarly, when you want to sell a stock, you don't have to look for buyers. The stock exchange takes care of these things.

"A stock exchange cannot and will not recommend a stock, but they are the backbone, ensuring a smooth flow of operations. At any point of time, you'll never come across a situation where your stocks are not being sold, because even if there is no buyer, the exchange has many specialists who will buy the stock and sell it later."

NYSE or NASDAQ

For some reason a pessimist always complains about the noise when opportunity knocks
Anonymous

Bill asked, "Are *NYSE* and *NASDAQ* the most common stock exchanges?"

Sam said, "Yes. The two most common stock exchanges are *NYSE*, which stands for *New York Stock Exchange*, and *NASDAQ*, which stands for *National Association of Securities Dealers and Automated Quotation*.

"A corporation might choose between *NYSE* and *NASDAQ*. The *New York Stock Exchange* was started in 1792, but *NASDAQ* didn't open until 1971.

"A company might choose *NYSE* because it has built a great name over the years. But if the company finds it difficult to meet *NYSE* standards, it might choose *NASDAQ* because the annual fee is a lot less. For a company to be listed in *NYSE*, it has to pay $35,000 to $500,000 per year, whereas NASDAQ charges only $21,225 to $60,000 per year.

"As of October 2003, the most valuable company listed in the *NYSE* was *General Electric*, and in *NASDAQ*, it was *Microsoft*."

Bill's mom said, "Interesting. Do you find bargains as you would in department stores?"

Sam said, "Absolutely. Say it's Thanksgiving, and you want to buy a new Sony 52-inch HDTV television. After researching its technical details, the next thing you would do is to compare the prices among various merchants. You visit stores like *Best Buy* and *Circuit City* and verify the prices. You might also go a step further and check the availability and price from www.buy.com or www.overstock.com.

"As a consumer, you have tons of places to choose the product from. Once you finalize your decision, you can easily verify the price from various merchants by visiting sites like www.edealinfo.com or www.pricegrabber.com, that list the best bargain prices at various stores.

"Like *Circuit City* and *Best Buy* that operate stores nationwide, brokerage firms operate nationwide to buy stocks. But the best way to buy a stock is to buy online using a discounted brokerage firm, because once you have identified the stock, all you need to do is to buy it.

"Stores make profits by selling products at a margin. In other words, if *Circuit City* buys a CD-Player for $100 from a manufacturer, they might add a $50 margin before selling it to the consumer. The profits are therefore added into the price."

Bill said, "That is the reason prices vary between stores. If *Best Buy* decided to increase their volume of business, they may sell their products at a lower price than *Circuit City* and vice versa.

"But stocks are traded differently, right?"

Sam said, "Yes, the price of the stock remains the same at any point in time across all firms, be it an online firm like www.scottrade.com, www.ameritrade.com, www.brownco.com, or a full brokerage firm like www.fidelity.com or www.vanguard.com, But these companies make money by charging their customer a fee called a 'trading fee' or 'transaction fee'.

"For example, as of today (10/01/2003) *Scottrade* charges $7 per trade (a buy or a sell), and *Ameritrade* charges $10.99 per trade. However, the full brokerage houses like *Vanguard* and *Fidelity* charge approximately $20 per trade."

Buying Stocks at Bargain Price

Bill's mom asked, "If stock prices don't vary among brokerage firms, how can we buy stocks at a bargain price?"

Sam said, "When you buy a Coke or Pepsi or a Sony Television, the prices may vary among stores, but not all the time. However, the price of a stock does not vary among the brokerage firms, but it varies almost every minute across the country.

"The stock price is determined in the stock exchange. As I already said, the two most popular exchanges are *NYSE* and *NASDAQ*, but many more exchanges are available. In these exchanges, stocks are traded and the prices are determined based on supply and demand. As more investors buy a stock, its price rises, and as more people sell a stock, its price drops."

The stock exchanges in the U.S. operate between 9.30 AM to 4.00 PM Monday – Friday, excluding major holidays.

"Since prices vary almost every minute during the exchange's operating hours, the best way to buy a stock is to look for a price that is lower than its actual value and buy it."

Bill objected, "But, I don't think it is possible for us to watch the price every second."

Sam said, "Well, the technology is so advanced, you can set the price in http://finance.yahoo.com, and Yahoo will send an alert message both to your cell phone and to your email address, when the price comes down lower than your set price."

Bill's mom said, "That's impressive. There is so much to learn. Thanks, Sam. I will see you later."

After she left the room, Bill asked, "When is your interview?"

Sam said, "Tomorrow, at the campus. I think it is going to last a couple of hours. This firm also offers educational services to common investors. They are looking to fill a position in that group. I thought it might be a good starting point before I decide where to go next."

Bill said, "Ok. Good luck. I am sure you will do very well. Try and talk to Jessica."

Impact of Buying Stocks at Various Prices

Give me a place to stand, and I will move the Earth
Archimedes

Sam entered the interview room. He shook hands with Alex Goodrich and Mark Townsend.

After an initial round of introductions, Alex said, "Sam, your resume is quite impressive. You listed 'teaching investment concepts' as one of your skills. Can you expand on that?"

Sam cleared his throat and began, "Sure, sir. I first taught a group of my friends about the importance of investing. Then I taught them certain formulae that can be used to analyze and measure a company's soundness before purchasing its stocks."

Mark asked, "Did your friends show continued interest?"

Sam said, "Yes, sir. They definitely did. I have a different way of explaining things. I use fictitious companies to explain financial concepts like debt or earnings per share."

Alex said, "Interesting. Why don't you explain an investing concept of your choice, in the same way you did with your friends?

Sam said, "Sure. I am going to explain how to determine the right price of a stock."

Mark nodded and said, "That should be good."

Sam began, "I will explain how to understand the impact of buying a stock at its lowest price. Say you have $10,000 to invest, and you have identified *Microsoft* as the best stock to buy. The best thing to do is to wait for the right price. How effective is it to wait for the right price?

"After applying all the formulas, we find out that *Microsoft* is an excellent company. It has no debt, and the profit margins are excellent with a very high return on equity.

"But can we buy *Microsoft* at any time? Definitely not. Let's go with the facts.

"The value of $10,000 invested in *Microsoft* in October 1993 would have been worth $233,136 by January 2000. Now that is very impressive.

"However, $10,000 invested in the same company in October 1998 would be worth only $10,053 around October 2003. Did the company stand still during those five years? Not at all. During this five year period, *Microsoft* introduced products from .NET to XBOX and went very big on Pocket PCs. "

Alex interrupted, "But why haven't the share prices gone up?"

Sam answered, "Well, that is due to the fact that from October 1998 through 2000, *Microsoft's* stock prices were very high. In other words, *Microsoft's* share price was much higher than its actual worth. Clearly, that was not a great time to buy *Microsoft* shares.

"To illustrate further, assuming you had invested $10,000 in *Microsoft* in 2000, the net worth of your investment would have been worth only $7,932 in 2003.

"There is nothing wrong with *Microsoft* shares. The only thing is that in October 1993, the share price was around $2.50 (split adjusted), but during January 2000, it was trading at $50.

"The only way to make killer profits in stocks is to buy shares of a great company like *Microsoft*, but at a lower price than its actual worth. If you like big screen TVs, you would want to buy the best projection TV at the lowest price. Along the same lines, it is not enough to buy a great company's shares. You need to buy them at a bargain price.

"Unlike consumer products like televisions, stock prices do not vary among different brokerage firms. The prices are always the same across brokerage firms at any point of time. After identifying a great company, the key is to buy its stock below their actual value. Paying a high price for a great company's stock is equivalent to betting on a horse with broken legs. You will certainly lose your original investment, even if you wait for years."

Alex said, "Good! I like the way you explain. Can you prove this with another company?"

Sam said, "Thanks, sir. Yes, let me take another example.

"*PayChex*, the most popular payroll processing firm, was trading around $3 during October 1993. An investment of $10,000 in *PayChex (PAYX)* at that time would have been worth around $183,505 in October 2000.

"The same $10,000 investment in *Paychex* in October 2000 would have been worth only $6,000 in October 2002. Why is that? Because *PayChex* was trading above its worth in October 2000, and it was definitely not the best time to buy. The company's stock was trading at $55, and the price came down to $28 in October 2002.

"The key is always to buy a stock below its actual worth. Whenever a great stock is sold below its value, it is a great time to buy, and sooner or later, the stock will meet or increase its net worth.

"For example, $10,000 invested in *PayChex* around January 2003 would have been worth $16,000 in October 2003. In less than a year, we made huge returns (60%) on our investment. Why is that? During January 2003, the stock was trading below its net worth, and after a few months, the stock price went up almost 60% due to heavy demand.

"It is neither the period nor the market timings that are important. The key is identifying a great stock and buying it at a price lower than its actual net worth.

"Just like we get promotional offers during Thanksgiving or discounted prices for travel to the U.K. during winter, stock prices will come down once in a while, and as investors, we have to determine whether its price is trading lower than its actual worth. A great stock trading below its worth is an indication that it is time to buy the stock."

Alex said, "Interesting. How does an investor know whether a stock's price is a bargain?"

Sam replied, "Well, two stocks may be traded at two totally different prices, but a $5 stock may be valued much higher than a $30 stock. One of the ways to find that out is by calculating the company's 'earnings yield'.

"Dell.com sells a *Dell* laptop with an *Intel* Centrino processor and 512 MB RAM for $5,000, but the nearby dealer sells a *Lexus* RX300 for $15,000. Which one is sold at a bargain price? Isn't it the *Lexus*?

"Just as a dealer sells a car at a bargain once in a while, a great company's stock sells at a lower price once in a while. An investor who hunts for bargain prices of a great company has the key to becoming a millionaire."

Earnings Yield

There are many ways of going forward, but
there is only one way of standing still
Anonymous

"Whenever we buy a product, we look at its net return. If you were replacing the tires on your car, you would be measuring how many miles the new tire will last. If you were buying a car, you would be measuring how many miles per gallon of gas the car would consume.

"Our first goal is to identify whether the company is capable of producing at least 20% returns in the long run.

"We have to find a company whose earnings to price ratio is more than the return you would otherwise get if you had invested in a bond. As of today (October 2003), from the website http://bonds.yahoo.com/rates.html, the yield of a 10-

year bond is 4.34. We therefore have to find a stock whose earnings yield is at least slightly above 4.34.

"As the earnings for previous years are already known, and only the current price varies, it is ideal to find a stock whose earnings to yield is higher than 4.34.

"To calculate the earnings yield, divide the earnings per share of the stock with its price. Once you get the earnings from websites like http://moneycentral.msn.com, type the ticker symbol, and you will see the 'quote' page with the current price and the earnings for the past 12 months.

"As of October 2003, *Yahoo (YHOO)*'s earnings were 0.336 and the stock price was \$43.93. The earnings yield of *Yahoo* can be calculated as follows."

Earnings yield = Earnings/ Price * 100

"Yahoo's earnings yield = (0.336 / 43.93)* 100 = 0.76.

"An earnings yield of 0.76 is way below the current bond rating of 4.34, and therefore *Yahoo* would not be a great company to buy, because it cannot produce a higher income than the returns from bonds.

"Let us also look at another famous company called *Orthodontic Centers of America Inc. (OCA)*. The earnings as of October 2003 for *OCA* were 1.101, and the current price was 8.98. Let us calculate the earnings yield of the company."

Earnings yield of *OCA* = (1.101/8.98) x 100 = 12.26%

"As a 12.26 earnings yield is much higher than a 4.34 treasury yield, *Orthodontic* is a great company to buy, provided it passes all the other formulas.

Alex said, "You have certainly done your homework."

Sam smiled, a little relieved, and said, "Thanks, sir."

Mark said, "Can you give us an example of a good company and the impact of buying its stock at various prices? You can take your time. You can use the laptop and Internet connections here. We will join you once you are ready."

Low Prices, High Returns

A pat on the back, though only a few vertebrae removed from a kick in the pants, is miles ahead in results.
Bennett Cerf

After 20 minutes, Sam told them he was ready, and knowing he was on familiar ground, began, "Over the last year, you had several opportunities to buy shares of *General Electric (GE)*. Because the stock price is always changing, let us assume the stock was trading at different prices last year, and you bought 1000 shares of *GE* at different prices.

"Also, let us assume that *GE* is currently trading at $50.

"Let us find out what your total profits earned and the percentage of growth in a year's time would have been."

Sam showed them a chart with different prices.

Figure 11.1: Comparison of GE's growth bought at different prices over a period of one year

Purchase price ($)	Total investment (Price * 1000 shares) ($)	Today's net worth (50 * 1000) ($)	Net profits / Losses made ($)	Growth %
10	10,000	50,000	40,000	400
15	15,000	50,000	35,000	233
20	20,000	50,000	30,000	150
30	30,000	50,000	20,000	66.66
50	50,000	50,000	0	0
60	60,000	50,000	(10,000)	(16.67)
80	80,000	50,000	(30,000)	(37.50)
100	100,000	50,000	(50,000)	(50.00)

"As you may notice, the company hasn't changed. It is still *General Electric*. Only the share price has changed and is trading at $50 today. If you had bought when it was trading at $10, you would have made a great profit of 400% in one year. However, if you had bought the same stock at $100, you would have lost 50% of your investment.

"It is very important to determine a stock's price before buying. Even if a company is solid, our investments will grow only if we buy its stock at a lower price. "

Alex said, "Well, you do have a knack of explaining concepts well."

They chatted for a couple of minutes, and Sam walked out of the interview room feeling completely exhausted.

Are We Paying the Right Price?

One man's wage is another man's price increase
Harold Wilson

Sam dialed Joe's cell phone. He said, "Hey, Joe."

Joe answered, "Sam, how did your interview go?"

Sam said, "I think it went well. Where is Jess? I have to talk to her."

Joe said, "I think she will join us at the deli where we were going to meet for lunch. She is not telling me anything. All I know is she is very upset."

Sam said, "Okay. I will see you guys later."

The group met at the deli and started on their favorite sandwiches.

Joe said, "Jessica asked me to tell you she will not be able to join us."

Troy opined, "Man, this is serious. Sam, you must talk to her."

Sam said, "I am trying to. But she is avoiding me. I think I will go over to her place tonight. She will definitely understand. She is a very sensible woman."

Bill added, "And very much in love with you, my friend."

Sam said, "I will take care of this, guys."

He gave them a blow-by-blow account of his interview.

Joe said, "Your next topic covers the price at which we should buy a stock, after we identify it as a good stock to buy, right?"

Sam replied, "Yes, everything in today's world is associated with measurement. Without measurements, the world wouldn't make sense. Imagine time without clock and calendar.

"Say you are running a big business, and you want to set up a meeting with your client to discuss a contract. Can you inform your client you will meet him 'sometime' without specifying the exact date and time? Is it possible to set up the meeting without the exact date, time and place?

"Just as we need a calendar and a clock to measure time, we also need to measure whether we are paying the right price before buying a stock.

"Say you have to drive from Washington to Boston to meet your client. How will you know the approximate time it will take to get there?"

Troy volunteered, "You will naturally take into account the distance between Washington and Boston and the approximate speed you will drive. Washington to Boston is approximately 450 miles, and if you drive at 60 miles per hour on an average, then you will reach Boston in about 7 hours and 30 minutes."

Bill added, "But you cannot drive non-stop for the entire stretch. You'll be taking breaks in between. If you have a meeting in Boston, you will need at least 8 hours to get there from Washington."

Sam said, "Right! Would you ever promise your client you would meet him in an hour's time in Boston? Of course not! Why? Because you know it is impossible to drive from Washington to Boston in an hour's time, even if you own a Lamborghini.

"Just as we measure time before setting a meeting with a client, we also need to measure a stock's value before buying.

"Owning stocks of *Microsoft* or *General Electric* doesn't guarantee great returns unless you buy them at the right price."

Sam's cell phone started to ring. His face lit up on seeing that the call was from Jessica.

Jessica said, "Sam, I am sorry I couldn't join you guys at the deli. How did your interview go?"

Sam said, "It went well, Jess. I was in fact, going to stop by your place. I will see you seven-ish?"

Jessica agreed and hung up.

Determining BiC Pen's Cost

Advertising is what transforms a yawn into a yearn
Anonymous

Sam continued, "OK, let's say you are the CEO of *BiC* World, and one of your main tasks is to determine the price at which your products must be sold. How would you do that?"

Joe said, "I would first calculate the actual production cost, including waste, advertising, shipping to retailers, etc., and then add in the required margin."

Sam said, "Right. Now, the challenge for any CEO is to find the exact margin at which he can bring in profits, so competitors cannot really break the company's monopoly.

"Assume every manufacturer publishes the company's actual production costs. As consumers, how much extra are we willing to pay? Naturally, the first reaction would be none. But it is difficult to run a business if you don't receive any profits. As consumers, we have to pay an additional cost above production costs to receive goods and services. But you wouldn't want the business to rip you off. On average, as a consumer, you may be willing to pay up to 20% more than production costs.

"Similarly, to buy a stock, you have to pay more than the actual income produced per share. Let me tell you the method to measure the cost of a share relevant to the income produced per share."

On an average, 14 million *BiC* pens are sold every day throughout the world.

Price to Earnings

People demand freedom of speech to make up for the freedom of thought, which they avoid
Soren Aabye Kierkegaard

"Before buying a stock, we have to determine the income generated by the company per share, because we want to pay a reasonable price per share."

Joe asked, "Isn't the income generated per share known as earnings per share?"

Sam said, "Exactly, and the price at which the stock is trading is known as price. The ratio between price and earnings is known as price to earnings ratio, or P/E ratio."

Bill said, "Oh! This is the famous P/E ratio I have always heard about but never understood."

Sam said, "Now you do! Historically, the price is a great buy if the stock is trading well below 20 times its earnings. Let's take the *GE* example I used during my interview. "

"Assuming *GE's* earnings per share a year before was $2, let's determine the actual price to earnings at which you could have bought the stock."

Stock: *General Electric (GE)*
Earnings: $2.00
No. of shares bought: 1,000

Figure 11.2: Finding the P/E ratio for the same stock at different prices.

Purchase price ($)	P/E ratio	Remarks	Net worth of GE's 1,000 shares at $50 per share ($)	Growth %
10	5	Excellent time to buy	40,000	400
15	7.5	Still a great price to buy	35,000	233
20	10	Well below our reasonable limit of 20	30,000	150
30	15	Close to our limit of 20.	20,000	66.66
50	25	Higher than our limit of 20	0	0
60	30	Higher than our limit of 20	(10,000)	(16.67)
80	40	Much higher	(30,000)	(37.5)
100	50	Definitely not a good time to buy this stock.	(50,000)	(50)

Troy said, "By just looking at the P/E ratio, we could have easily determined whether it was a great buying opportunity."

Joe said, "Let me get this straight. A great stock is not worth buying if it is too expensive."

Bill summarized, "The P/E ratio should be less than 20, and the earnings yield should be greater than the yield from bonds."

"Bingo!" Sam exclaimed

"When everyone starts realizing that a stock is expensive, they'll avoid buying it, and naturally the price will crash to a very low level. This is what happened to all the technology companies between 2000 and 2001.

"The P/E ratio is a key factor in making and losing millions. However great a company may be, if you determine the bargain price and wait for it before buying, you'll have learned the art of making money in stocks."

Troy said, "Looks like anyone can determine the bargain price of a stock."

Sam said, "Absolutely!"

Prepare for the Worst

> Nothing worries the pessimist like the optimist who
> says there's nothing to worry about
> *Anonymous*

Bill asked, "Okay, what if everyone buys at a P/E ratio of 15, and there comes a time when I want to sell. How will I make a profit if the price has not appreciated?"

Sam said, "Good question. If you remember the first formula, we identified companies whose earnings grow consistently, which means naturally the prices also appreciate."

Joe added, 'Okay, this means the P/E ratio is still somewhere less than 20, because as the earnings grow, the price also grows. You are going to make a profit if you sell it and it is also a good buy."

Sam said, "Right. If you want to understand this better, take a look at a fictitious situation."

He showed them a table of Price and Earnings.

Figure 11.3: Price of a stock with the same P/E ratio

Company ABC	For 2002 ($)	For 2003 ($)	For 2004 ($)
Price	15	30	45
Earnings	1	2	3
P/E ratio	15	15	15

Bill said, "Now I understand."

Sam said, "Good. Companies like *PayChex (PAYX)*, *Bed, Bath and Beyond (BBBY)*, and *CDW Corporation (CDWC)* are very good companies to buy from if their price per earnings is between the range of 15 to 20.

"Let us do the calculation. You spent $10,000 for each of these stocks and bought them at a P/E ratio of 15.

"These earnings are taken from 1995 and they are actual data. However, the prices are fictitious. I assume you were able to buy these stocks at a great price."

Figure 11.4: Result of investing in companies with consistent growth

Ticker	Earnings per share for 1995 ($)	Earnings per share for 2003 ($)	Growth of $10,000 invested in 1995 ($)	Annual compounded growth %
BBBY	0.11	1.00	100,077	33.36
CDWC	0.24	2.03	213,324	46.59
PAYX	0.11	0.78	134,526	38.38

"We should identify companies whose earnings grow much higher every year. Every time their earnings grow, naturally their stock prices go higher.

"We'll compare the price of the stock with the same P/E ratio of 15 between 1995 and October 2003.

"Once again, the earnings are actual data, and I'm assuming the price is always trading at 15 times the earnings. In reality, the price will be much higher than 15 times its earnings, and you would make much higher profits."

Figure 11.5: Price of a stock with consistent earnings but with the same P/E ratio

Ticker	For 1995 EPS ($)	Price (At P/E ratio of 15) ($)	For 2003 EPS ($)	Price at P/E ratio of 15 ($)	Difference in price per share ($)	Growth of $10,000 invested in 1995 ($)
BBBY	0.11	1.65	1.00	15.00	13.35	90,900
CDWC	0.24	3.60	2.03	30.45	28.42	84,583
PAYX	0.11	1.65	0.78	11.70	10.05	60,909

"Since the earnings for these great companies also grow consistently, we would have really made tons of money.

"However, in reality the price of the stock occasionally comes down, which is a clear indication it is time to buy. As soon as a few bargain hunters start buying these great companies, the price will start trading at a P/E ratio much higher than 15.

"The following table illustrates the actual growth of the following companies as of October 2003."

Figure 11.6: Actual growth of investing in companies with consistent earnings

Source: Morningstar, Inc.

Ticker	Earnings per share for 1995 ($)	Earnings per share for 2003 ($)	Actual growth of $10,000 invested in 1995 ($)	Annual compounded growth %
				Period 1995 - 2003
BBBY	0.11	1.00	100,077	33.36
CDWC	0.24	2.03	213,324	46.59
PAYX	0.11	0.78	134,526	38.38

Joe said, "You are saying that we should not only find a company that passes all the criteria you discussed, but you should also buy it at a low price. If we buy companies whose earnings grow consistently, the stock price will always appreciate, even if everyone buys stock at the same P/E ratio."

Sam said, "Yes, to make our stocks grow at 20% per year, always buy stocks whose earnings grow at an average 20% per year. This ensures the price will be really growing irrespective of all economic factors.

"See the actual data from companies whose earnings grew at least 20% per year."

Figure 11.7: Companies with consistent earnings per share growth

Source: Morningstar, Inc.

Ticker	EPS for 1999 ($)	For 2000		For 2001		For 2002	
		EPS ($)	Growth of EPS vs. 1999 %	EPS ($)	Growth of EPS vs. 2000 %	EPS ($)	Growth of EPS vs. 2001 %
BBBY	0.34	0.46	33.8	0.59	29.7	0.74	25.4
CDWC	1.11	1.79	61.3	1.89	5.6	2.10	11.1
PAYX	0.37	0.51	36.6	0.68	33.3	0.73	7.4

Stock Market's Global View

It is better to have a little ability and use it well than to have much ability and make poor use of it
Anonymous

Sam's cell phone buzzed again. After his telephone conversation, he joined his friends.

Sam said excitedly, "Guess what, guys! I cleared the first round."

Troy said, "Congrats, man! When is the second round?"

Sam said, "Not sure. Maybe tomorrow. Tonight, I am meeting them at dinner for an informal chat."

Bill said, "Okay, this calls for a *partay!*"

Joe asked, "Do you want to continue or prepare for your interview?"

Sam said, "This job will require me to teach investment concepts to novice investors. After a year, I will be required to join the analyst team. I guess explaining the concepts to you guys is preparation in itself."

Bill said, "Lady Luck is definitely smiling on you."

They finished their lunch and decided to go to Joe's place, since Sam wanted to meet Jessica.

Jessica opened the door and asked, "What are you doing here?"

Joe wanted to leave them alone and asked the guys to join him in the backyard.

Sam gave her the news.

Jessica said, "I am happy for you, Sam. The next interview will also be a breeze."

Sam said, "Thanks, Jess. I guess we need to talk about our situation here."

Jessica said, "I think it is pretty clear. I guess we will just remain friends."

Sam said, "C'mon, Jess. Are you breaking up with me because I am going to live on the east coast if I get the job?"

Jessica said, "I am not so sure, Sam. Let's discuss this later. We have some more time before you leave. I need to think about this."

He said, "Jess, I have to meet with the interviewers tonight. Can we postpone our dinner date?"

Jessica just said, "Not a problem."

Sam said, "Thank you so much. You are the best."

The guys interrupted them. Bill asked, "Okay, Sam. Now that your time in L.A. is running out, we had better squeeze all the financial knowledge out of you."

Troy joked, "How refined!"

Bill said, "Okay, how do we find out whether the prices of stocks have gone up in the past two years or two days or two months?"

Sam replied, "We always need a global indicator for the stock market. A global indicator generally measures the price movement of the stocks. This helps us understand the stock market in general.

"Having a global indicator has two major merits. The first one is to get a general view, and the second one is to compare.

"For example, the *New York Times* headlines might say, 'East Coast had 12 inches of snow yesterday', meaning the average snowfall was 12 inches in one day on the east coast. But Buffalo might have had 25 inches, meaning it had more snow than the average, and New York City might have had only one inch, meaning it had much less snow.

"Along the same lines, a global indicator for stocks helps us measure whether our stocks have performed higher than the average."

Global Indicator for Stocks – S & P 500

Many people doubt their ability, but few have any misgivings about their importance
Anonymous

Jessica asked, "Okay, is this where the *S&P 500* comes into the picture?"

Sam was both surprised and pleased to see Jessica participating in the discussion. "Yes, Jess. It is widely regarded as the best gauge of the U.S. equities market. The index includes 500 leading companies in various industries of the U.S. economy. Because *S&P 500* covers all the major industries and major companies within each industry, the index is widely accepted across the U.S. as the single best source of verifying the general trend in the stock market.

"A team of *Standard & Poor's* economists and index analysts called the *S&P* Index committee meets on a regular basis and maintains the *S&P 500*. The committee's purpose is to ensure that the companies listed are great ones and *justify a single index for measuring the U.S. market.*

"The *S&P 500* lists only U.S.-based companies as part of its index. This is to ensure the accounting methods used are common across all the companies within the index. Also, the companies that are part of the *S&P 500* should have a market capitalization of more than 3 billion dollars. This is to ensure only the major companies participate.

"Some of the leading companies in the *S&P 500* Index are

- *Microsoft (MSFT)*
- *General Electric (GE)*
- *Wal-Mart stores (WMT)*
- *Intel Corporation (INTC)*
- *Pfizer Inc (PFE)*
- *Citigroup (C)*
- *Johnson & Johnson (JNJ)*

Bill asked, "Has there ever been a company that was removed from the *S&P 500* list?"

Sam said, "Yep, if a company doesn't meet the requirements, it will be removed from the index. For example, *Rational Software (RATL),* the company that developed Rational Rose, was removed from the *S&P 500* because it failed to meet the standard requirements."

Comparison Between the S&P 500 and Individual Stocks

Executive ability is a talent for deciding something
quickly and getting someone else to do it
Anonymous

Troy summarized, "If an individual stock performs higher than the *S&P 500*, it is considered to be performing well.

"On the contrary, if a company's returns are lower than the *S&P 500*, it has not been doing well at all."

Joe said, "I think the *S&P 500* is more like Mass Body Index (MBI). Like the way we compare our weight with the average MBI, we can use the *S&P 500* index to compare our stock's performance with that of others."

A good stock always performs better than the global indicator.

Sam said, "Okay, assume we invest $10,000 in some good stocks. Let's compare their performance against the *S&P 500* over a 10-year period."

Figure 11.8: Growth of companies compared with S&P 500

Source: Morningstar, Inc.

Company	Growth of $10,000 invested in 1993 as of 2003 ($)	Compared to S&P 500	% of growth higher than S&P 500
S&P 500	23,838	NA	NA
General Electric	43,369	19,531	81.93%
Medtronic	99,590	75,752	317.78%
Bed, Bath and Beyond	100,522	76,684	321.69%
Microsoft	109,585	85,747	359.71%
Hot Topic	114,051	90,213	378.44%
Paychex	127,347	103,509	434.22%
CDW Corporation	248,872	225,034	944.01%
Dell	961,202	937,364	3932.23%

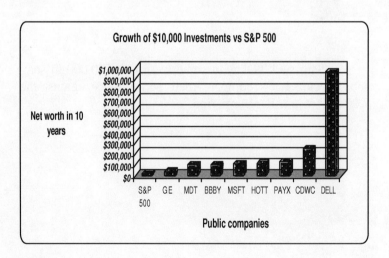

Shopping Before Buying

Bill said, "This is what we should ideally be doing. Once we identify a great stock with a P/E ratio of less than 20, the next thing is to compare it against the P/E ratio of the *S&P 500* as well as the P/E ratio of the industry to which the company belongs. Right, Sam?"

Sam said, "Yes, take a look at the comparison of the P/E ratio of some great companies with the *S&P 500* and with the industry average."

Figure 11.9: P/E ratio of companies vs. S&P 500 and Industry's average

Source: Morningstar, Inc.

Company	Current P/E ratio	P/E ratio of S&P 500	Industry's average P/E ratio	Remarks
	As of October,2003			
NVR	9.3	24.84	13.47	Reasonably priced but not at low price
Harley-Davidson	21.14	24.84	21.12	Not at its low price
Orthodontic Centers of America	8.50	24.84	20.16	Great time to buy as the price is very reasonable
Home Depot	19.3	24.84	20.78	Reasonably priced but not at low price

"A great investor will make every effort to verify not only whether the price to earnings ratio of a company is less than 20, but also whether it is less than the *S&P 500* and the industry's average."

They chatted for a while and left.

Book Value

Sam met the guys on campus the next evening. He said, "Guess what! I have to teach my first class right here in L.A."

Bill said, "You have not even joined the company yet."

Sam said, "Yeah! That is the second round of the interview. The firm wants me to talk to a couple of people about 529s and IRAs. You guys are welcome to attend."

Bill laughed, "Yeah, right!"

Sam said, "You get lunch."

Bill asked, "What time?"

They all laughed.

Sam said, "I have three days to prepare. This class is in front of a live audience. Of course, my recruiters and potential managers will be attending the class, too."

Joe said, "Sam, if you have a couple of minutes, may I ask you a question?"

Sam agreed, and they walked to the campus cafeteria. Joe asked, "What is price to book ratio? Do we need to look at that ratio too, apart from the P/E ratio?"

Sam said, "Yes. I was going to explain that next. The actual shareholder's worth of a company is determined by 'book value per share'. Assuming a company decides to close its operations today, the first and foremost thing it needs to do is to pay off its debt to banks and financial institutions. Only after clearing its debt would it be able to pay its shareholders.

"How much would the company pay its shareholders? It is based on the book value of the company. If a company gets liquidated, the shareholders are not eligible to receive anything, because a company gets liquidated only when it has no money left.

"Investors need to determine the book value of the company and confirm they are not paying too much for the stock."

Bill asked, "What is the average price an investor should pay before buying a stock?"

Sam replied, "Once the P/E ratio is determined, the next thing to determine is price to book value per share, or P/B ratio.

"A P/B ratio of two or less is considered to be very good. A price/book value per share of five and above is not worth considering.

"To summarize, once an investor decides on the right company with the right P/E ratio, he or she needs to look at the price/book ratio to know whether the company's stock is at the right price.

"Take a look at some companies with their P/E ratios and P/B ratios as of October 2003."

Figure 11.10: P/E ratio and P/B ratios of companies during April 2004.

Source: Morningstar, Inc.

Company	Price ($)	Earnings ($)	P/E ratio	Price/ Book ratio	Remarks
		As of 4/8/2004			
Western Digital	11.42	0.75	15.20	5.75	P/B ratio is high. So wait for the price to come down.
Q Logic Corp.	32.13	1.35	23.80	3.52	P/B ratio is reasonable but P/E ratio is high.
Lincare Holdings	30.69	2.22	13.80	3.68	Both P/E ratio and P/B ratio are reasonable.

Comparison

Troy asked, "Is it sufficient if we find a great company with an excellent price/book value?"

Sam said, "Well, to get the ultimate satisfaction, the best thing would be to compare it with the global average and the industry average.

"Once we determine the right stock at the right price, we can determine whether the price is lower or at least equivalent to the global average. If the price/book value is lower than two but much higher than the *S&P 500* average, then the price is much higher than the market average.

"Along the same lines, we have to compare the industry average before buying an excellent stock. A great stock picker like Warren Buffett or Peter Lynch would wait and buy a stock only if the price was much lower than the industry's average book value per share.

"Let's compare the stock's current price with the *S&P 500's* Book Value per Share and the industry's average Book Value per Share.

Figure 11.11: Price to Book value of different companies vs. S&P 500 and Industry.

Source: Morningstar, Inc.

Company	Price/ Book value per share	S&P 500's Price/ Book value	Industry's Price/ Book value	Remarks
			As of 4/8/2004	
General Electric	3.95	4.52	4.28	Reasonably priced to buy
Home Depot	3.70	4.52	3.90	Not at its low price
Best Buy	5.11	4.52	4.85	High priced
Microsoft	4.02	4.52	4.87	Reasonably priced to buy
Intel Corporat ion	4.82	4.52	4.94	Not at its low price

Consistent Earnings but Not Comfortable Earnings

Bill said, "I have a question. Do companies like *Wal-Mart*, *General Motors*, and *General Electric* also make income from borrowing and investing in stocks?"

Sam said, "Good question. Sure they do. Money generated from non-investments is also counted as part of earnings. Let me give you an example.

"Say John lives in Austin, Texas and rents out condos all over the U.S. He owns condos all the way from Atlanta to California. However, they are all run down. Every time a tenant comes in, they stay in the condo for a few days and then leave, because they keep facing problems. In spite of his irregular income, he is able to produce consistent earnings. How is that possible?

"In addition to getting money from rent, he also invests in the stock market and borrows from banks heavily.

"Money generated from non-investments is also counted as part of earnings. His income statement looks as follows.

Income from rent:	$10,000
Borrowed from bank:	$100,000
Income from stock investments:	$200,000
Total income	$310,000

"By simply looking at this figure, the total income looks very impressive, but actually he makes only $10,000 from his main business. The income from his main business is also known as sales.

"Even corporations like *Wal-Mart*, *General Motors*, and *General Electric* generate income by borrowing and investing in stocks. But unlike John, their true income comes only from sales and not by borrowing. Why?

"Sales are relatively more consistent than borrowing. A company like *General Motors* might decide to borrow money a particular year to introduce a new model and to open a new plant, but the next year they may not need to borrow any money. The money they borrow from banks and other financial institutions is a debt.

"In addition to comparing the stock's current price with average price to earnings and price to book value, the best way to figure out if the price is reasonable is by measuring price to sales.

Price to Sales

"Now, let us go back to John's example. His business is called '*John's Estate*.' Let us assume he has issued 10,000 shares to expand his operations. Comparing the stock's current price with average price to earnings and price to book value, it appears a share price of $50 is good. The company's earnings are high, and the book value is also very high.

"But in reality, his main source of income, namely rent, is only $10,000.

"Now, let us calculate the actual sales made for every share he sold."

Total sales	: $10,000
Number of shares	: 10,000

Sales per share: $1

"He can produce only $1 for every share he sold, yet the stock is currently trading at $50.

"The actual price of the stock per sales per share is $50. That is

Current price / Sales per share = $50/$1 = $50

"By stock market standards, a price to sales of 50 is very high. A reasonable price to sales figure should be less than two.

"When earnings look good, the stock's price should appreciate. But the main source of income for 'John's Estate' is from rent, and this is very low. When the stock price is trading at $50, a sales per share of $1 is very suspicious. Once the public realizes its earnings were not from rent but from borrowed money, its share price will plummet.

"As an investor, you always want to buy shares of companies that are capable of producing consistent earnings, but the earnings should also come from sales and not from borrowed money. The best way to decide is by verifying the price to earnings and price to book value, and most importantly, we should make sure the price to sales ratio is well below two.

Joe said, "The best time to buy a great stock is:

"When earnings yield is greater then the yield from bonds.

"When the price to earnings is less than 20.

"When the price to book value is less than 2.

"When the price to sales is less than 2."

Sam "Yes. Now that you have identified a great company whose price ratio meets all these criteria, is it the right moment to buy? Not necessarily."

52 Week High and Low

Bill exclaimed, "Oh man!"

Sam laughed, "Well this is the final check. Every stock price varies, and the price range during one year is defined as a 52-week range. Stock prices vary between a 52-week low and a 52-week high.

"For example, if a particular stock's 52-week low were $5 and the 52-week high were $15, the stock price in the past year would have been between 5 and 15."

Joe said, "I assume that the 52-week range can be obtained from websites like *Moneycentral* and *Morningstar*, right?"

Sam said, "Yes, Joe. Also, if the current price of the stock is close to its 52-week high, it means the stock has already reached its highest price for the past year.

"In theory, when it reaches its 52-week high, the price will start to fall. It is not good to buy a stock when it is close to its 52-week high."

"To avoid losses, the best time to buy a stock is when it is close to its 52-week low.

"For example, if the 52-week low is $5 and the price is $6, it is a good time to buy. If the price is $30, it is not a good time to buy."

Bill said, "Neat. Okay, I am gonna take off. Sam, thanks again, man."

Troy left with Bill.

Joe hesitatingly told Sam, "I don't know if I am acting like an interfering brother here, but what did you and Jessica decide? You both really seem perfect for each other. She is not the same person since you told her about your east coast move."

Sam sighed and said, "Yes, Joe. I understand your concern. I will finish my second round and think about this."

Sam's Sprinkles

- NYSE and NASDAQ are two different stock exchanges. NASDAQ is 100% computerized, whereas trading at NYSE takes place on the trading floor.

- Making money in the stock market depends not only on the company chosen, but also the price at which the stock is bought.

- The key to finding the right price is to find the company's worth and buy the stock when it is trading below its worth. This doesn't happen very often, so an investor should spend more time to find the right stock and then wait until it trades below its worth.

- Earnings yield is the ratio of earnings to the stock price. The earnings don't differ often, but the price of the stock varies every time the stock is traded. Hence, the earnings yield changes.

- It is always wise to buy a stock whose earnings yield is higher than a 10-year treasury bond.

- Buying a stock at a low price increases the investment's growth. However, buying a stock at a high price reduces the investment's growth.

- The ratio between earnings per share and the current price is known as P/E Ratio.

- Buying a good stock at a low P/E Ratio and selling it at a high P/E Ratio is the first secret of making great money in stocks.

- If a company has good earnings that grow consistently, the stock price will naturally grow as well.

- One of the most common indexes is known as the S&P 500. Standard and Poor's index measures the price and calculates the index of 500 companies from various industries.

- Before making an investment, compare the P/E Ratio of the stock versus the P/E Ratio of the S&P 500 and in the industry to which the company belongs. A good company whose P/E Ratio is below the S&P 500's and the industry's average ratio is a great bargain.

- The company's actual net worth for shareholders is determined using Book Value. The Book Value is calculated after deducting all liabilities, goodwill and other intangible goods from the company's assets.

- A stock with a Price to Book Value Ratio of two or less is a great bargain.

- Compare the P/B Ratio of a stock with the S&P 500's and the industry's. Make sure the price paid is not too high.

- The source of earnings is sales. It is very important to identify companies whose sales are also consistent.

- Identify stocks whose Price to Sales Ratio is reasonable, compared to its industry and the S&P 500.

- A stock is a great bargain if its Price to Sales Ratio is less than two.

- Since a stock's price keeps changing almost every minute, its price range over the past year is measured as 52-week low and 52-week high.

- The 52-week low for a stock gives the lowest price it was trading in the past year. Along the same lines, the 52-week high gives the highest price the stock was trading in the past year.

- Identifying a good stock and buying it closest to its 52-week low is a bargain.

- Websites like http://finance.yahoo.com, http://moneycentral.msn.com, etc., alert you through your email and cell phone whenever the stock price either goes below or above a number you choose.

True or False

- Making money in stocks is solely based on picking the best company and nothing else.

- There is no way to measure the right price for a stock.

- The price of a stock remains stable if the company's earnings are consistent.

- It is enough to measure only the P/E Ratio before buying a great stock.

- Buying a stock at its 52-week low and selling it at 52-week high is the best way to make money in stocks.

Self Explorer

- Find the current price of your favorite stocks and check the difference in yield between buying them at their 52-week low and their 52-week high.

- Identify the list of competitors for your favorite companies and decide which stock is worth owning.

- Identify the average sales or income a company makes per employee and decide whether it is running efficiently.

- Identify companies that pass the criteria discussed in the chapter and set an alert both in your mobile phone and in your inbox for the right price.

- Who is an insider? Find an insider's recent activity for a particular stock.

Interruption by the Authors

Whew! That was some learning of many a formula. Well, we decided to give you a break. There are three topics remaining, and we would like to dish it out to you in three flavors.

How would you like to see Sam and Jessica's future?

Chapter XII

Part 1: It's a fairy tale romance, like investing in Microsoft.

Part 2: It's neither fairytale nor disaster.... like investing in General Electric.

Part 3: It's an absolute disaster ... like investing in Enron.

Pick and choose any part of chapter 12, or read them all...and you decide the fate of our dollar-wise couple, Sam and Jess...............

Chapter XII-Part I

Who is Dollar Wise, Penny Foolish?

Education Planner or College Dropout?

Not to know is bad; not to wish to know is worse

Unknown

Varsity Blues

*Education is the ability to listen to almost anything
without losing your temper or your self-confidence*
Robert Frost

Alex Goodrich welcomed Sam to the lecture hall.

Sam said, "I am going to answer questions about college education, right?"

Alex nodded and said he would join him in a few minutes.

Sam's cell phone buzzed. He said, "Hello Jessica. I am rather busy now. Can we talk later?"

Jessica was puzzled by Sam's cold response. She said to Joe, who was with her, "That's odd. He never answers my call so coldly. I guess I don't even know him anymore."

Joe said, "Maybe he is really busy. Are you coming with us?"

Jessica nodded and joined him.

The lecture hall was quite full. Bill, Joe, Jessica and Troy also went as promised. Sam was dressed in formal wear.

Sam took Jessica aside for a minute and said, "Jess, I want to tell you something very important after the class. Will you have time?"

Jessica said, 'Why are you so formal? Of course I have time."

Alex Goodrich introduced Sam to the group.

The first question was from a man in his forties. He said, "My name is John. I have a question on something I came across in the newspaper. I saw several advertisements under the section 'College Education' with a catchy title '529 plans – The way to save for college education.' What are they?"

529 Vs. Bank Investments

Education is when you read the fine print.
Experience is what you get if you don't
Pete Seeger

Sam answered, "Well, as you are aware, investing in banks is 100% secure. Your investments are FDIC insured, and you'll never lose your principal investment. However, because of inflation, your investment loses its value. To protect against inflation, your money should earn more than the inflation rate. In other words, the interest rate from the bank must be more than 8% to 9% to beat inflation and taxes.

"Because bank accounts do not earn these levels of interest rates, the states have come up with a special plan for people who have children and who want to help them get a good education."

Another person asked, "How do 529 plans compare with bank accounts?"

Sam said, "There are tons of differences between 529 plans and bank investments. The main difference is that 529 plans are only for college savings. The money you save in the bank can be used for anything."

John asked another question. "Who offers these plans?"

Sam answered, "529 plans are offered only by your state. However, banks can offer other types of investments, such as certificates of deposit or money market programs.

"529 plans also differ from IRAs. Any financial institution can offer IRAs, but only the state can offer a 529 plan."

Someone from the audience said, "Well, I saw the newspaper article about 529s too. I remember a big financial firm advertising it."

Sam replied, "Even though 529 plans are offered only by the state, they use the help of financial institutions to administer the funds and market them. The states may not have the expertise to manage the fund, so they rely on financial institutions to do that for them."

John asked, "Are there only 50 plans, offered by the 50 states?"

Sam replied, "Not really. Each state can offer any number of 529 plans. You as an investor can choose from any plan offered by the state."

A woman said, "My name is Cynthia. I am curious to know why a state offers more than one plan."

Sam acclaimed, "Good question. Each plan caters to specific needs of individuals. One plan might be for a person who has a son or daughter who will be in the college in the next seven years. Another might be for a person who starts a plan as soon as a child is born. There are a variety of plans based on when your child is going to start college, and also based on your level of risk tolerance."

Bill said to Joe, "Tell me, why am I here, again?"

Joe laughed, "To eat!"

Cynthia asked, "Risk tolerance. Aren't investments with the state safe?"

Sam replied, "Not necessarily. 529 plans are no different from mutual funds. The state, either on its own or in association with a financial institution, invests the money in different securities such as stocks, real estate, bonds, etc. The returns are not guaranteed like bank deposits, and you have the potential of losing your investments."

John said, "I am confused now. Didn't you say 529 plans are better than bank investments? If 529 plans are not safe, then why can't I invest in a bank directly?"

Pros of 529 Plans

One's first step in wisdom is to question everything
and one's last is to come to terms with everything
Georg Christoph Lichtenberg

Sam replied, "Even though 529 plans are not guaranteed like bank deposits, they offer much higher growth potential. If you are getting only 2% from bank deposits, a 529 plan may return 6%. The advantage of 529 plans is that you have a higher potential to earn more money over a bank deposit, but the disadvantage is that the returns are not secured. You may even lose your investments."

Cynthia asked, "Hm! Even though 529 plans are not 100% safe, they may offer better growth than bank deposits. Should I give up safety to earn better returns?"

Sam asked, "At the end of the year, do you get to keep 100% of the interest from bank deposits?"

John smiled and said, "The IRS comes knocking, for sure."

Sam said, "Well, you need not answer the door if the interest is from 529 plans. They offer tax-free growth.

"In other words, if you earn $1,000 in interest from the bank, you have to pay taxes on the interest, but if you earn $1,000 in interest from 529 plans, you don't have to pay taxes. The dividends also grow like regular investments."

Cynthia said, "Fantastic. Are you saying I do not have not to pay taxes at all on the earnings?"

Sam said, "Not exactly. While you are investing in 529 plans, you don't have to pay taxes on the dividends. But as soon as you make a withdrawal, you have to pay taxes. As of now, the federal government won't collect taxes if the returns are used for education before 2010. The law may change in 2010 or it may stay the same. We are not sure at this moment."

Cynthia summed up, "In other words, a 529 plan offers tax-free growth and may give better returns than banks in the long run, even though that is not guaranteed. If I withdraw before 2010 for education expenses, I don't have to pay federal taxes."

Sam continued, "Correct. One more thing, it also offers flexibility. For example, you may open the plan in your child's name, but you can subsequently change the designation to anyone, including yourself, without incurring any penalties. You have entire control over the plan, not your child."

John asked Sam, "So, for whom do you think 529 plans are ideal?"

Sam said, "People who don't have time to manage their own investments or who would like to rely on financial professionals to decide their investment goals should find 529 plans to be ideal."

Control Your Destiny

A lot of people have gone farther than they thought
they could because someone else thought they could
Zig Ziglar

Bill asked a question, "What if I know how to pick stocks, and I want to make my own financial decisions? Is there a way to invest in stocks for educational expenses?"

Sam replied, "Good question, Bill. The answer is a big yes. The best way to save for college education is to invest wisely in appropriate stocks and allow the money to grow tax-free. The younger the child is when you start saving, the better, because the money will have more time to grow.

"In memory of the late Senator Paul Coverdell, our country offers an excellent plan for those who know how to choose stocks and make the most out of the market. This is known as the 'Coverdell ESA,' which stands for 'Coverdell Education Savings Account'.

"If you are familiar with stock-picking skills, it is fun not only to save a little for education, but also to make big returns from your investment using stocks as a tool.

"But the only constraint is that the maximum allowable contribution is only $2,000 per year. If you were a prudent investor, you would invest $2,000 per year as soon as your child is born and invest in the right stocks until he or she is ready to go to school. The biggest advantage of the Coverdell ESA is that the money can be used even for elementary schools and not necessarily for college.

"The 529 plans have no limitations on the contribution, but the state invests the money through financial firms. Growth is not guaranteed, but there is no limit on the contribution.

"On the other hand, the Coverdell ESA offers complete flexibility to parents who are savvy investors. Instead of investing thousands of dollars in 529 plans and receiving only paltry returns, smart investors will find all the choices they need in a Coverdell ESA."

John was astonished. "I have a question. How did you get this knowledge despite being so young?" he asked Sam.

Sam smiled. Alex Goodrich volunteered to answer. "He is one of a kind!"

Sam smiled and said, "Thanks. I will draw a comparison table so you can get a better idea. "

Figure 12.1.1: 529 Plans vis-a-vis Coverdell ESA

Description	529 Plans	Coverdell ESA
Purpose	For college education and other qualified higher-education expenses.	Money can be used for elementary as well as higher education.
Administrated by	States, usually through investment firms like Fidelity or Vanguard.	The investors themselves.
Growth limitations	Limited by the plan's growth. Investors have no control over the investment's growth.	Growth and control are entirely dependent on the investors. They can invest in stocks, mutual funds, or even bonds.

Description	529 Plans	Coverdell ESA
Dividends - tax implications	Dividends grow tax-free.	Dividends grow tax-free.
Federal tax implications at withdrawal	Until 2010, the federal government will not charge taxes on the investment's growth.	There are no taxes on the investment's growth.
State tax implications at withdrawal	Varies between each plan and state.	No state taxes on the investment's growth.
Maximum allowable contribution per year	Varies between each state, but generally a maximum of $250,000 per beneficiary per year.	A maximum of $2,000 per beneficiary per year.
Targeted to	Individuals who need help in planning their college education expenses.	Individuals who clearly know how to invest their money and who want 100% control of their finances.

After the presentation was over, the group asked several questions during lunch.

Alex told Sam, "Well, you handled the class well, and I think it is safe to say you have nothing to worry about. You are one of us now."

Sam was thoroughly pleased. He thanked Alex and went to find Jessica and the guys to pass on the news.

Bill said, "Congrats, Man! You totally deserve it. You forgot one thing, though."

Sam was surprised, "What?"

Bill said, "You forgot to take down the phone numbers of some of the parents who may already have daughters in college."

Sam laughed, "I am sure gonna miss you, Bill."

They all left. Sam told Jessica he would pick her up later for dinner.

Closing Bell

Love makes the wildest spirit tame, and the tamest spirit wild
Alexis Delp

That evening, Jessica was surprised when Sam drove her to his house. They went to his patio and he plugged the wireless card to his laptop.

Sam asked, "Jess, can you do me a favor?"

She said, "Yeah. What is it?"

Sam asked, "Can you write on a piece of paper the ticker symbols of the companies I tell you?"

Jessica, "What! Sam, I am not in a mood for that. Let's just go and eat."

Sam said, "Please, Jess."

Jessica thought Sam had gone completely crazy. She finally yielded to his request.

Sam said, "Okay, please write down the tickers for *Wilmington Trust Corporation*, *Lucent*, *Marriott International*, *Royal Bank of Canada*, and *Massey Energy Company*."

Jessica painstakingly found the ticker for each company Sam mentioned. She wrote, *"WL LU MAR RY MEE."*

She looked at it deeply and was taken aback by what she read. The drift of Sam's cryptic message dawned on her. She looked at Sam.

Sam said softly, going down on bended knee, "Jessica Calderone, will you marry me?"

Some moments passed in silence, before she said, "Sam, would you write down the first letter of your first name?"

Sam was puzzled, but it took him just a second to realize she said "S".

He hugged her, and the two were locked in an embrace for what seemed an eternity. She then asked, "What about your job?"

He said, "Well, I asked them if they had an opening here in L.A. They said I could work here for a year and then decide about New York later. But without knowing all this, how come you accepted my proposal?"

Jessica smiled and said, "I am no fool to refuse a million dollar offer!"

Sam's Sprinkles

- Investing in banks is very secure. However, due to inflation, the investment value goes down.

- 529 plans are state-sponsored programs, designed exclusively for college education purposes.

- The state may use a financial institution for implementing its 529 plan.

- You do not need to choose a 529 plan only from your state. You can choose from any of the fifty states, and each state has multiple plans.

- 529 plans work like mutual funds. A financial institution manages your money. Unlike bank deposits, the returns from your money are not guaranteed.

- Unlike bank deposits, 529 plans offer better growth. The returns from bank deposits are guaranteed. However, the bank's interest rate is limited. Although 529 plans do not have guaranteed returns, in the long run they are likely to provide better returns.

- The dividends from 529 plans are known as capital gains. The investor does not need to pay taxes on capital gains every year.

- The federal government does not tax the returns on 529 plans, if used for college education purposes before 2010.

- Under 529 plans, the individual investor cannot make any decisions on where the investments are made. The financial institution controls it. Investors who want to pick their own investments can choose an Education IRA instead of a 529 plan.

- The Education IRA is also known as the Coverdell ESA. Under this scheme, investors can choose any investment they desire. They can directly invest in stocks for college purposes. The returns from a Coverdell ESA are not taxed.

- Both Coverdell ESA and 529 plans offer the flexibility of withdrawing money for non-educational purposes. However, investors must pay taxes on the returns, and a fine is levied if they use it for non-educational purposes.

True or False

- You can invest in a 529 plan from your local bank.

- All 529 plans have a risk of losing the investments.

- The laws for Coverdell ESAs may change after 2010.

- There is no limit on the amount you can invest in a Coverdell ESA, but a 529 plan has restrictions.

- Neither 529 plans nor Coverdell ESAs offer the flexibility of early withdrawal.

Self Explorer

- Determine your state's and other states' 529 plans. Understand the different types of investment methods available under those plans.

- Visit your local financial institution and ask for the different 529 plans they offer. Measure the performance on a yearly basis as well as over a five-year period.

- Call different brokerage firms and find the costs of opening and maintaining a Coverdell ESA account.

- Based on the age of your child and the amount you can allocate on a yearly basis, decide an investment plan that suits your needs.

- Find the differences between opening a Coverdell ESA account in your local bank versus a discount brokerage firm.

Chapter XII-Part II

Who is Dollar Wise, Penny Foolish?

Early Retirees or Forever Workers?

Action springs not from thought, but from a readiness
for responsibility
Dietrich Bonhoffer

Plan Early or Suffer Late

The ladder of success is never crowded at the top
Napoleon Hill

Alex Goodrich welcomed Sam to the lecture hall.

Sam said, "I am going to answer questions about retirement plans, right?"

Alex nodded and said he would join him in a few minutes.

Sam's cell phone buzzed. He said, "Hello Jessica. I am rather busy now. Can we talk later? I have something important to tell you."

Jessica was puzzled by Sam's cold response. She said to Joe, who was with her, "That's odd. He has never answered so coldly. I guess I don't even know him anymore. I guess its time to move on."

Joe was stunned by her reply. He said, "Maybe he really is busy. Okay, are you coming with us?"

Jessica replied she wasn't.

The lecture hall was quite full. Bill, Joe and Troy also went as promised. Sam was dressed in a suit.

Sam obviously noticed Jessica's absence. He just thought she was upset.

Alex Goodrich introduced Sam to the group.

A young man asked the first question. He said, "Hi! My name is Josh. My father wanted me to attend this session. I didn't quite expect to see a person my age talking about retirement plans. My question is, why should we think about retirement at our age?"

Sam smiled and said, "Good question, Josh. Most of us react only to immediate necessities but completely forget about needs we have to fulfill in the future.

"Our mind is trained to react only when a need arises. That is why many people go to a fitness center only after they gain weight. However, if they exercised regularly and controlled their eating, they would be exercising to keep themselves fit and not to lose extra pounds.

"The same thing goes for retirement. Even though the government and your employer take a certain percentage out of our paychecks for social security, it is not sufficient to meet even our basic retirement needs. So we need to plan at an early stage in our lives."

Practice with Social Security

You can often gauge a man's ambition by whether he hates his alarm clock or considers it his dear friend
Anonymous

"The best way to experience retirement is to practice it right now. Try to live for a couple of months on the assumption that your only income was social security. You can call the local social security office to find out how much you would receive. They should be able to give you an approximate amount you will be receiving once you retire.

"Living on social security income is like wearing a sweatshirt. A sweatshirt alone is good for the spring but not for the winter, especially if you happen to live in Buffalo or Alaska. Living on social security alone is like spending the winter in Buffalo with just a sweatshirt and a pair of trousers. The social security income sounds good when we are in our twenties or thirties. However, once we are into retirement, the average inflation rate would have made everything much more expensive. The only solution is to buy realizable stock at a bargain price."

Nostradamus – Can you help us?

> *God gives every bird its food, but he does not*
> *throw it into the nest.*
> J. G. Holland

Josh said, "Hmm! Interesting. Do you think it is difficult to predict what our expenses would be when we retire?"

Sam took a sip of water and replied. "You know Nostradamus, don't you? At first, when he made some predictions, he was denounced as a fraud and lunatic. But when one after another became true, everyone's opinion about him changed. He became very popular, and today he is known all over the world. His name became associated with predicting the future.

"Even today, people around the world open the pages of *Quatrains* by Nostradamus and interpret their own meaning. He is famous for knowing things well in advance, but what even he could not predict was the cost of retirement and how much money that we'll need to retire worry-free. Even if Nostradamus were alive today, there are some things we wouldn't be able to predict, such as tax rates, the cost of medical insurance, auto insurance, home insurance and utility bills."

Everyone laughed.

Sam continued, "The U.S. is facing a huge deficit, especially after borrowing billions of dollars from Japan and China. The only way it can handle the deficit is to increase taxes and get more money from its own people. You may be 25 years old now, and it may still be 40 years before you retire. What makes predicting retirement really difficult is a combination of many things. We may get money from social security, but that will not be enough to pay the bills. We may get Medicare, but that may not be sufficient to take care of our long-term needs. Even though we will not be spending money for work clothes, we will still have to pay our heating bills. We will not be spending money for commuting to work, but we will still have to pay for auto insurance. We will not be spending money for work lunches, but we will still be spending money to go out with the family.

"*Verizon* might say, 'We never stop working for you,' as long as we pay our phone bills. *McDonald's* may say, 'We love to see you smile,' as long as we pay for their burgers. Life after retirement is really fun, but it requires a lot of money to enjoy the fun. It requires millions of dollars to have a comfortable retirement without worrying about anything."

Business – Is It In You?

It's easier to get rich than it
is to explain not getting rich
E. James Rohn

Another member of the audience asked, "What are the options available, so we can start saving right now?"

Sam answered, "To accumulate wealth for retirement, you have several options. The most common ones are 401-K, IRA and Roth IRA. I'll explain the difference among the retirement plans based on the way a business is run. I need two volunteers."

Joe and another person from the audience, Pat, came forward.

Franchise and 401-K

Sam began, "Thanks. Let's say that both of you are given an opportunity to run a business. But before you do anything else, you need to decide between creating your own business and franchising an operation. Which option would you choose?"

Pat answered first. "If I have a great idea and am confident I can sell it to the entire community, then I would start my own business."

Joe said, "Well, I would like to take advantage of someone who has already established a name and style, and franchise an operation. I think that is much more effective."

Sam thanked them and asked, "Okay, can each of you tell me how you would go about establishing the business of your choice?"

Joe answered, "Well, let's say I decide to open a sandwich shop franchise. I would meet the franchise manager, who would help me choose the location and set up the shop. I would be given all the support I need. If my business does well, I can also expand the shop with the franchise manager's help. Of course, I would have to pay a large initial fee."

Sam asked, "How will your profits be divided?"

Joe said, "Well, obviously I would get the lion's share of the profits, but I would also have to pay the owners. They supported me by helping me start the business. I did not have to spend time creating a new product. The company also supplied me with an established name known to customers around the world. If I had started my own shop, no one would be familiar with it. In short, I would be responsible for paying an initial fee and sharing a percentage of my sales with the franchise owners."

Sam said, "Thanks, Joe. Investing in a 401-K plan is exactly like opening a franchise store. Big corporations like *General Electric (GE)*, *General Motors (GM)*, or *American Express (AXP)* offer retirement plans known as 401-K. Now the biggest advantage of using your employer's 401-K plan to save for your retirement is that you don't have to pick the investments. The company either has its own financial planner or hires an outside firm to help. A financial firm has a list of investment possibilities you can pick from for your retirement. The amount deducted from your paycheck goes directly to your 401-K account.

"A financial institution administers a 401-K plan. A 401-K account is a lot like your bank account, except a financial institution manages it. The biggest advantage is you don't have to worry about managing the fund yourself. As an investor, you don't have to worry about whether the economy is doing well, what would happen if a stock weren't doing well, and so on. The financial institution manages everything for you. Once you decide to invest in a 401-K, a financial planner would explain the different investment possibilities. If you are quite young, you may decide to invest in stocks and mutual funds. If you are in your upper 40s, you may want to invest in safer instruments such as bonds and treasury bills. The financial advisor would explain the pros and cons of investing in each option."

A member of the audience added, "My company offers 401-K plans, and I get an additional contribution from my employer."

Sam said, "Right. Many companies will also contribute to your retirement funds, matching up to a certain percentage of your contribution. For example, if you are contributing $250 from your paycheck to your 401-K plan, your employer may also contribute an additional $250. That is like getting bonus money from your employer without having to work long hours for it. Most corporations do this in the hope their employees will continue working for them."

Joe said, "It would make me feel secure to know that my company is taking care of me and providing me more opportunities for my money to grow."

Sam said, "When you invest in a 401-K plan, the financial institution takes a certain percentage of your investment as a management fee. Assume the institution is taking 1% of your investment as a management fee. Every time you invest $250 from your paycheck, 1% of $250, or $2.50, goes to the financial institution for managing your money. This is like Joe, the franchise owner, paying a percentage of his profits to his parent company every time he makes a sale.

"Some financial institutions charge either front-load or back-load fees. This is like the initial fee Joe paid to open his franchise. The charge is predetermined and varies among the financial institutions."

Sam turned to Pat. He said, "Now, let's see what Pat has to say. Why would you run your own business instead of running a franchise?"

The whole group was very impressed. Most of them thought the seminar would be another monologue. But it was interactive and interesting.

Pat answered, "Well, I would like to start my own business. Maybe run a big restaurant. I know running a business always involve risks, but I would have complete control in making the decisions. I would want to decide my company's name, logo and location, and I would want the freedom to choose my own staff. On the other hand, if I wanted to operate a franchise, I wouldn't have a lot of control."

Do-It-Yourself

*The world is moving so fast these days that the man
who says it cannot be done is generally interrupted
by someone doing it*
Elbert Hubbard

Sam said, "Thanks, Pat. Planning for your retirement using an IRA is no different from Pat's situation. IRA stands for 'Individual Retirement Account.' It is designed to help people who want absolute control over their retirement goals. Under a 401-K plan, even though it is designed for employees who want to have a sufficient cushion for their retirement, your employer's financial institution has total control over you plan. In other words, you may have better ideas on how to invest your money, but you cannot implement them under a 401-K plan. An IRA, which is also designed to meet your retirement goals, offers you full control over your retirement goals.

"An individual investing in an IRA is like Pat's business. You have absolute control over your retirement account. Just as Pat can chose any location, you could invest your hard-earned retirement money any way you like.

"You can invest your money in stocks, bonds or mutual funds, or you can even put the money in bank deposits. The choice is absolutely yours. You are not bound by the limited options provided by just one person or one firm. That is the power of an IRA. When you implement your retirement goals through an IRA, you take full control of it. You are free to shop around and decide the best way to manage your IRA."

Joe was puzzled. He asked, "Are you saying that IRAs are better than 401-Ks?"

Sam smiled and replied, "Not exactly. Let me illustrate some of the differences between the two. Let me ask you a question. You were interested in operating a franchise. If you wanted to make changes to the way your shop looked, or if you decided to change the menu because customers wanted something different, would you have the option to do it?"

Joe shook his head. He said, "That would be difficult. The management team would need to approve even a small change."

Sam said, "Exactly. Your parent company's management team could not approve every one of your suggestions, because a small change would affect the entire chain of stores operating in their name."

He continued, "Similarly, even though employees have individual 401-K accounts, any change the financial institution makes to the plan would affect everyone enrolled in it. The financial institution would not make a change lightly because of the potential consequences. You may have a better solution to manage your money, but if you are investing your retirement money in a 401-K plan, then you have no control over the plan except for contributing to it.

"In addition, even if you have been contributing for a long time, if your financial institution fails to provide good growth, no one can be held responsible. The retirement fund is fully administered and managed by the financial institution, and the fund's success is fully dependent on it."

One person from the audience asked, "Can you explain that with numbers, please?"

Sam said, "Sure. For example, you may contribute $100 per month for five years. The total contribution from your end was $6,000, and your employer contributed an equal amount. So the net contribution was $12,000. Now, if the financial institution doesn't manage your money well, your contribution may potentially decrease from $12,000 to $10,000, $5,000, or even just $1,000. However, if it does well with your money, your $12,000 may grow to a higher amount. The biggest advantage of a 401-K is that people manage it on your behalf, but the biggest disadvantage is that you are affected if they don't manage the money well.

"When you choose to invest your retirement savings through an IRA, you have all the freedom to visit and talk to many financial institutions including banks, mutual fund firms, and brokerage firms, and decide your own investment method. If you are not comfortable with investing your entire money in one firm, you can divide your retirement account into as many firms as you want. For example, you can invest part of your retirement savings in a bank's Certificate of Deposit, and you can invest the rest in stocks. You can take advice and opinion of as many books, friends, and relatives as you want, but the final decision is in your hands.

"Along the same lines, an IRA offers much more flexibility than a 401-K account. Under an IRA plan, you are free to change your financial planner or institution at your own discretion. Your current financial planner or institution may offer only mutual funds, even though you might be interested in investing in stocks. Or your financial institution may charge a higher fee for maintaining your accounts, but you discovered that working with discount brokers might be a better choice if you are comfortable with investing in stocks."

Josh said, "Let me get this straight. Employees who put their money in 401-Ks are dependant on one financial institution to make sure their money is handled well, like Joe who is dependent on his parent company to see to it that the entire business is profitable."

Sam confirmed, "You are absolutely right, Josh."

An elderly person got up and asked, "Son, what about the tax breaks offered by 401-Ks?"

Sam said, "Yes, sir. I was going to address that next. 401-K plans offer a big tax break during your working years. Contributions are taken out of your paycheck before taxes are taken out, so you do not pay taxes on the money when it goes into the account. When you invest in your 401-K account, you not only accumulate wealth over a period of time, you also ensure that you have plenty of savings when you are ready to retire. So at the time of retirement, you can start withdrawing money from your 401-K account to meet your needs.

"Once you retire and start withdrawing money out of the account, you will have to pay taxes on that money. The tax impact would be minimal because you no longer have a regular paycheck, and any income you may have from occasional work is not likely to be much. The tax percentage for retired people is also much less. You therefore have the advantage of paying no taxes at the time of contributing and paying very little taxes at the time of withdrawal after retirement."

Tax Break

Behind every successful man stands a woman and the
IRS. One takes the credit, and the other takes the
cash
Anonymous

Alex Goodrich, who was quite impressed with his potential hire, intervened, "Don't IRAs also offer tax breaks?"

Sam replied confidently, "Yes, Alex. An IRA offers several tax benefits. Once you choose an IRA, you don't have to pay taxes, even if the IRA makes a huge profit. The reason is that you are not withdrawing any money while you are working. You will start withdrawing money from the IRA only after you retire. A person can invest just $1,000 in an IRA and turn it into $100,000 by choosing the right stocks. But an investor doesn't have to pay taxes on the growth as long as it stays in the account."

Bill, who was silent until now, summed up. "Looks like both retirement options are fine. If you know how to diversify and make the right investment decisions, you can choose to put your money in an IRA."

Sam said, "Yes. You have to know clearly what you want to invest in, since you make your own decisions as the prime investor. Investing your money in stocks can be tricky. You may be careful in the beginning as you start to take control of your investments. As you watch your money grow, you may decide you want to grow your money very fast so you can retire early. You then end up making bad decisions and losing money in the stock market."

Pat asked, "I have heard of Roth IRAs. What are they?"

Sam said, "There are two different types of IRAs. One is a regular IRA, and the other is known as a 'Roth IRA'. The key difference between a regular IRA and a Roth IRA arises when you pay the taxes.

"A regular IRA works similarly to a 401-K plan for tax purposes. In other words, your contributions are completely tax-deductible, since you are not using the money for your personal expenses. If you had contributed $3,000 in one year to your IRA, you get to deduct the taxes on it when your file your returns. However, the money you invested may grow very well, since you control the investments.

"Let us assume the $3,000 you invested had grown to $150,000 over a period of 30 years, and now you are ready to retire. When you retire, you will be withdrawing from your IRA for your personal expenses. Now, when you withdraw from your IRA after you retire, you have to pay taxes on the amount you withdrew. If you withdrew $150,000 in one year, the entire $150,000 would be treated as income, and you would have to pay taxes. But since you would have no additional income and the tax percentage for seniors is comparatively low, you would end up paying less tax on the $150,000 than you would have before you retired. The IRS gives you the benefit of deducting taxes when you make an

IRA investment, but it collects taxes at the time of withdrawal.

"The Roth IRA was named after late Senator William V.Roth Jr. It is one of the best schemes available for people who can take advantage of it. It has all the advantages of an IRA, with one major difference. Under the regular IRA scheme, you deduct taxes at the time of contribution and pay the taxes at the time of withdrawal. However, with the Roth IRA, you pay taxes at the time of contribution, but you don't have to pay taxes at the time of withdrawal.

"For example, assume you deposited $3,000 under a Roth IRA in a discount brokerage house. You learned the art of investing wisely, and your money grew to $300,000 by the time you were ready to retire. Now, you get to withdraw the entire $300,000 without having to pay taxes. At the time you contributed, though, you didn't have the advantage of saving taxes.

"I have copies of a handout here that I prepared. It has a detailed table, showing the comparison of the various retirement plans we discussed. If you have any questions, please feel free to ask me."

He distributed the handouts. The entire group was going through the table carefully as they headed for the lunch buffet.

Figure 12.2.1: Comparison between different retirement planning options

Description	401-K	IRA	Roth-IRA
Eligibility	Sponsored by the company. The company sets the eligibility requirements.	An individual or married couples who are not enrolled in a 401-K. An individual or a married couple who are enrolled in a 401-K with limits on gross income.	
Fund deposit	Usually deducted from the paycheck and sent to the 401-K account.	Account holders either can pay a lump sum every year or allow the financial firm to withdraw from their checking accounts regularly.	
Maximum contribution	Up to $12,000 or 100% of compensation, whichever is less.	$3,000 for an individual under 50 and $3,500 for an individual above 50. $6,000 for a married couple filing jointly and $7,000 for a married couple above 50.	
Contribution by whom	Employer contributes to the retirement funds. The employer sets the contribution rate.	No contribution from the employer. The employee makes the entire contribution.	

Description	401-K	IRA Roth-IRA
Managed by whom	Financial firm sponsored by the employer.	The employee who owns the account. Employees may choose a financial planner or firm to manage the account on their behalf.
Allocation of funds	Employee may choose to divide the money among a limited number of investment options.	The employee has entire control over the allocation. The employee can even allocate part of the retirement funds in one financial firm and the balance in a different firm.
Choice of investments	Limited to the investment options available within the plan.	No limitations. Employees can choose from a wide variety of investments, including bank deposits, stocks, mutual funds and bonds.
Growth	Restricted to the growth of the investment options in the plan.	Employees can choose the best growth options to meet their requirements.

Description	401-K	IRA	Roth-IRA
Withdrawals	Employees can withdraw either after they reach 59½ or if they retire after 55.	Eligible to withdraw after 59 ½.	
Penalty	Early withdrawal may be subject to a 10% penalty.	Early withdrawal is subject to a 10% penalty.	
Tax	Calculated on entire withdrawal.	Calculated on entire withdrawal	Since the tax is paid at the time of contribution, no taxes need to be paid at the time of withdrawal. The earnings grow tax-free.

Description	401-K	IRA	Roth-IRA
Ideal for	Employees who prefer to take advantage of their employer's contribution and don't have time to manage their retirement goals.	Employees who prefer to save money on taxes when they contribute; the employer doesn't offer a 401-K plan. Employees who prefer to manage their retirement goals on their own without being restricted by their employer's investment options.	Employees who prefer to pay money on taxes during their employment but prefer to take the entire growth tax-free at the time of retirement. Employees who prefer to manage their retirement goals on their own without being restricted by their employer's investment options.

Closing Bell

> *The heart has its reasons of which the mind knows*
> *nothing*
> *Blaise Pascal*

While they were having lunch, Alex told Sam, "Well, you handled the class well, and I think it is safe to say you have nothing to worry about. You are one of us now."

Sam was thoroughly pleased. He thanked Alex and told his friends about Alex's offer.

Bill said, "Congrats, man! You totally deserve it."

Sam said, "Okay, guys. I have an important thing to do. I have to go."

Joe hesitated before saying, "Jessica is not around. In fact, she has a date tonight."

Sam was shocked. "What! I don't get this. I have to talk to her anyway."

He dialed Jessica's cell phone. She answered, "Yes, Sam. How was your seminar?"

Sam said, "It went well. I need to talk to you, Jess. Can I come over in an hour if you have some time?

She said yes. Sam spent some time with Alex and the group and then dashed off to Jessica's house.

Sam said, "Jess, I got the job and I want to take it."

Jessica congratulated him.

He continued, "I also love you very much, Jess. Tell me, what do we do about this? Joe told me that you have a date. C'mon, Jess, give us another chance."

Jessica said, "I don't think long-distance relationships work out very well. I think we have to move on with our lives."

Sam said, "How do you know without trying? Why don't we give it a shot? You are giving up way too easily."

She hesitated. "I don't know. In spite of living in the same town, we have so many communication gaps. I don't think we can maintain this relationship if there is so much distance between us."

Sam said, "Jess, what we have is something special. I think we can work this out. Tell you what. Sleep on it and give me a call tomorrow. I will be waiting."

Sam went back home riding on a roller coaster of emotions. He couldn't sleep thinking about his bittersweet day.

Early next morning he heard the phone ring and he groggily picked it up to hear Jessica ask, "Sam, quick question. Which cell phone provider gives the best nationwide plan?"

Sam's Sprinkles

- The amount you contribute towards social security and 401-K plans is not sufficient to handle your retirement expenses.

- It is difficult to predict the exact cost of retirement. At this point in time, it is impossible predict the tax rates, health care costs and inflation rates in the long run.

- Some of the different retirement schemes available are Roth IRA, 401-K and traditional IRA.

- Corporations offer 401-K plans. The company you work for must have a partnership with a financial institution to offer 401-K plans.

- The money you contribute to a 401-K plan is tax deductible at the time of contribution. However, taxes must be paid when withdrawing the money after retirement.

- Since the tax percentage and income after retirement will be relatively low, taxes on 401-K withdrawals are also likely to be very low.

- Under 401-K plans, the employer may also contribute money to your retirement account. This in turn allows you to get extra income from your employer in addition to your salary.

- A financial institution sponsored by your company manages the 401-K account. As an investor, you have very little control over the account. The fund choices are also very limited.

- IRA stands for Individual Retirement Account. Under this plan, investors choose a financial institution suited to their needs. It could be a bank or a financial institution specializing in mutual funds, or a brokerage firm offering the flexibility of both mutual funds and stocks.

- The two different types of IRAs are traditional and Roth IRA.

- Under the traditional IRA, you need not pay taxes at the time of contribution. This allows you to deduct taxes during your years of employment.

- Under a Roth IRA, you do not get to deduct the taxes at the time of contribution. However, when you retire, you do not need to pay taxes for either the contribution or the growth.

- Investors personally manage both traditional IRAs and Roth IRAs. They have the opportunity to invest as little or as much as they want to allow their investments to grow.

True or False

• Under 401-K plans, the employer's contribution is taxable.

• The growth of 401-K retirement funds is limited by your stock-picking skills.

• IRA schemes offer the flexibility of investing in stocks as well as mutual funds.

• You need the consent of your employer to open an IRA account.

• You can invest in multiple institutions under 401-K plans.

Self Explorer

- Now that you have multiple methods to invest for your retirement, decide which scheme is ideal for you.

- Assuming you are able to contribute $3,000 per year for your retirement, find out how much you would save for retirement under each scheme.

- Assume you are contributing $3,000 regularly for your IRA, is it ideal to open a traditional IRA or Roth IRA? Find out the tax implications of both types.

- Assuming you are not contributing to any retirement scheme, calculate the amount that you would get from social security. Calculate if social security would be sufficient to handle your retirement needs.

- Calculate how much you will need for your retirement. Decide on a plan that fits your retirement needs.

Chapter XII-Part III

Who is Dollar Wise, Penny Foolish?

Sellers with High Profits or Sellers with No Profits?

Change your thoughts and you change the world
Norman Vincent Peale

One Among Many or One in Many

Courage is saying, "Maybe what I'm doing isn't working; maybe I should try something else."
Anne Lappe

Bill and Troy met Sam at the college campus. Bill asked, "How did your second round go?"

Sam smiled and replied, "I think it went well, guys."

Bill exclaimed, "Wow! Congrats, man. When do you have to leave?"

Sam said, "Not sure. If I get the job, I am assuming I will have two weeks' time. By the way, there is just one more thing I have to tell you guys about investing in stocks."

Bill joked, "C'mon, man! I thought we already graduated from 'Sam's school of stocks'."

Sam laughed. They decided to meet at his place. Bill promised to inform Joe and Jessica.

Sam called Jessica. "Hi, hon! How are you?"

Jessica replied curtly, "Doing all right! How was your interview?"

Sam asked, "It went well. Haven't heard from them yet. I hope you are coming to my place for the last lesson in investing."

Jessica said, "Sorry, Sam. I have a date."

Sam was dumbfounded. He let out a nervous laugh and said, "Jess, are you joking?"

Jessica retorted. "You were, with my life. Talk to you later."

Sam opened the door, and the very first words from Bill were, "Who died, man?"

Sam told them about his conversation with Jessica. He added, "Well, that's life. Anyway, you guys ready for attaining 'stocks nirvana'?"

Joe politely asked, "Sure you want to continue?"

Sam said, "Yep. Don't worry! I can handle this."

Bill said, "Okay. Will you tell us when to sell a stock, assuming we bought a stock after filtering it with using your formulae?"

Sam said, "Yes. Grab a soda if you want and let's go to the basement."

Once they had settled down, Sam began, "Owning a stock is like running your own business. To run a business successfully, you have to invest your money, hire the right people, maybe even fire some employees at the right time, and most importantly know how to run a business.

"Okay, someone tell me: what is the most important thing a person should do to run a successful business?"

Troy said, "Interesting question. I would say, to run a successful business you have to do things differently.

"For example, Howard Schultz built a business no one would have thought of. He built a chain of coffee stores and made *Starbucks* the world's most popular coffee shop. He didn't build another burger chain or another donut chain. He simply made coffee, a rich and tasty experience for his customers, and they loved it. "

Sam agreed, "Right! Good example. Let me give another one. When everyone was renting DVDs from stores like *Blockbuster* and *Movie Gallery*, Reed Hastings decided to rent DVDs by mail. He offered the flexibility of receiving DVDs in your mailbox, instead of having to drive to the video store. Even though this was a new concept, it took less than four years for *Netflix* to reach one million subscribers.

"Like *Starbucks* and *Netflix*, a business needs a unique strategy to thrive. Similarly, investing requires a unique strategy to succeed.

"Most investors are momentum or short-term investors. Investors buy and sell a stock based on a conversation in a bar. If they read good news about a company, they buy the stock. Within the next couple of days, if the stock's price goes down, they sell it. By investing in this fashion, their profitability is likely to be very small since they haven't adopted a strategy.

"For a business to be successful, it needs a goal. For example, if someone else copies the *Netflix* or *Starbucks* model, it may not be possible for them to succeed like *Netflix* or *Starbucks* did. The reason is that a business needs objectives for its existence, what it is aiming to do, and how it is catering to its customers' needs. A business cannot simply emulate another business' success.

"Similarly, an investor cannot simply buy and sell based on momentum. An investor should have solid reasons to buy or sell a stock."

Rule 1: Sell Low Performing Stocks

*The art of being a
good guest is to know when to leave*
Prince Philip

"Now, after a lot of analysis, you know the right techniques to buy a stock. But when should you sell it?

"There is a major difference between momentum investing and objective long-term investing. Say, for instance, you buy a stock and the price comes down drastically. What should you do?"

Bill answered, "Make a phone call to Sam Cohen in New York."

Sam laughed, "Just to avoid that, my friend, I will tell you what to do when the price comes down.

"A momentum investor panics as soon as the price comes down. However, an objective long-term investor analyzes the reasons before making a decision to buy or to sell.

"When you run your business, you may possibly get into a cash-crunch situation. How do you get out of that situation? You expected to sign lots of contracts with your customers. You hired quite a few people and trained them to handle future requirements. Suddenly the business takes a 180-degree turn, and quite a few customers are choosing to go with someone else instead of you. Keeping all the employees on board would be a big revenue loss for you, since you don't have enough business to keep all of them busy. Also, you don't have enough money to pay all of them. So, what would your first move be? Lay off certain poorly performing employees.

"Along the same lines, after investing your money in stocks, you might get into a cash crunch situation. How? You might decide to buy a house, which requires a hefty initial payment. You might decide to get married, which requires paying for all those wedding expenses. Now you need to get some cash, and you've decided to sell some stocks. The simplest solution is to sell the stocks that have either performed below your expectations or performed poorer than the other stocks you own."

Joe said, "Assuming I bought the stock at a low price, I am likely to make a profit when I sell it. I have to pay hefty taxes on them, right?

Sam said, "Yes. But there is a way to avoid that. If you had placed the stocks in non-taxable accounts such as IRAs or Coverdell ESAs, then selling them wouldn't require paying any taxes. However, when you need cash to meet your personal expenses, you are likely to end up selling from your regular brokerage account. So whenever a stock is sold for a profit, you'll end up paying taxes.

"It is certainly not possible to predict a stock's exact price in the future. But after you have analyzed a great stock and bought it at a low price, it will definitely do well in the future.

"Sometimes our personal reasons might force us to sell a stock before it reaches its full potential. In such situations, it is only prudent to sell a stock that has not met your expectations."

Rule 2: Sell When Price is High

Underpromise; overdeliver
Tom Peters

Bill said, "Okay, I have a question. Say I bought a stock that is performing extremely well. Now, when should I sell it? How do I know this is the maximum it can reach?"

Sam replied, "Good question, Bill. Okay, you run a great business and you hire some excellent people to help you design a great website. Once you start engaging them in work, one of your key employees asks for huge raise. Even though you can afford to keep him, you certainly feel the salary he is asking for is unreasonable. How do you reach this conclusion?"

Bill replied, "Well, maybe his skills are not unique, or maybe he has been offered another job with a higher salary and he is demanding a still higher salary from me."

Sam said, "Right! Along the same lines, after you buy a great stock, chances are good the price will go high. The simple reason for that is other people would realize a good stock is trading at a low price and would start buying, naturally causing the price to increase.

"There are plenty of reasons a stock price might be really high. If the company is part of the pharmaceutical sector, the *FDA* might have approved one of its key drugs. If the company is part of the technology sector, it might have released a new gadget that is completely unique and very useful. Investors might like the new product and buy additional shares in the company. This simply results in a higher price for the stock.

"Every product on the market should have a reasonable price. A stock should also be reasonably priced. But due to momentum investors, a stock may be overpriced. For example, *Yahoo* was being traded at $216 during 1999, and that was definitely a very high price for a company with a presence strictly on the Internet. So a smart investor would not only pick great companies but would also sell the stock once its price is fairly high compared to the industry."

Troy asked, "How do we know the price of a stock is trading too high?"

Sam replied, "Like the way we found out whether our employee was being paid too high. You compare the employee's skills and experience with the rest of the industry. For example, the CEO of a multibillion-dollar company might be paid a base salary of $10 million, but if the CEO of a competitor is paid $100 million per year, then he or she is overpaid. A guy working at *Starbucks* may be paid $10 per hour, but if he demands $20 per hour, he is asking to be overpaid.

"Similarly, find the price to earnings ratio of a stock. If the P/E ratio is much higher than that of the industry, the stock is trading at a high price. If you happen to own a stock whose price is much higher than the industry standard, it is time to sell it.

"For example, let us compare the P/E ratio of a few stocks as of February 27, 2004."

Figure 12.3.1: P/E ratios of some public companies versus Industry's P/E ratios

Source: Morningstar, Inc.

Company	Price	P/E	Industry's P/E ratio
As of February 27,2004			
Bed, Bath and Beyond	$40.93	34.40	31.30
Best Buy	$53.25	90.30	45.50
General Electric	$32.52	21.80	25.40

Joe observed, "From the table, it looks like the price of *Best Buy* was trading much higher than the rest of the industry. Even though it is a good sign for current stockholders, it is very possible the price will come down in the near future."

Sam said, "Right! Even though there is no rule that says the price must come down, the possibility is very remote for a retail company to continue trading at a P/E ratio of 90. It is wise to sell the stock if you owned it."

Rule 3: Sell When Sales are Low

Regimen is superior to medicine
Voltaire

Troy asked, "Is it enough if we look only at the P/E ratios before selling?"

Sam said, "Well, there is one more important thing: Price to Sales ratio. For example, who is a good salesperson? A person who brings in maximum profits, a person who generates maximum revenues, or a person who does both? There is a distinction between these two.

"Profit is the income generated after deducting all expenses. A sales person might bring in an order worth one million dollars, but the expenses involved in completing the order might be around $500,000. So the net profit is 50%.

"Now, another salesperson may bring in orders worth ten million dollars, with total expenses of more than six million dollars. In this case, the company's profit is 40%. So which one of these two salespeople is better? For a company to make sufficient profits, it has to generate not only a great volume of business but also a sufficient profit margin."

Joe asked, "Are you saying that earnings alone may not be the true reflection of a company's performance?"

Sam said, "Exactly. Even if a company has a reasonable price to earnings ratio, that doesn't mean its stocks are worth holding.

"In addition to the P/E ratio, another method to measure the performance is price to sales ratio. If a company's Price to Sales ratio is much higher than the industry, it is an indication that its stock price is trading much higher than normal. That is a time to sell.

"Let us analyze the price to sales ratio of the following two companies as of February 27, 2004, and decide which one to sell."

Table 12.3.2: Price to Sales ratio of some public companies versus Industry's P/S ratio

Source: Morningstar, Inc.

Company	Current stock price	Price to sales ratio	Industry's price to sales ratio
As of February 27,2004			
Netflix	$34.40	7.06	0.71
Western Digital	$11.39	0.80	2.46

Joe concluded, "Hmm! *Netflix* is trading at a much higher price compared to its sales. When the entertainment industry is trading at a ratio of 0.71 compared to its sales, it is unusual for *Netflix* to trade at a much higher ratio of 7.06."

Their session was interrupted by Jessica's arrival.

She greeted them. "Hello, guys. Mind if I join?"

Bill whispered to Troy. "This situation is more confusing than P/E ratio or Price to Sales Ratio."

Sam simply said, "Jess, I didn't expect to see you here. "

Jessica replied, "Me neither. We need to talk, Sam."

The rest of the group made an attempt to leave the room.

Jessica said, "Oh! Sorry. I don't want to interrupt. Finish your session and we can talk later."

Objective Analysis

Success seems to be largely a matter of hanging on after others have let go
William Feather Doug Larson

Sam was confused and didn't know where to continue. Bill rescued him with a question. "If a company's price is trading higher, the natural expectancy is for future earnings to be really high. Why would I want to sell when I expect it to grow even more?"

Sam, back in full throttle, said, "I will give you another scenario. There could be two sales executives joining the same level in the organization, but one of them might be paid much higher than the other. How is that possible?

"The natural expectancy is for the higher paid sales executive to bring in more business. It could be that he or she has contacts with some of the best-known names in the industry. For example, a person who worked with an envelope corporation has contacts with companies like *Office Max*, *Citicorp*, and *Staples*, and is expected to bring in more orders. However, another sales executive may not have contacts with such big companies and is not expected to bring in more orders initially. Naturally, the sales executive with the major contacts is paid much higher.

"Let us compare this to *Netflix*. Why is *Netflix* trading at a much higher price than *Blockbuster*? The brick and mortar store, *Blockbuster Inc.*, is trading at a price to sales ratio of 0.53. However, the online DVD rental store *Netflix* is trading at a price to sales ratio of 7.06. Why there is such a remarkable difference?

"The difference is in the expected earnings. It is equivalent to the sales executive who is expected to bring in more orders.

"*Netflix* is expected to grow its earnings at 112%, whereas *Blockbuster* is expected to lose 10% in its future earnings. Just as sales executives are paid based on the future earnings they are expected to bring, a company's stock price reflects the future earnings it is expected to earn.

"A higher stock price does not necessarily mean it is a solid company and will continue to grow. If the stock's price is not proportionate to its earnings and its future growth, the best way an investor can profit is to sell the stock and cash in on the profits."

Bill remarked, "Interesting!"

Rule 4: Sell When You Foresee Danger

To know the road ahead, ask those coming back
Chinese Proverb

Troy asked, "Is there anything else we should know? For instance, how do we monitor a stock we bought? What should we monitor?

Sam said, "Okay. Let me tell you some of the things you should look out for. At the time you buy a stock, the company's debt level might have been low, which would have made it a great stock to buy. However, it may need to borrow money to meet its financial needs, and that is not a good sign. A company that accumulates debts instead of repaying them is a company to avoid. The most common reason a company files for bankruptcy is that its debts are too heavy to repay. So if its debt level is growing, simply avoid it or sell its stocks if you already own them.

"Another thing to look out for is that a company may fail to produce great earnings for one quarter. Of course, when it fails to produce earnings as expected, its stock price falls drastically. However, the price will recoup once its earnings are better in the next quarter."

Figure 12.3.3: Companies with growing debt level

Source: Morningstar, Inc.

Company	Total Liabilities ($ in Millions)		
	For 2000	For 2001	For 2002
Continental Airlines	7,799	8,387	9,727
Lyondell Chemicals	5,902	5,954	6,269
Waste Management	13,764	14,098	14,323
RF Micro Devices	41.5	344.4	339.3
Kohl's Corporation	1,229	1,652	2,138

Rule 5: Negative Cash Flow

He who asks is a fool for five minutes, but he
who does not ask remains a fool forever
Chinese Proverb

"The other important thing is negative cash flow. If poor performance is a main factor for an employee to be fired, a company's negative cash flow is a factor that prompts investors to sell their stocks.

"Debt is dangerous for a company. Negative cash flow will hurt in the long run as the company spends more money than it receives. It uses loans and other means to raise required capital.

"It is time to sell a stock when the cash flow for the recent several quarters is turning negative."

Figure 12.3.4: Companies with receding cash flow

Source: Morningstar, Inc.

Company	Ticker	Free cash flow ($ in Millions)		
		For 2000	For 2001	For 2002
Falcon Products Inc.	FCP	5.1	(4.6)	(11.6)
Max and Erma's Restaurants	MAXE	(5.6)	(7.9)	(10.3)

Closing Bell

Grief is the agony of a moment; the indulgence of
grief the blunder of a life
Benjamin Disraeli

Bill asked, "Great! Now we know when to sell. Can I have your home, mobile and work phone numbers, just in case I need to consult you, any time of the day or night?"

Everyone laughed. They went upstairs, leaving Sam and Jessica alone.

Sam asked, "Tell me, Jess. Can't we work this out? We have a great thing going on. Can't we have a long-distance relationship for a while?"

Before Jessica answered, Sam's cell phone rang. He spoke for a few minutes.

He told Jessica, "Well, I have good news and great news. I got the job, and I can work here for six months and then leave for New York. What do think? Is that great timing or what?"

Jessica waited for a few minutes before she answered. "I am happy for you. But, let me put it in your own terms. If our relationship is a stock I bought, it is performing way below my expectations, and I want to sell before I get hurt more."

Sam's Sprinkles

- A momentum investor buys and sells stocks based on the market's direction. However, long-term investors want to make money in stocks, and they have a clear goal and reason behind their actions.

- Buying and selling stocks does not incur taxes if done in tax-deferred accounts such as IRAs or Coverdell ESAs.

- If a stock is sold for a profit in a regular account, taxes must be paid.

- Sell a stock only if the Price to Earnings Ratio is much higher than the industry standard.

- Sell a stock if the Price to Sales Ratio is much higher than the industry standard.

- Sell a stock if the company's debt level is growing instead of shrinking.

- Sell a stock if the company spends too much money on capital investments.

- Sell a stock if the company's cash flow is negative.

True or False

- Listening to the news and making a decision to sell or buy is the best way to pick stocks.

- It is wise to sell a stock when its price is going down, and it is wise to buy when it is going up.

- A good company's stock price never comes down if you buy it near its 52-week low.

- It is time to sell a stock if a company's Debt to Equity ratio is lowering.

- It is time to sell a stock if a company's free cash flow is rising.

Self Explorer

- List all the formulae and the minimum ratios a company should pass before buying its shares.

- Use the stock screeners found on various websites including http://moneycentral.msn.com and www.zacks.com, and list various companies that pass the criteria.

- Find the pros and cons of buying and holding a stock for a long time versus buying and selling frequently.

- Find the pros and cons of a public company versus a private company.

- Find the rules companies must follow to become listed on the NYSE and NASDAQ.

INDEX

C

D

E

F

G

H

I

investor   5, 8, 45, 52, 80, 93, 94, 149, 178, 180, 203, 204, 209, 212, 224, 232, 237, 246, 247, 248, 249, 261, 262, 270, 271, 274, 275, 281, 289, 298, 301, 302, 303, 306, 307, 309, 313, 315, 322, 323, 335, 356, 357, 362, 365, 374, 377, 382, 391, 396, 397, 405, 412, 413, 415, 419, 423

K

key ratios   164

L

lawsuit   13, 299
lend   44, 45, 46, 48, 49, 147
lenders   134, 283
liabilities   161, 162, 173, 366
life span   69
linear progression   24
loan   8, 9, 47, 69, 109, 132, 143, 150, 162, 189, 195, 245
long-term   149, 174, 248, 283, 286, 389, 412, 413, 423
long-term debt   174, 283, 286
long-term investing   412
loss   21, 87, 100, 121, 299, 306, 312, 313, 413
lottery   39, 78, 265, 269

M

management   9, 24, 132, 189, 275, 296, 392, 394
management fee   392
margins   207, 208, 209, 212, 218, 220, 223, 233, 236
market capitalization   352
market share   118, 273, 275
market value   17, 284
measuring profits   106
medicine   69, 70, 416
merger   99, 301
miles per hour   107, 340
million dollars   28, 39, 40, 41, 42, 52, 55, 58, 59, 60, 61, 68, 71, 75, 76, 78, 129, 148, 179, 224, 265, 267, 279, 280, 288, 306, 417
millionaire   27, 58, 75, 76, 94, 137, 335
momentum investors   294, 415
money market   9, 38, 41, 42, 44, 373
monthly deposits   39
mortgage   9, 47, 69, 187, 243

S

T

U

V

W

Y